CULINARY FICTIONS

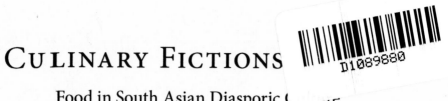

Food in South Asian Diasporic Culture

ANITA MANNUR

Temple University Press

PHILADELPHIA

Temple University Press
1601 North Broad Street
Philadelphia, PA 19122
www.temple.edu/tempress

♾ The paper used in this publication meets the requirements of the American National Standard for Information Sciences—Permanence of Paper for Printed Library Materials, ANSI Z39.48-1992

LIBRARY OF CONGRESS CATALOGING-IN-PUBLICATION DATA

Mannur, Anita.
 Culinary fictions : food in South Asian diasporic culture / Anita Mannur.
  p. cm.
 Includes bibliographical references and index.
 ISBN 978-1-4399-0077-2 (cloth : alk. paper)
 ISBN 978-1-4399-0078-9 (pbk. : alk. paper)
 1. Food in literature. 2. Food habits in literature. 3. South Asians in literature.
4. Cookery, Indic. 5. English literature—South Asian authors—History and criticism.
6. English literature—Women authors—History and criticism. I. Title.
PN56.F59M36 2009
820.9'3564—dc22

                                                                2009017460

    2 4 6 8 9 7 5 3 1

THE
AMERICAN
LITERATURES
INITIATIVE

A book in the American Literatures Initiative (ALI), a collaborative publishing project of NYU Press, Fordham University Press, Rutgers University Press, Temple University Press, and the University of Virginia Press. The Initiative is supported by The Andrew W. Mellon Foundation. For more information, please visit www.americanliteratures.org.

For my family, and, in memory of Carmina Fugaban

CONTENTS

Acknowledgments ix

Introduction: Food Matters 1

PART ONE Nostalgia, Domesticity, and Gender

1 Culinary Nostalgia: Authenticity, Nationalism, and Diaspora 27

2 Feeding Desire: Food, Domesticity, and Challenges to Heteropatriarchy 50

PART TWO Palatable Multiculturalisms and Class Critique

3 Sugar and Spice: Sweetening the Taste of Alterity 81

4 Red Hot Chili Peppers: Visualizing Class Critique and Female Labor 114

PART THREE Theorizing Fusion in America

5 Eating America: Culture, Race, and Food in the Social Imaginary of the Second Generation 147

6 Easy Exoticism: Culinary Performances of Indianness 181

Conclusion: Room for More: Multiculturalism's Culinary Legacies 217

Notes 227

Bibliography 235

Index 249

Acknowledgments

Growing up in various nodes of the South Asian diaspora, I came to appreciate the intimate connections between food, gender, and ethnicity through my mother's efforts to teach me how to cook Indian food. Disciplining me into becoming a good Indian woman by teaching me how to cook was perhaps an extended exercise in futility. But as someone who loved to eat and loved to cook, I rejected the idea that I needed to learn how to make naan and chapattis and taught myself how to make baguettes and bagels instead. I found a way to satisfy my mother's wish to see me cook while maintaining a critical distance from the notion that I needed to cook Indian food in order to affirm my Indianness. After becoming a college student in the United States, I learned to cook Indian food with the help of my able instructor Madhur Jaffrey. Today if I eat Indian food, it is not so much to remind me of India, a place where I have never lived. Rather, Indian food is saliently connected with my various homes in Malaysia, Australia, Papua New Guinea, and the United States.

Three generations of women in my family view food in radically different ways. When my mother cooks, it is to feed loved ones and to nourish our palates and bodies in the same ways she takes care of our souls; when her mother cooked, it was a form of sustenance. My grandmother supplemented the family income by teaching cooking classes in her home; and following the death of her husband (my grandfather), she generated income by publishing two cookbooks in English and Kannada, respectively. And when I cook it is certainly about feeding my friends and family. But it is also about nostalgia, performing cultural identity, and establishing alternative networks of intimacy not circumscribed by lines of blood and filiation. This book is my effort to understand the stories we tell about food. It maps how food matters, tracing what happens when we put food at the center of critical inquiry.

One of the wonderful things about writing a book about food is that good conversations and meals are never in short supply. Precious few among us do not hold strong opinions about food, and I wish to thank the people with whom I have cooked, shared a meal, and talked about food. I have benefitted immeasurably from the richness of these conversations about matters culinary; and while there isn't enough space to thank everyone, I remain grateful for the kindness of all who have lent an ear to the work that comes together in this book.

Though this volume represents work completed after earning my Ph.D., the influence of my teachers and mentors dating back to the early 1990s (when I was a high school student in Papua New Guinea) can be detected throughout it. I thank John Smith, my history teacher at Port Moresby International High School, for instilling a love for engaged critical praxis and a passion for the histories of colonized subjects and spaces. Luis Madureira, Jane Tylus, and the late Amy Ling introduced me to the rich array of postcolonial, ethnic, and Asian American literature while I was an undergraduate student at the University of Wisconsin, Madison. I am happily indebted to my mentors at the University of Massachusetts, Amherst—Cathy Portuges, David Lenson, R. Radhakrishnan, and Sunaina Maira—for encouraging me to build a strong foundation for my research, which would eventually branch into this work. Cathy's unwavering support and encouragement have guided my intellectual and personal growth. David's enthusiasm, humor, and friendship have been vital; Radha's sheer brilliance, love of all things gastronomic, and probing questions have helped me to articulate important questions; and finally, Sunaina Maira's incisive feedback gently nudged me into becoming a better—or at least more self-reflexive—writer, and thinker. The Five Colleges of Western Massachusetts is a vibrant intellectual space, and I am grateful to the many students, faculty, and Five College fellows—too numerous to mention here—who make Amherst such a rich and layered place to think and work. I want to mention Carolyn Porter, Bunkong Tuon, Sejal Shah, Lucy Burns, Nina Ha, Stephanie Dunson, Amy Cheng, Ignacio Lopez-Vicuña, Jana Evans Braziel, Karen Cardozo, Jennifer Rodgers, Neil Hartlen, Liz Fitzpatrick, Sonny Suchdev and Jonathan Sadow, my graduate school compatriots, for countless hours of engaged and thoughtful conversations. Sharing cosmopolitans in the late 1990s while discussing cosmopolitanism rates among my most cherished of graduate school memories.

Postdoctoral fellowships in the Asian American Studies Program at the University of Illinois, Urbana-Champaign, and two years of a Freeman Postdoctoral Fellowship at Wesleyan University gave me the time to think about food and race without the pressure of publishing. I wish to thank Kent Ono at UIUC and Claire Potter, Ann Wightman, Tricia Hill, Su Zheng, and Steve Angle at Wesleyan for their support. I am grateful to Denison University for providing research support to work on this book. I wish to thank the staff at the Doane Library at Denison for helping me track down several sources.

Former students at Wesleyan University and Denison University have been a wonderful source of inspiration. I am grateful to their commitment to thoughtful and rigorous critical inquiry. I thank Ada Fung, Justin Leroy, Tara Fickle, Pia Sahni, and May Kyi at Wesleyan and Ayesha Venkataraman and Emily Toler at Denison for several rich conversations about food, race, fashion, and popular culture. At Denison I had the good fortune of teaching a senior seminar titled "Culinary Fictions," and I want to acknowledge the students in that course for their persistent and engaged passion and for thinking critically about food (especially at nine thirty in the morning). Amanda Dever, Hope Justice, Jennifer Luebbers, Brian Crush, Halle Murcek, Nick Bailey, Brynn Lewallen, Luke Gelber, Jonathan Lydon, Elizabeth Whitman, Dawn Cunningham, Dan Sweatt, Jon Gardner, Jayme Hughes, and Gail Martineau are among the most talented and thoughtful group of students I have had the privilege of teaching; in many ways, this book is for all of you.

Among my former colleagues at Denison, I want to thank David Baker, Eric Saranovitz, Isis Nusair, Toni King, Veerendra Lele, and Barbara Fultner for the feedback they have provided at various faculty colloquia. My weekly writing sessions with Joanna Mitchell were invigorating and effective. Mary Tuominen and Marlene Tromp inspire me with their unflagging energy, commitment to social justice, and concern for the intellectual and emotional lives of junior faculty of color. The pages of this book bear the traces of their generous and astute critiques. I am grateful to my colleagues at Miami who have welcomed me into the English Department and the Program in Asian/Asian American Studies. I look forward to many lively conversations and scholarly exchanges.

Stephen Sohn, Paul Lai, Tara Fickle, Fred Porcheddu, Allan Isaac, and Gladys Nubla all read drafts of this book at various stages. Their friendship, collective wisdom, and willingness to engage my work has been immeasurably valuable. I thank Martin Manalansan, fairy godmother to this book, for his continued belief in the relevance of food within Asian American studies. His recent work on the anthropology of the senses has been foundational to my understanding of food, race, and affect. I remain grateful to Nilesh Patel for sharing his wonderful film, *A Love Supreme*, and for allowing me to use images from his film. Thanks to Sandeep Sood for allowing use of the comic strip *Queer Eye for the FOB Guy*. I also wish to thank the Singh Twins for granting permission to use their painting *Pupoo in the Kitchen* for this book's cover image. Their artwork updates the style of Indian and Persian miniature paintings to provide compelling commentaries on the effects of globalization and migration as they take root in the everyday spaces of South Asian diasporic lives.

The many others, near and far, whose thoughts and feedback I have appreciated include Henry Abelove, Evelyn Hu De Hart, Kandice Chuh, James Kyung-Jin Lee, John Vincent, Greg Mullins, Jeffrey Santa Ana, Rich King, David Leonard, Jose Alamillo, Bakirathi Mani, Maeve Adams, Min Song, Floyd Cheung, Shilpa Davé, Khyati Joshi, Nila Bhattacharjya, Kehaulani Kauanui, Anu Sharma, Terry Kawashima, Nancy Inouye, Jenny Robertson, Jon Okamura, Christine Yano, Nitasha Sharma, Sangeeta Ray, Julie Sievers, Wenying Xu, Fred Gardaphe, Rafia Zafar, David L. Eng, Betsy Traub, Moon-Kie Jung, Sugi Ganeshananthan, Laura Lindenfeld, Suvir Kaul, Ania Loomba, Simona Sawhney, Kumi Silva, Robert Ji-Song Ku, Tseen Khoo, Sita Ranchod-Nilsson, Stephen Hong Sohn, Dennis Read, Molly O'Neill, Gladys Nubla, Paul Lai, Shirley Lim, Martha Cutter, Sanda Mayzaw Lwin, Jennifer Ho, Joe Ponce, Asha Nadkarni, Patti Zimmerman, Yu-Fang Cho, Kaara Peterson, Susan Morgan, Nalin Jayasena, Vaishali Raval, Rajini Srikanth, Julie Minich, Jason Palmeri, Gita Rajan, Susan Muchshima Moynihan, Gabe Wettach, Victor Mendoza, Peter Feng, LuMing Mao, Mindy Chen and Leslie Bow.

None of this would be possible without the tireless efforts of my editor at Temple University Press, Janet Francendese. Thank you for believing in this project. This book is the better for the suggestions provided by the two anonymous reviewers. Heartfelt thanks to Emily Taber, Charles Aulit and Gary Kramer at Temple University Press and to Tim Roberts with the American Literatures Initiative for all their efforts.

My closest friends and family sustained me throughout the writing process. Dale Hudson has been a continued source of support since our days in graduate school. I am grateful for his friendship through the years. I thank Chris Vials for his sage advice and for many compelling conversations about work, class, and ethnicity in American popular culture. Allan Isaac has been a staunch ally, and I am grateful to him for his sharp critical insight, his willingness to always accompany me on eating adventures, and for passing his love of buffets on to me. Bill Johnson Gonzalez's unmatched generosity has been a source of comfort. I have benefitted tremendously from his expansive knowledge of all things literary and his willingness to always feed me. Amy Scott-Douglass helped keep my spirits up during the writing process. I appreciate her support during times of adversity and for always believing in the importance of leading an ethical life. I am most grateful to Cathy Schlund-Vials for her energy, wit, and intellect. Her friendship and generosity of spirit have been a constant as we have journeyed from being graduate students to assistant professors. Not only did she read every word of this book in draft stage, but she has been a consistent believer in the relevance of my work. Words cannot express how much I value her unwavering friendship and generosity.

I thank my parents, Hanumant and Shobana Mannur, for their support and love. Their home in Mangalore, India, became a writing sanctuary in which to complete the first draft of this book. My mother's capacity to love has inspired me at each turn. She read every text I wrote about, clipped every article in newspapers about food in South Asian contexts, and listened to every idea percolating in my head. From her willingness to engage my ideas about food, domesticity, and diaspora, to cooking delicious food while in India and stocking my American freezer full of delicious curries and idlis, she, more than anyone else, has taken good care of my mind, palate, and spirit.

Michael Needham came into my life as I was struggling to give shape to this manuscript. His unwavering support, love, and, most important of all, his journalistic respect for deadlines helped me bring this book to its completion. He nourished my mind and soul during the writing and editing process by joining me on scores of eating adventures, eventually becoming my personal barista, brewing endless cups of coffee to keep me alert and focused. For this as well as his assiduous reading of multiple drafts of this manuscript, I remain grateful; all mistakes, however, remain my own. And, of course, I am most grateful to him for bringing Keith into our lives.

I dedicate this book to the memory of Carmina Fugaban (1974–2006), a brilliant young mind who passed before her time. A dear friend from Port Moresby International High School and my compatriot in our International Baccalaureate Higher English class, Carmina brought her writerly eloquence and beauty to everything she wrote. I would read Carmina's essays and be in awe that someone so young could write with such elegance and maturity. I think she would have been proud of me for realizing my dreams. For that, and so much more, I remember her with respect and love.

CULINARY FICTIONS

Introduction: Food Matters

It is difficult, if not impossible, to think of immigrant Indian existence in the United States without at the same time thinking of Indian food.
—KEYA GANGULY, STATES OF EXCEPTION

CARRIE BRADSHAW: *When a girl gets backed up against a wall she can't afford, she has to consider renting others (sniffing through open window). Do . . . Do I smell curry?*
REALTOR: *There's an Indian restaurant downstairs.*
CB: *Delia, I ask you, how can this apartment be $2,800 a month? I pay $750 for something that's twice the size and it don't smell like takeout.*
REALTOR: *You have a rent-controlled apartment. I suggest you stay there.*
CB: *Unfortunately, that's not an option. Now what other shit holes are you showing me today?*
—"RING A DING DING," SEX AND THE CITY

I was looking for some kind of symbol which would represent the success of Indians abroad, something that would symbolize what they have gone through in their long history . . . But look at it metaphorically. Indians have gone abroad, have lived in the most challenging environments in the world and they have done well. Indian coconuts have done very well abroad. Now, what is the coconut famous for? It grows on sandy soil, requires very little water, and requires virtually no maintenance. In other words, send an Indian anywhere, just let them be, with minimum nourishment and watch the tree grow taller and taller until it dominates the landscape. That is what I think the Indian Diaspora is like.
—LALIT MANSINGH, "THE STORY OF THE INDIAN DIASPORA IS COMPELLING AND INSPIRING"

On December 12, 2003, Lalit Mansingh, former Indian ambassador to the United States, delivered a speech to a crowd of Indian Americans at the annual awards banquet of the weekly news magazine *India Abroad*. During his speech, Mansingh spoke in no uncertain terms about the lofty achievements of the Indian diaspora, especially the strand of the diaspora located in the United States. In speaking about the purported resilience of the Indian character, Mansingh suggests the coconut is an apt metaphor for Indians because "it grows on sandy soil, requires very little water, and requires virtually no maintenance" (S16). Here, the coconut stands in for all that rings stereotypic about Indian Americans: the notion that the community is uniformly flourishing and has made the better of often hostile environments. Mansingh's narrative, to be sure, privileges the experiences of upwardly mobile and middle- to upper-class Indian Americans, ignoring the experiences of those Indian Americans who do not flourish in the United States—Indian Americans located on the lower rungs of society's ladder: the working class, the undocumented, and the disenfranchised.

Mansingh's use of the term "coconut" is intriguing. Typically used to reference assimilatory moves among Indian Americans and South Asian Americans, the term "coconut" is more colloquially used to name individuals who might identify as "white." With its hints of a racial ontology, the term suggests there are authentic and less authentic ways of being Indian. Looking Indian, being brown on the outside, and having a particular set of tastes and preferences that don't necessarily correspond to predetermined notions of what it means to be Indian may lead to one being labeled a coconut—white on the inside and brown on the outside. Other communities of color frequently apply culinary metaphors to speak of similar forms of racialized performance. Within the African American community, the favored term is "Oreo"; among East Asian Americans, the terms "banana" and "Twinkie" are analogues to the Oreo, and for Native Americans, the term "apple" serves a similar function. Woven through each of these metaphors is a narrative of ethnic betrayal: the notion that one might be colored brown, black, yellow, or red on the outside, and act in a way to suggest one is "white" on the inside.[1] To capture the sentiments of South Asian youth who do not identify with whiteness, but choose instead to mark their alliance with Blackness, KB, a member of the hip-hop Indian group Karmacy, presents the term "rotten coconut," brown on the outside but black on the inside. Nitasha Sharma argues that such seemingly simplistic metaphors are actually more complicated; while bananas and coconuts are healthy fruit, connoting positive identification with whiteness, the image of rotten coconut carries a negative stigma. While these metaphors are context-specific, they hint at the dynamic nature of racial categories, deconstructing the idea that race is "something 'natural'—whether biologically or culturally so" (Sharma 30–31). Surprisingly, Mansingh's speech seems ignorant of this complex and sullied history behind the term "coconut," whether in a state of presumed "freshness" or "rottenness": instead, he identifies the coconut in the most positive terms as a symbol of potent upward mobility, one which would ignore the appalling effects of race and class discrimination that are more salient for those without access to the education, social services, and adequate language skills necessary for survival in an increasingly monolingually driven cultural and political economy.

Underlying Mansingh's glib assertions about Indianness is a rather simple truism: when it comes to thinking about South Asian diasporic bodies, food is never far. Outside of Mansingh's assertions, much of the positive valorization of Indianness is linked to the growing popularity of Indian food and the popularity of India-inspired clothing, fashion, and commodities within spaces and communities that have become South Asian diasporic sites. Discursively the terms by which "Indianness" is imagined almost always mobilizes a culinary idiom; more often than not food is situated in narratives about racial and ethnic identity as an intractable measure of cultural authenticity. While Mansingh's assertions may take on a unique character insofar as he actively seeks out the realm of the culinary to metaphorize U.S.–based Indian diasporas, he is by no means the only political figure to link food with cultural and ethnic identity, particularly as it relates to Indian bodies.

Only two years prior to Mansingh's speech, another political figure—this time on the other side of the Atlantic Ocean—connected culinary symbols with race and ethnicity. In the now infamous "chicken tikka masala" speech, Robin Cook, then foreign secretary for Britain, famously claimed chicken tikka masala (also popularly referred to as "CTM") for Britain, proclaiming the popular spicy chicken dish as Britain's national dish. The speech, not surprisingly, spurred wide interest among the British public, food critics, and Indians around the world. Purists among the critics decried chicken tikka masala as an inauthentic imitation of a culinary item with no antecedent in India, while activists among Black British communities were aghast that a British political leader might so willfully ignore the complex historical conditions which have led to Indian restaurateurs creating CTM for consumption in their restaurants.

As legend has it, the dish was born to satisfy the bland palate of an English diner. Iqbal Wahhab, a journalist and restaurateur, suggests that CTM was invented by a Bangladeshi chef in an Indian restaurant. As the story goes, upon being served chicken tikka, a traditionally dry preparation of meat, an irate customer demanded to know where the gravy was in the dish he ordered. To placate the customer, the chef whipped up a sauce made of Campbell's cream of tomato soup and some spices, and thus was born chicken tikka masala. While the origins of the dish are certainly elusive, especially for its purist detractors, the debate around chicken tikka masala is fascinating for it chronicles the ways in which food becomes indelibly grafted onto the national psyche, at the same time that the larger debate functions as an index of apparently changing cultural norms. In its current usage, CTM is more frequently consumed as post-pub fare: a spicy concoction to satisfy the appetite of inebriated individuals. But while the consumer market may have legitimized CTM as a "British" dish to the point that it, along with a number of other Indian foods, has "arrived" and been packaged for the frozen-meal market, one cannot overlook the role played by entrepreneurial innovators such as Indian immigrant Ghulam Noon. His company, Noon Products, specializes in prepackaged frozen Asian meals and is widely available in supermarkets. The products are so popular that some credit Noon for making CTM a household name in Britain. And yet a more clear history that might account for how an immigrant of Indian origin might have been able to successfully foment a career by selling CTM to a largely white public, a brilliant entrepreneurial move by most estimations, does not emerge in Cook's speech.[2]

For Robin Cook, chicken tikka masala represents a new form of multiculturalism, notably one in which the British national character is praised for its ability and willingness to "absorb" from and adapt the culinary histories of its immigrants and formerly colonized subjects. Left out of Robin Cook's praise is the notion that the CTM version of Indianness is malleable enough to be reinvented by Britons without any rigorous interrogation about what enables British consumers to have access to CTM in the first instance. Indeed, the very conditions of colonialism that brought Indians to Britain, the conditions of race and class in Britain which made it necessary for South Asian immigrants to enter into the business of making Indianness palatable to Western tastes, and the question of who, or what, is responsible for making Indianness available to the mainstream British palate form a narrative that is wholly submerged in Cook's fantasy of British-style multiculturalism. Put another way, what makes CTM acceptable on British tables when the same Indian bodies that produce CTM are not welcome to sit at the table with the British?[3] Whatever the origins of the dubious dish might be, one thing is certain: the CTM debate has ceased to be (if it ever was) exclusively about food. The CTM debate is as much, if not more, about anxieties about cultural admixtures, race, and ethnicity as it is about accurately chronicling the etymology for a dish comprised of tandoori-style meat drenched in masala sauce: something that seems so quintessentially "British" that British persons may claim to know good Indian food better than Indians, for instance.

Read together, Mansingh's and Cook's speeches speak to the cultural continuum linking migratory subjects from South Asia. The "contributions" of South Asian bodies, separated by oceans, can be made to best resonate if apprehended through culinary metaphors and symbols. Left out of both their glowing statements is any sense of how the culinary practices and preferences of the South Asian diasporic subjects they both celebrate might also be connected to the racism and tension that South Asian bodies with ever greater frequency experience on a daily basis. Where, for instance in either of these celebratory utterances is a sense of how food odors, often indelibly grafted onto bodies of racialized subjects, serve to negatively racialize South Asian bodies? Here, various forms of popular culture in the United States and the United Kingdom illustrate the multiple complexities and conflicts enmeshed with culinary rhetoric. One might recall the scene from the hit television series *Sex and the City* in which Carrie Bradshaw turns her nose up at an apartment that, to her, reeks of Indian food; something that identifies the apartment to her as a "shit hole." The 2007 racial controversy emerging from the British reality show *Celebrity Big Brother* offers yet another example of South Asian food carrying a negative stigma. When one of the contestants, Jade Goody, entered into a protracted argument with Bollywood actress Shilpa Shetty, the former launched her tirade against the actress in culinary terms, calling her "Shilpa Poppadom," referring to the customary appetizer served in Indian restaurants. While the British and Indian publics quickly came to Shetty's defense, lambasting Goody for her racism couched in culinary terms, it quickly became apparent how seamlessly Goody's racism dovetailed with a negative rendering of Indian food. Amid Cook's and Mansingh's rhetoric of culinary multiculturalism, where are the narratives that bear witness to the often horrifying work conditions of those who labor in restaurant kitchens in the United States and Britain to serve CTM?

Take, for example, a powerful scene from the film *The Guru*, in which familiarity with Indian food buttresses a stunning moment of racial abjection in the otherwise unspectacular film. A Bollywood-inspired film that hit North American screens in early 2003, *The Guru* centers its narrative on Ramu, a young Indian immigrant who arrives in New York in search of the American Dream. Ramu, a stylish young man who makes a living instructing middle-aged women in India in the techniques of the macarena dance, discovers his first days in the United States to be anything but dreamlike. Like many immigrants who find themselves ethnically "downgraded," upon his arrival in the United States Ramu is unable to procure employment and finds his first viable job opportunity as a waiter in an Indian restaurant. Early in his days of working at Gandhi, a nondescript Indian restaurant in New York, Ramu finds himself confronting obnoxious customers who find fault with the food Ramu delivers to their table:

(Scene setting: Gandhi, an Indian restaurant in New York)

Ramu, a part-time waiter, approaches a table of three white male diners who are jovially chatting. He places the platter of chicken tikka masala down:

MATT: What is this? I ordered chicken tikka masala.

RAMU: That is chicken tikka masala, sir.

MATT (*affecting a stereotypical Indian accent*): That is *not* chicken tikka masala.

RAMU: That is *definitely* chicken tikka masala.

MATT: Dude, I know chicken fucking tikka masala, and that's not it. So how about you take your skinny brown ass back down to the kitchen and get me some?

Friend's voice in background: Come on, Matt . . .

RAMU: Yes, sir (*pauses as he takes the dish back*). I'm sorry (*pours the dish over Matt's head*), Dude.

Shot through with threads of a violent racism, the scene's humor is based on the notion that white bodies have the right to put racialized immigrants in their place for not serving them on the terms they demand. In the exhortation to "get your skinny ass back down to the kitchen," the customer marks his intolerance for the brown body serving his food by offering a variation on the tired phrase which reminds immigrants of their place or lack thereof within the racialized landscape of the restaurant. Here racism and anti-immigrant sentiments emerge against a purported affinity for Indian food, becoming legible through the immigrant waiter's refusal to accept the racial taunts of the customer he is serving. Reading this scene from *The Guru* against Cook and/or Mansingh's assertions, one cannot divorce the racism and intolerance for brown bodies from the seeming ease with which Indian food has been placed at the tables of populations that look askance at nondisciplined South Asian bodies.

An episode of *Goodness Gracious Me*, the Indian-British sketch comedy show, unrelentingly mocks the British public's ritualized consumption of Indian food in a sketch titled "Going out for an English." Lampooning the now masculinized British custom of gorging on Indian food after a night of heavy drinking, the sketch focuses on a group of Indians ordering food at an "English" restaurant. Reversing the now familiar pattern of patrons demanding the spiciest dish on the menu, they want to know what "the blandest thing on the menu is." The brilliance of this particular sketch lies in its ability to articulate the racism in considering Indian food as the means by which to purge after a night of excessive drinking. In positioning the abject immigrant as the subject, the sketch wrenches power away from what Nirmal Puwar dubs "the terror of whiteness" (264) to castigate the forms of consumption rendered normal within the cultural imaginary of English pubgoers such that bland English food, rather than "excessively" spiced Indian food, comes to occupy the space of abject culinary matter.

This overview of the culinary in U.S.- and U.K.-based popular culture signals the multiple ways in which everyday Indianness is scripted within the language of consumption and culinary practices. Such forms of cultural representation also set the stage for what is at stake in this book: how a culinary register becomes the most salient, and often most palatable, index of managing difference in South Asian diasporic literary and cultural production. Rather than affirming the terms of culinary ontology that French gastronome Jean Brillat Savarin proffers—"tell me what you eat, I'll tell you what you are"—this book seeks to repudiate these benign culinary symmetries in which culinary tastes isomorphically align with bodies. I am less invested in examining the culinary foodways of South Asian diasporic populations than I am in negotiating how narratives about food make palatable the inclusion of selective aspects of South Asianness. This book inserts itself strategically within the gaps and lapses produced in Mansingh and Cook's collective musings about the South Asian diaspora and food to ask why culinary practices are enfolded into the image of multiculturalism, when South Asian bodies so often are not enfolded into the same vision of inclusion? My contention here is that the culinary idiom mobilized by South Asian diasporic cultural brokers is both strategic and conjectural: the use of food is more than an a priori affirmation of palatable difference; it is also a way to undermine the racialized ideologies that culinary discourse is so often seen to buttress. For South Asian diasporic cultural texts, the "culinary" most typically occupies a seemingly paradoxical space—at once a site of affirmation and resistance. Affirmation, because food often serves to mark defining moments in marking ethnicity for communities that live through and against the vagaries of diasporized realities, marred by racism and xenophobia. Resistance, insofar as the evocation of a culinary register can deliberately and strategically disrupt the notion that cultural identity is always readily available for consumption and commodification and always already conjoined to culinary practices.

In its mapping of South Asian American culinary fictions, this book examines cultural production from the Anglo-American reaches of the South Asian diaspora. While South Asia is politically composed of seven countries—India, Pakistan, Sri Lanka, Bangladesh, Bhutan, Nepal, and the Maldives—the cultural and political hegemony of India has often led to a conflation of South Asia with India. This book works against that logic while being mindful of the ways in which the diasporic experience, both in American contexts and elsewhere, is shaped through and against this logic of Indocentrism. While this book focuses primarily on texts and cultural forms produced within the United States, it also examines diasporic texts which travel to form part of the larger corpus of diasporic South Asian texts in North America. This is not to subsume cultural production from Britain, Trinidad, or Canada under the behemoth umbrella of "Asian America," but rather to recognize the vital ways in which cultural productions from other national spaces have shaped, energized, and refracted the contours of debates around food, race, and ethnicity in a North American context. As Rajini Srikanth so persuasively argues in *The World Next Door*, the "South Asian American experience is one of diaspora. One cannot discuss South Asian American literature without considering the numerous geographical locations this diaspora comprises" (2–3). I take inspiration from Srikanth's mapping to argue for a definition of South Asian America patently aware of the borders which circumscribe the lives, cultures, and literatures produced within the United States and Canada, at the same time that it takes into account how the workings of the imagination, to borrow from Arjun Appadurai, situate South Asian diasporic cultural production outside of a purely national framework. The imagination, as Appadurai reminds us, is "central to all forms of agency, is itself a social fact, and is the key component of the new global order" (31). Food, as a central part of the cultural imagination of diasporic populations, becomes one of the most viable and valuable sites from which to inquire into the richly layered texture of how race is imagined and reinterpreted within the cultural arena, both to affirm and resist notions of home and belonging.

Culinary Fictions situates South Asian diasporic culture within the purview of Asian American studies not to suggest the experience of diaspora can be conflated with Americanness or that Asian American narratives are necessarily diasporic, but to more rigorously interrogate the conceptual frameworks we use in theorizing Asian America, especially as the transnational acquires ever greater urgency in framing Asian American cultural critique. At stake in understanding how the culinary shapes the contours of South Asianness in a diasporic frame is a larger set of questions about how—perhaps where—to situate South Asian transnationalisms in relation to Asian American studies. Certainly "Indian American," "Indian," and "South Asian" are not overlapping terms, nor should South Asian diasporas be conceived so loosely as to allow for all iterations of South Asian transnationalism to be considered Asian American. *Culinary Fictions* offers a synthetic approach, concerned with the micro- and macroepistemologies of food in South Asian diasporic cultural texts. Part of the more exciting developments in the current state of Asian American studies comes from the multiple methodologies that orient and reorient the field. I do not attempt in this work to conflate British and Canadian cultural productions with Asian American ones but rather to attend to the complex ways in which texts from these diasporic spaces converse with works from the United States.

I press these connections by weaving together my analyses in each chapter to unearth connections between these texts and to suggest an alternative methodology for reading the South Asian diaspora, one that is cognizant of the dynamic interchange between the United States and other diasporic nodes. We might also conceive of this kind of intellectual work through the rubric offered by Shu-Meh Shih and Françoise Lionnet. Proposing an alternative mode of understanding the transnational in ethnic studies, one that would lead us to conceive of transnationalism outside of the polarities of "homeland and origin" wherein transnationalism is framed in vertical terms, they propose that scholars in U.S. ethnic studies "look sideways to lateral networks that are not readily apparent" (1). Thus, the archive of South Asian culinary texts I draw upon is built upon lateral and rhizomic connections that do not always center on an "experience" that can be discernibly marked as Asian American. A more vibrant, historically and aesthetically relevant way of theorizing the place of the culinary in South Asian American fictions would reach out laterally to works in conversation with another; as such, this book seeks to articulate a vision of South Asian Americanness that is attentive to the crisscrossing networks that connect Sri Lankan–British, Indo-Caribbean, Pakistani-American iterations of subjectivity. Part of this book's archive, then, comprises texts that are not so easily labeled

"Asian American"; instead, the book also interrogates South Asian trans-national texts that situate how an understanding of home, diaspora, and migration become complexly intertwined with food and belonging within gendered hierarchical structures.

Food Studies and Literary Studies

A study devoted to food within the larger field of ethnic studies poses some unique challenges and possibilities for cultural inquiry. For some years, food has been garnering interest as a subject for cultural and lit-erary inquiry. Despite the flourishing interest in foodways, there is a relative dearth of critical analyses of film and literature about food that moves critical engagement out of representational analyses and into in-terrogative spheres which would trouble the very ways in which food is used to buttress narratives about belonging, kinship, and dissent. Twenty years after the publication of Susan Leonardi's landmark *PMLA* article "Recipes for Reading: Summer Pasta, Lobster à la Riseholme, and Key Lime Pie," some literary and cultural critics remain ambivalent about the status of "food studies."[4] This ambivalence speaks more to the anxi-ety about placing something as seemingly superficial as food into the center of critical analysis (Dunphy, Walker, Schumann et. al 903–8) than it does to the seriousness of food per se.

Equally stringent within the field of food studies has been an almost indignant insistence on labeling the field as "scholarship lite," a critique lodged within a well-publicized op-ed piece published in the *Chronicle of Higher Education*. While such charges are crucial, my thinking about food, as someone anchored within literary studies, has led me to fol-low a slightly different trajectory than have some of my interlocutors in food studies. Instead of countering charges of "scholarship lite" with the response that food is a serious and valid area for academic inquiry, we would do well to attend instead to the contradictory perplexities which animate the doubts leveled against "food studies." Why, for instance, is it the case that within the academy food scholarship has typically fallen within the purview of anthropology and sociology, and by extension, outside of literary studies? Carole Counihan and Penny Van Esterik, edi-tors of the seminal collection *Food and Culture*, understand this to be a function of anthropology's status as a discipline that is "holistic by defi-nition" (2). But if anthropology has been a particularly fitting home for what we might schematically refer to as "food studies," this has less to do with the social sciences being a natural fit with food studies, and more to do with the fact that literary analysis of food takes multiple forms, with critical analyses often occurring in parallel though nonoverlapping critical spaces. When we think about food, it is often to discern some truthful fictions or fictive truths about group identity. Such interest in linking discourse with cultural contexts almost always leads to an automatic assumption that food studies is exclusively concerned with the material realm of food culture, and more suited for anthropological or sociological modes of inquiry, rather than literary studies. When literature does feature into cultural texts, more often than not it is to buttress theoretical formulations emerging from the social science–oriented disciplines.

While it is not an overstatement to suggest that food poses particular challenges for literary studies, this not for lack of interest among literary and cultural critics. The difficulty of imagining food scholarship to be about the "literary" and thus to be a natural fit for the social sciences can be better understood if we think about historical developments within literary studies that have steered literature away from its moorings within "an ahistorical and largely immanent formalism or thematics" and toward analyzing literary and cultural texts as part of wider discursive formations, to loosely paraphrase the U.S. cultural studies pioneer Cary Nelson (165).

Food studies, which emerged during the 1970s, owes an unquestionable debt to the work of structuralism and to the sociologists and anthropologists at the forefront of that methodological orientation. Since the 1970s, this corpus of critical literature has placed special emphasis on understanding the role of food in social and group relations. Among the most important theorizations are those that consider how taste for certain foods can be seen as to reflect social and cultural patterns and how culture, in turn, shapes food preferences (Claude Levi-Strauss, Pierre Bourdieu, and Mary Douglas); the relationship between food, colonialism, and power (Sidney Mintz); the ceremonial uses of food in religion (Claude Levi-Strauss); the development of table manners (Norbert Elias); the symbolic meaning of food (Herbert Gans and Roland Barthes). These theoretical formulations owe no small debt to the popularity of structuralism in the 1970s. Structuralism's attention to semiotics, thematics, and the formalist dimensions of culture provided a logical script through which to navigate the alimentary symbols and motifs in literature. In 1984, when the literary critic James W. Brown published his seminal study about the function of the meal in the nineteenth century, there was little scholarly work within literary studies devoted to the place of food in literature. Though this is certainly no longer true,

Brown's foundational text, which masterfully maneuvers through the multiple culinary symbols in nineteenth-century French literature, continues to be regarded as the ur-text for what I am loosely defining here as literary food studies, long after structuralist and formalist analyses have been jettisoned for more historically grounded, politically valent modes of textual analyses. I do not mean to suggest that there is not a critical literature on food within literary studies, but rather to emphasize that this critical literature has not adequately emphasized the importance of viewing food as a discursive space able to critically interrogate the nostalgic and affective rendering of food in relationship to racial and ethnic identity. This critical literature, published primarily since the 1990s, has emerged in the footsteps of liberal multiculturalist discourse that sees food as affirming ethnic and racial difference wherein the real import of food derives purely from its symbolic functions in expressing group or cultural identity.

Sau-Ling Cynthia Wong's cogent extension of Brown's methodology has for some time now been the only literary map available to literary critics navigating the idiosyncratic and affective culinaryscapes of Asian American writing.[5] Wong's careful delineation of food as metaphor deftly maneuvers through a wide-ranging selection of canonical Asian American novels to better understand how culinary practices animate the enactment of literary tropes within Asian American literature. She is rightfully wary of the illusory promises of literary metaphors rooted in formalist analysis. Against a literary methodology that might overemphasize the validity and applicability of monolithic images, she cautions, "alimentary images being so context-sensitive, students of non-mainstream literature must guard against too facile a reliance on axiomatic principles" (19). Such an overreliance on this kind of methodology presents culinary literary discursive structures as "immanent," and the overuse of culinary-based literary axioms colludes with the tenets of liberal multiculturalism precisely because it mobilizes a language of inclusions anchored in an aestheticization of difference that too carefully sets the parameters for what can be considered "knowable."

While the years since the advent of multiculturalism have given birth to a proliferation of culinary-themed novels in Asian American literature and within the larger American publishing market, even a cursory glance through many recent collections and monographs yields similar results—food is rarely considered a serious topic of academic inquiry within literary studies. Asian American literary studies is plagued by similar anxieties, though for necessarily nonequivalent reasons. With the notable exception of Sau-Ling Wong's landmark essay, there have been few systematic attempts to map the study of culinary narratives onto studies of race and gender in Asian American literary studies. If, as literary critic Wenying Xu suggests, "a healthy and secure community does not agonize over its cuisine and rituals" ("Sticky Rice" 51), Asian America, cognitively and psychically, is a decidedly unhealthy and insecure community. As a community of scholars, readers, and writers, Asian Americans and Asian Americanists are only just beginning to formulate a critical vocabulary to think through the multiple significations of food and representations thereof within the Asian American cultural imaginary.

And yet ironically, for communities of immigrants who often find that restaurant kitchens, doughnut shops, fruit picking, and working in canneries are their first stops in America, food is more than just a source of psychic sustenance; it also feeds into the literary rendering of Asian American subjectivity. Food provides a language through which to imagine Asian alterity in the American imagination. The recent proliferation of food writing by South Asian authors, including Chitra Bannerjee Divakaruni's *Mistress of Spices* (1998), Bharati Kirchner's *Pastries: A Novel of Desserts and Discoveries* (2003), Shobha Narayan's *Monsoon Diary: A Memoir with Recipes* (2003), Amulya Malladi's *Serving Crazy with Curry* (2004), and *The Mango Season* (2003), as well as Asian American and Arab American writers more broadly—Diana Abu-Jaber's *Crescent* (2003), Linda Furiya's *Bento Box in the Heartland: My Japanese Girlhood in Whitebread America* (2006), T. C, Huo's *Thousand Wings* (1998), SunHee Kim's *Trail of Crumbs: Hunger, Love and the Search for Home* (2008), Don Lee's *Wrack and Roll* (2008) , David Mas Masumoto's *Epitaph for a Peach: Four Seasons on My Family Farm* (1995), Mei Ng's *Eating Chinese Food Naked* (1998), Bich Minh Nguyen's *Stealing Buddha's Dinner* (2007), Ruth Ozeki's *My Year of Meats* (1998) and *All Over Creation* (2003), Monique Truong's *Book of Salt* (2003), and David Wong Louie's *The Barbarians Are Coming* (2000)—suggests that a variegated literary idiom, rooted in culinary discourse, has begun to find a foothold within the literary marketplace.

In addition, there are a number of culinary scenes within staples of South Asian diasporic cultural fare, ranging from maligned works such as Bharati Mukherjee's *Jasmine* to the much-celebrated novel *The Namesake* by Pulitzer Prize–winning author Jhumpa Lahiri. For Jasmine, the title character of Mukherjee's novel, food becomes a cultural conduit connecting her with the white community surrounding her. In almost celebratory terms, she notes: "I took gobi aloo to the craft fair last week. I am subverting the tastebuds of Elsa County. I put some of last night's matar panir in the microwave. It goes well with pork, believe me" (19). Jasmine, an Indian American living in a predominantly white American rural area in Iowa, becomes the mediator of all things Indian, disciplining the white community into integrating other tastes into their palatal preferences. At the same time, she chides her Indian American relatives in immigrant enclaves in Queens, New York (where she spends an early portion of her first days in the United States), for taking pleasure in maintaining cultural norms by keeping their foodways alive.[6] Jhumpa Lahiri's first novel, *The Namesake*, on the other hand, poignantly evokes a sense of immigrant nostalgia for tastes of home from the outset of her novel. *The Namesake* begins with a scene in a kitchen in which Ashima Ganguli, the protagonist's immigrant mother, is combining Rice Krispies, Planters peanuts, red onion, salt, lemon juice, and green chili pepper as a "humble approximation of the snack sold for pennies on Calcutta sidewalks" (1) to evoke the character's location in United States, as well as her nostalgic connection to India. For Tanuja Desai Hidier and the controversial Kaavya Viswanathan, writers who target adolescent and young adult literary markets, culinary scenes emerge as an easily recognizable index of cultural alterity for the figure of the "ABCD"—American Born Confused Desi.[7] Though none of these works fall within the genre of "food writing," food emerges as a vital textual modality, one that becomes a means of articulating one's sense of ethnic or national identity.

Cursory examinations of many ethnic-themed novels will demonstrate how a visual rendering of food on novel covers is frequently also the means by which publishing houses market Asian Americanness to a readership hungry to consume delectable renditions of alterity even when the narrative may have little to no actual content focused on food and foodways. Increasingly it is also the means by which Asian American authors speak to mainstream reading publics. But this explosive interest in food writing has not been met by much interest in the topic within Asian American literary studies. Outside of Sau-Ling Wong's chapter on food and Wenying Xu's and Jennifer Ho's books, few paradigms exist for navigating the relevance of food in Asian American psychic and material lives despite the fact that food often functions as a multivalent symbol within Asian American literature. Such an omission seems particularly egregious because there is ample historical and sociological research to document how Asian American material, cultural, and political life is closely intertwined with the business of food production and the consumption of racially coded foods. Whether it is the Chinese waiters, cooks, or bus boys who populate restaurants; Vietnamese shrimp boat operators in Galveston Bay, Texas; Hmong meatpackers in northern Minnesota; Filipino and Japanese labor in the plantation economy in Hawaii in the 1930s; Chinese labor in Alaskan salmon canneries; Bangladeshi waiters in Indian restaurants in New York City; or Cambodian owners of doughnut shops in California, Asian American laborers have played a pivotal role in agribusiness, food service, and the food and beverage industry. It is through their labor that Asian Americans have become and continue to be racialized in the political and literary imaginary. Wenying Xu phrases it best in observing, "there is nothing natural or culturally predetermined about Asian Americans' vital relationship with food. Harsh circumstances made such work one of the few options available . . . they did what others wouldn't, and did it with pride and dignity" (*Eating* 12). But the absence of any serious engagement with immigrant foodways cannot be understood as an intellectual sleight against the gravity of food studies per se, or similarly, as a refusal to attach primacy to the importance of food as a vector of critical analysis. Within the specific purview of Asian American literary studies, the inattention to foodways can be better understood as an epiphenomenon of several disciplinary anxieties, elisions, and omissions that closely emanate from the ambivalence within Asian American studies toward according an overly important place to food.[8]

Some of this ambivalence is best understood with reference to Frank Chin, one of Asian American studies' most controversial authors and cultural critics. Within his expansive literary oeuvre, culinary writing— what he dubs "food pornography"—occupies a curiously abject position. Chin's militations against food writing stem from a desire to banish from Asian American rhetoric any evocation of the culinary—as psychic or real sites. His targets, most typically women authors, are those who deliberately use a culinary idiom to anchor depictions of racialized life for Asian Americans. Despite stringent critiques against Chin's bombastic rhetoric, a similar distrust of the very narratives he decries can be found within the larger body of South Asian literary studies. The critical reactions against Chitra Bannerjee Divakaruni's novels, many of which deploy "food pornography," illustrate this point well. I thus delve into questions about South Asian American texts and their relationship to food pornography in further detail in chapters 3 and 4; each chapter analyzes how food pornography operates to both buttress and dismantle narratives of racial abjection.

But while social and labor historians and anthropologists have documented the pivotal role that Asian immigrant labor played in the development of American agribusiness, the place of food in the imagination and the discursive strategy of using food to imagine race have been largely left unexplored. Without a theory to articulate how we discursively imagine those worlds through culinary tropes and alimentary images, we run the risk of replicating this logic that views Asian American literary works merely as portals into sedimented and buried histories and material realities. While there are useful and politically compelling reasons to read literary fictions for what they tell us about histories and stories of marginalized experience, Asian American literary studies too frequently resonate at the level of understanding what Asian American literature tells us about lived Asian American realities and how we might reconstruct fragmented histories through literary narratives. But writing about food, in particular, can never be exclusively an ethnographic project adhering to the principles of mimetic realism. It is seductive and not always misplaced to navigate the Asian American literary landscape by examining how representations are social facts (Rabinow) or contrarily how ethnographies are partial fictions (Clifford), but to legitimize Asian American literature solely on the basis of its ability to uncover submerged histories and fill in ethnographic details about obscured realities is to perpetuate a false divide between the aesthetic quality of "Literature" and the social relevance of "Asian American literature." We need theory and literary theory to organize how we imagine Asian America and Asian American literary and cultural production.

To frame literary analyses anchored in literary theory—structural, poststructural, psychoanalytic—as inimical to the conventions of material analysis foundational to Asian American studies is to perpetuate a false divide between Asian American literature and "Literature." To bring theory into Asian American literary critiques, as in much of the recent scholarship in Asian American literary studies, is an ethical-political project for it recognizes that Asian American literature is aesthetic and political; in "refusing the subject/structure dichotomy," literary critics can complicate the terms by which we understand subjectivity and the notion of "experience." Histories of the field have been cautious about, even suspicious of, including "high" theory for fear that theory's obfuscatory language and "gatekeeping" tendencies runs counter to the very tenets at the heart of Asian American intellectual and critical inquiry, but as David Palumbo-Liu succinctly puts it, "one cannot but 'borrow' theories and apply them to Asian American studies; however, one has to do so cautiously and critically" (55). My aim is not to supplant the methodologies and epistemological orientation of Asian American studies. Rather it is to supplement these analyses by arguing that discourse is not inimical to the material. Asian American literary and critical discourse cannot gain legitimacy solely because it happens to shed light on the material. How literary discourse epistemologically maps the material is equally important. As Kandice Chuh compellingly argues, "to underscore the literariness of "Asian American" is to argue for studying the ways that it aestheticizes and theorizes the social relations and material conditions underwriting the resistance and racism to which it refers" (28).

Culinary Fictions suggests that food organizes the discursively constructed worlds of the South Asian diaspora in more ways than we have been willing, or able, to acknowledge, either in literary studies, postcolonial studies, or Asian American studies. And yet to fully flesh out the valences of food, I take an approach to reading the place of the culinary that is both thickly descriptive and theoretical. Descriptive, because it attempts to construct a narrative that tells us how we might use food to chart a path through the complex terrain of South Asian American literature and culture, finding on the way moments that confound how we script alterity through culinary discourse. Theoretical, because it also acknowledges how we utilize food as epistemological device to navigate the imagined worlds of Asian America while simultaneously countering the notion that the only productive way to engage with food is to do so while opening a window onto the ethnic and racial lives of minoritized subjects.

I want to be clear in noting that *Culinary Fictions* is not providing an overarching theory about the relevance of food for literary studies, Asian American studies, or the confluence of the two. Instead I take on the challenge of examining the epistemological parameters for defining what is knowable about food in terms of ethnicity, race, class, and gender. The workings of the "culinary," the production of various kinds of fictions modulated by discourse about cooking, eating, and the relationship of the food to the self and communities become places to consider why it is that Asian American studies is so deeply distrustful of the culinary as mode of representation, but comfortable with thinking about food as an enduring index of ethnicity. Likewise, thinking through food allows us to consider why as critics we are more comfortable with thinking about food through its *absence*. Why, for instance, are we comfortable in theorizing hunger, collective or individual, but less able to think about consumption and desire? At the same time, what is it that as readers we are hungry for? Why do we find pleasure in consuming narratives about difference, almost as a guilty pleasure, at the same time that we are so ill at ease with navigating the contradictions inherent in the culinary narrative? I am cognizant of the importance of creating a methodologically consistent way to approach the culinary text, but also recognize that to study food, discursively or materially, is to implicitly embrace an interdisciplinary methodological and theoretical formation.

Food studies cannot be bound by a set methodology, nor can it be firmly wedded to a single discipline. Whether or not one fully agrees with Counihan and Van Esterik's assertion, it cannot be denied that literary critics interested in food engage in what Brad Epps has termed a form of "promiscuity," turning to anthropological and sociological literature on food for the ways in which it compellingly articulates food and politics while continuing to maintain a commitment to thinking about literary and cultural forms. The scant attention paid to the literary rendering of culinary practices and the popularity of the culinary as a mode of signifying difference, and rendering ethnicity and race palatable suggests that South Asian diasporic and Asian American studies might do well to take a page from African American studies, where works by Doris Witt and Larry McKee have turned to the culinary as a site of racialization, suggesting that such forms of disciplinary "promiscuity" can be vitally transformative. Where Witt hones in on the political contexts of African American material culture to render salient her readings of race and the cultural politics of food in African American culture, McKee's research into the foodways of plantation-era slaves employs methodology from archaeology to "map the range of possibilities available within the system of plantation food supply" for slaves and masters (McKee 219).[9]

Through thick readings of the varied cultural texts, *Culinary Fictions* signals how Asian American literary criticism might tap into the largely unexplored terrain of food writing in order to produce relevant analyses concerning representations about everyday encounters with food, race, and gender, thereby shifting the epistemological and methodological orientation of the existing body of Asian American literary criticism, so that is less about understanding what the literature tells us about how and what South Asians in diasporas eat, and more about how food serves as an idiom to imagine subjectivity while being attentive to the peculiar problematics the study of food poses. In focusing on the fictions of South Asian diasporic culinary works, I am not suggesting that the literary-cultural realm produces "transcendental guarantees" separable from their moments of historical conjecture. Instead, I focus on the culinary as a space for literary conjecture in order to insist that these culinary works, as fictive texts, are merely one constellation of texts within a wider series of discursive formations that enable us to better negotiate the limits of the knowable, furthering our understanding of how material practices are written about in South Asian culinary-inspired works.

Recipes for Reading

Culinary Fictions argues for the importance of understanding food not as an exclusively sociological or anthropological enterprise and asks how studying food offers insight into the discursive construction of South Asian bodies through its sustained analyses of South Asian diasporic literature and culture. The book deliberately militates against reading strategies which might seek to establish benign symmetries between food and different identitarian vectors. But it also aims to confront the perplexities of difference that animate much of recent South Asian diasporic cultural production. Food, I should stress, is not necessarily the sole focus of this study but a necessary path through which to reimagine the terms by which South Asian American subjectivity has been imagined in the wake of multiculturalism's ostensible interest in navigating "difference"—racial, ethnic, cultural. Taking stock of multiple generic forms—the short story, novel, cookbook, television show, and feature-length film—*Culinary Fictions* navigates through recent South Asian diasporic cultural production produced in the wake of multiculturalism's interest in palatable difference as a first step in better orienting Asian American studies and literary studies toward understanding the centrality of food, as an organizing thematic, as well as a theoretical point of entry into the construction of South Asian diasporic subjectivity within the recent corpus of writings, by and about South Asian diasporic formations. This book is organized into six chapters, each of which engages a particular culinary problematic—nostalgia, palatability, and fusion. Each of these chapters is then organized in pairs placed in conversation. In each chapter, I focus on the fictiveness of these culinary writings to guard against the notion that these works can allow access to immutable cultural truths about immigrant life and foodways, and to emphasize instead how writing about food is always contingent and conjectural: what food offers, I will argue, is an alternative register through which to theorize gender, sexuality, class, and race.

Part 1, ""Nostalgia, Domesticity, and Gender," includes two chapters, each of which engages with the notion that the home site produces gendered subjects. Food and cooking are among the rituals most associated with domesticity; as chapters 1 and 2 show, the culinary functions as a site of cultural negotiation: both disciplining subjects into gendered roles and buttressing an alternative rendering of sexuality and gendered performance that cannot be contained by the structures of heterosexual patriarchy. Recognizing that among the most common of the complex emotions food engenders for diasporic subjects is a sense of nostalgia, I begin with a chapter that is centered on immigrant nostalgia, asking what it means, discursively, affectively, and politically, to be nostalgic for foods coded in national terms. As this chapter suggests, the desire to remember home by fondly re-creating culinary memories cannot be understood merely as a reflectively nostalgic gesture; rather such commemorative acts must be read as a commentary on what it means to inhabit different diasporic locations while constantly battling the implications of routing memory and nostalgia through one's relationship to culinary practices. By delineating the varied logic of what I describe as "culinary citizenship," that which grants subjects the ability to articulate national identity via food, I explore how "Out on Main Street," a short story by the Toronto-based Indo-Caribbean author Shani Mootoo, and Pakistani American literary critic Sara Suleri's *Meatless Days* use food to chart viable alternatives to "official" and "traditional" models of national definition, ones that question the validity of discourses about authenticity and purity. Toward this end, I explore how each text negotiates related but divergent models of "culinary citizenship," casting food into a complex web of affiliations mediated by class and sexuality.

With greater attention to the figuration of food preparation and sexuality within the home space, I turn my attention in the next chapter to queer diasporic fictions that deliberately reimagine the terms of culinary production to accommodate how a queer vision of kinship might transform the logic of culinary practices within the home. Looking at works such as the novel *Reef* by Sri Lankan British author Romesh Gunesekera, films like Mira Nair's *Monsoon Wedding*, Deepa Mehta's *Fire*, and Shani Mootoo's *Cereus Blooms at Night*, I suggest that the queering of the home space reconfigures the meanings ascribed to culinary practices within the heterosexual home site. By exploring how food plays a role in enabling antinormative relationships to emerge within the sexualized, gendered, and classed domestic space, I argue that the relationship between food and queerness challenges the apparently seamless links between food, home, nation, and (hetero) sexuality. Collectively, these two chapters focus on the place of food in the intimate lives of diasporized communities, tending to the notion that food evokes a complex set of emotions about home, longing, and belonging.

Following Sau-Ling Wong's point that eating and food cogently illustrate patterns of subjectification and objectification in Asian American literature, I argue that culinary narratives fall within the range of "acceptable" interventions—safely ethnic, and nonpolitical because they figuratively serve marginalia up on a platter. Often, more overtly political forms of writing are less visible on the Asian American literary landscape because Asian Americans must "find a frame of reference accessible and acceptable to 'mainstream' Americans" (Chu 15). In Asian American literature, narratives about food occupy a similar position to the mother-daughter tale, or the tale of the displaced immigrant's nostalgia. Such narratives have been viewed with suspicion because they are an appealing form of writing that appears to be ethnically affirmative and "merely" cultural. Their apparent lack of "hard" political content, and attention to the social and cultural, make these thematic interventions "acceptable" to the mainstream. With this in mind, chapters 3 and 4 focus on the genre—anathema to most Americanist critique—of the "food porn" novel. Chapter 3 examines two such novels frequently omitted from literary studies which have found their way into the hearts of the North American reading public—Bharati Kirchner's *Pastries: A Novel of Desserts and Discoveries* and Chitra Bannerjee Divakaruni's *Mistress of Spices*. Through lush evocation of spices and sugared treats, each novel mobilizes a culinary idiom sweetened or spiced with the taste of otherness. By engaging the texts' use of Orientalism to render race palatable, I ask if it is possible to wrest a novel's surface-level sugariness from the weighty issues lodged within the narratives. My reading of *Mistress of Spices* and *Pastries* suggests that belying the spicy-sugary exterior of these popular novels are surprisingly trenchant critiques of racial politics and capitalism in the United States. I therefore examine the very packaging of novels as "commodity-comestibles" to ask if there are generic limitations to the food novel, and its ability to advance a critique of class and labor.

My optimism for finding enabling narratives within this much maligned genre is further developed in the next chapter, which maintains its focus on Chitra Bannerjee Divakaruni by turning to her poem "The Makers of Chili Paste," anthologized in her largely overlooked poetry collection *Leaving Yuba City*. Long considered one of the South Asian diasporic writers who too easily fabricates diasporic worlds, Chitra Bannerjee Divakaruni has often been critiqued within South Asian and

Asian American studies. I implicitly engage this body of criticism by considering how the poem triangulates with a series of other cultural forms, inspired by the film *Mirch Masala* (Chili Masala), a film about women employed in the chili trade in India. This same film provides critical fodder for a short experimental video, *Unbidden Voices,* about restaurant workers in Chicago. Placed in conversation with each other *Unbidden Voices, Mirch Masala,* and "The Makers of Chili Paste" reveal how a visual aesthetic, geared toward focusing on the conditions of labor, deprivileges an aesthetic of visual consumption in order to advance a critique of the genre of food pornography. Through this deterritorialization of the genre of the "food film," these works collectively augur a class critique attuned to the exigencies of labor, class, and capital in the business of food production.

In a book that troubles the logic of understanding the relationship between food and different types of conjectural subjectivities for South Asian Americans at the same time that it negotiates how and why food becomes a way to anchor cultural identity, it is fitting to include a section on the meanings food occupies within the social and cultural imaginary of second-generation South Asian diasporic cultural brokers. The final two chapters of the book focus almost exclusively on visual media and literature from the United States. Each chapter is structured around an engagement with legislative acts that have vitally impacted the tenor and nature of immigration from India and concomitant changes in the position of South Asians as we enter an era of increasing xenophobia, marked by ever more punitive forms of legislation against persons of South Asian or Muslim origin. Centering on the types of inclusions that the 1965 Immigration and Nationality Act ostensibly enabled, chapter 5 focuses on short fiction by second-generation Indian Americans such as Jhumpa Lahiri, Pooja Makhijani, and Geeta Kothari; a cooking show featuring Maya Kaimal; and the film *Harold and Kumar Go to White Castle.* These works are not bound together by content but by an implicit awareness of how culinary identities have been vitally shaped and reshaped for the first generation to come of age in the United States after the 1965 Immigration and Nationality Act.

Consistent with the notion that the second generation of Indian Americans is often represented as harbingers of a new form of cosmopolitanism, arguably even a new form of racial fusion, I examine a version of culinary culture that is often celebrated as the first "postnational" cuisine, befitting the second generation—fusion cuisine. When we consider that historically South Asians have been excluded from psychic, juridical, and social definitions of citizenship, because they are seen to be too "alien," or "foreign" or "inassimilable," how can we interpret the vogue in fusion cuisine that celebrates the coming together of so called "Asianness" and "Westernness"? To ground my analysis, I explore several fusion cuisine cookbooks authored by Raji Jallepalli and Floyd Cardoz. In the case of the latter, I also offer a reading of the restaurant Tabla, where Floyd Cardoz is executive chef. Within the context of U.S. multicultural and racial discourses about Asian Americans as model minorities who are to be emulated because they have so readily assimilated, what does it mean to celebrate fusion cuisine while the U.S. state apparatuses and governing bodies such as the Bureau of Citizenship and Immigration Services (BCIS) actively foment a culture of suspicion that renders those very brown bodies producing the food so suspect. To examine these questions, I look at how second-generation cultural brokers renovate the concept of fusion cuisine to advance a critique of U.S. multiculturalism. My objects of study here are a novel by Denmark-based Indian author Amulya Malladi titled *Serving Crazy with Curry*. Malladi's novel, set in Southern California, examines how a version of fusion cuisine takes on a quasi-therapeutic function for a suicidal Indian American. Yet far from viewing fusion as a palliative for cultural schizophrenia, Malladi's novel stages the difficulties involved in ascribing an ameliorative psychic capability to cooking. I read cooking shows and cookbooks featuring Padma Lakshmi's versions of fusion cuisine against this novel as a way to suggest that the trope of fusion expands the vision of the second generation to accommodate narratives which speak to moments of racial abjection, produced against the experience of negotiating the muddy and often complex terrain of cultural schizophrenia.

* * *

The widely different contexts evoked by each chapter signal to the ways in which the culinary is imbricately layered into the cultural imagination of the South Asian diaspora. In my attempt to provide a consistent way to think through food, I want to suggest that we need to be careful how we negotiate the terrain of culinary fictions. To merely call for placing food at the center for critical analysis—literary, anthropological, historical, or sociological—is to recast the terms of this age-old debate about the relevance of food studies into a simple dualistic model of "inclusions" and "exclusions" that has arguably worked to the detriment of a politically transformative approach to Asian American literary studies. Models of Asian American studies that position South Asians at the center of critical analyses in order "to correct for under-representation without critiquing its basic assumptions," as some have argued, "leads to the replication of the model, with new centers, and perhaps slightly altered margins" (Davé, Dhingra et al. 76). Analogously, it is inadequate to merely call for a realignment of food studies by countering the argument that food scholarship is not serious and by demanding its inclusion within critical conversations about race, gender, and ethnic studies. For that matter, it is not enough to protest charges against food studies as "scholarship lite" by signaling to the numerous texts offering rigorous engagements with food and culture. It is important to examine how food is an equally important vector of critical analysis in negotiating the gendered, racialized, and classed bases of collective and individual identity. It is with this caveat in mind that this book examines the culinary as an enunciative space, one that vitally articulates race, food, class, labor, and culture.

PART ONE

NOSTALGIA, DOMESTICITY, AND GENDER

1 / Culinary Nostalgia: Authenticity, Nationalism, and Diaspora

Culinary practices situate themselves at the most rudimentary level, at the most necessary and the most unrespected level.
        —LUCE GIARD, "THE NOURISHING ARTS"

The diaspora women who thought Culture
meant being able to create
a perfect mango chutney in New Jersey
were scorned by the visiting scholar
from Bombay—who was also a woman
but unmarried and so different.

                        —SUJATA BHATT, "CHUTNEY"

Behind the assiduous documentation and defense of the authentic lies an unarticulated anxiety of losing the subject.
        —REGINA BENDIX, *IN SEARCH OF AUTHENTICITY*

In her short autobiographical essay "Food and Belonging: At 'Home' and in 'Alien' Kitchens," Indian American cultural critic Ketu Katrak suggests that culinary narratives, suffused with nostalgia, often manage immigrant memories and imagined returns to the "homeland." Narrativizing her own migratory journey from Bombay to the United States, she remarks, "my own memorybanks about food overflowed only after I left India to come to the United States as a graduate student. The disinterest in food that I had felt during my childhood years was transformed into a new kind of need for that food as an essential connection with home. I longed for my native food as I dealt with my dislocation from the throbbing Bombay metropolis" (270). Food becomes both intellectual and emotional anchor for her as an immigrant subject, psychically transporting Katrak to her geographically and temporally distant childhood home and giving her a sense of rootedness in the United States. And yet, she also acknowledges how the experience of dislocation, modulated by a nostalgic longing for the familiar, is deeply rooted in the creation of imaginary fictions that distort the lived realities of her pre–Asian American life:

Food was not pleasurable to me as a child. Thinking about this now as an adult, I can say that food was an overdetermined category for me in my childhood years; it tasted of the heady tropical environment, it delineated who was in and out of favor with my father. I tasted anxiety in the onions fried a bit too brown and tension in the too many dark burned spots on the roasted papad. One never knew what would be considered faulty at a particular meal, and the uncertainty overwhelmed any pleasure in what was eaten. (266–67)

Katrak's honesty registers the affective value of food and smells and, in the process, reflects the nostalgia that structures memories of home for the immigrant subject. Recalling Salman Rushdie's take on nostalgia and historical memory in his now classic essay "Imaginary Homelands," she cautions against a tendency to transform nostalgia for the ineffable into an idealization of the past. In "Imaginary Homelands," Rushdie sets in motion a complex investigation into the condition of the diasporic exilic writer. As he so eloquently puts it, "It may be that when the Indian writer who writes from outside India tries to reflect the world, he is obliged to deal in broken mirrors, some of whose fragments have been irretrievably lost" (9). Seeing the past through the shards of a mirror inevitably distorts the idealized memory one has of a "homeland": owing to the exigencies of displacement and dislocation, certain memories are remembered, while others, literally, are re-membered. As Rushdie moves us through the problem of memory and mimetic fidelity, he tells a story about returning to India after an absence of many years. He draws an analogy between an old black-and-white photograph of his childhood home taken prior to his birth and his perceptions of his childhood. With the passage of time and movement to different spaces, "the colours of history had seeped out of my mind's eye" (9): nostalgia intervenes to colorize, or, in this case, decolorize, the past, reducing it to a pale imitation of what it might have been to the mind's eye.

I begin this chapter with this brief, but necessary trail through these two short essays to highlight how nostalgia is always already predetermined, indeed overdetermined, in scripting immigrant attachment to the past. Further, both essays highlight some fundamental "truths" about the immigrant condition—the desire to simultaneously embrace what is left of a past from which one is spatially and temporally displaced, and the recognition that nostalgia can overwhelm memories of the past, allowing, as Rushdie so appropriately puts it, the colors of history to seep out of the mind's eye. Katrak's essay draws attention to the imprecise rendering of personal memory by using a culinary idiom to reflect familial tensions in her childhood home. She traces the contours of her ambivalence and shows how food takes on a nostalgic significance only upon her migrating to the United States. Such distortions of actual memories, normatively coded as an unconscious desire to attach primacy to the purity of childhood memories, underscore how the immigrant's memories of the past are always contingent: reflected in, and refracted through, the fragmented shards of a mirror, one in which nostalgia restructures how memories are seen.

As its focal point, this chapter examines the discursive and affective place rather than the symbolic or semiotic value of food in nostalgic narratives of dislocation. The desire to remember home by fondly re-creating culinary memories cannot be understood merely as reflectively nostalgic gestures; rather, such nostalgically framed narratives must also be read as a metacritique of what it means to route memory and nostalgic longing for a homeland through one's relationship to seemingly intractable culinary practices which unflinchingly yoke national identity with culinary taste and practices. By elaborating on the varied logic of what I call "culinary citizenship"—that which grants subjects the ability to claim and inhabit certain identitarian positions via their relationship to food—I explore how reinterpretations of official and traditional models of national definition are scripted in a culinary idiom. To negotiate how divergent but related models of "culinary citizenship" cast food into a complex web of affiliations mediated by class and sexuality, I consider how vestigial nostalgia for homelands among communities of recent immigrants who maintain financial and affective ties with their "homelands," for instance, can lead to the creation of distorted fictions, which imagine cuisines as discrete, immutable, and coherent expressions of unfaltering national essences.

Drawing on what may seem like an eclectic group of texts, this chapter works through and against those gaps in Asian American literary studies to bring to the table narratives that mine the potential of establishing food as an idiom for expressing nostalgic desire. The works I examine are a short story by Indo-Trinidadian Canadian author Shani Mootoo titled "Out on Main Street"; *An Invitation to Indian Cookbook* by Madhur Jaffrey, the prolific author of numerous cookbooks who has been described as "the virtuosa of Indian cooking in the West" (P. Roy 477); as well as Sara Suleri's memoirs, *Meatless Days*. All use food to fashion critiques of nostalgic longings for home, and, in the process, each text positions culinary discourse as an always available script for negotiating the pangs of migratory displacement. I route my reading of these tales about food and diasporic memories by exploring the entangled web of affiliations created between the language of food, nostalgia, and desire, foregrounding how memory itself is distorted and re-created in the diasporic imaginary of subjects who are multiply located and ambivalent about their own tenuous connections with a "home" contiguous with the geographic parameters of South Asia. Autobiographically speaking, Suleri and Mootoo's own relationships with "home," and a "homeland" are complicated by their status as bicultural and multiracial subjects. Sara Suleri, who was born to a Welsh mother and a Pakistani father and currently lives and works in the United States as a professor at Yale University, offers a poignant glimpse into her fractured subjectivity as she comes of age within an upper-class household in postcolonial Pakistan. Oscillating between life back "there" in Pakistan, and "here" in the United States, *Meatless Days* is a complex attempt to both retell the author's experiences of growing up bicultural and biracial, and to cast asunder the categories and mechanisms used to construct an autobiographical narrative of one's life from a temporally and spatially distanced present. With her multiracial status (Irish and Indo-Caribbean), South Asian Canadian author Shani Mootoo earned literary fame with the publication of her novel *Cereus Blooms at Night* (1996) as well as her earlier collection of stories, *Out on Main Street* (1993). The texts by Jaffrey and Mootoo have rarely entered into Asian American literary criticism. *Meatless Days*, a favorite text in postcolonial and diaspora studies, has enjoyed greater visibility, but the intellectual fodder provided by this text infrequently emerges from the culinary dimensions of the work. While foodways and representations thereof are not the only narratival axes in Suleri's or Mootoo's work, they play an important role in each narrative and intervene into debates about displacement and plural subjectivities rendered legible when food is placed at the center of critical analysis.

Fabricating Authenticity: Madhur Jaffrey's
Invitation to Indian Cooking

As hinted at by the lines from Sujata Bhatt's "Chutney" quoted in the epigraph to this chapter, diasporic women—diasporic married women—are often wedded to the belief that the faithful reproduction of "culture" inheres in accurately replicating, for instance, the perfect mango chutney. The domestic arena, so frequently associated with femininity, also becomes a space to reproduce culture and national identity. Immigrants, as Katrak's essay demonstrably illustrates, are invested in an image of the homeland as an unchanging and enduring cultural essence and are often singular about the ontological coherency of their national cuisines, despite the fact that memories are fragmentary, partial, and "irretrievably lost" (9). The mirror as a symbol of the reflective is powerfully resignified in Rushdie's essay such that it is not simply a surface to reflect reality, but one that distorts and tempers realities. Anthropologist Kathleen Stewart unravels the bases of these distortions which lead individuals to unconsciously nostalgize fragmentary knowledge of the past. Stewart defines nostalgia as "a cultural practice, not a given context; its forms, meanings, and effects shift with the context—it depends on where the speaker stands in the landscape of the present" (252). For upper-class Indian immigrants located in the United States such as cookbook author and culinary aficionado Madhur Jaffrey, cooking is one such cultural practice resignified, reinterpreted, and even distorted within the diasporic imaginary. In her autobiographically organized cookbook *An Invitation to Indian Cooking,* cooking "Indian" food stands in as a signifier of a connection with a place "back there." Concurrently, the desire for Indian food is mediated by a form of nostalgia that can only exist once she has left the physical borders of "India." The conditions of becoming diasporic, or living diasporically, produce a fundamental and affective longing for Indian-coded comestibles. In words reminiscent of Katrak's critical ethnographic essay, Jaffrey candidly observes: "It was when I was twenty and went to England as a student that I started to learn how to cook. I was extremely homesick, and this homesickness took the form of a longing for Indian food" (4). If India is reified as that mythic space "back there," the originary point from which the Indian immigrant to the United States emerges, it is because the recipes contained in cookbooks such as *An Invitation to Indian Cooking* strategically mobilize nostalgic memories of the past to enhance the value of the recipe for a readership hungry to consume "authentic" difference. In a recipe for eggplant bharta, a smoked eggplant dish typically found on menus of Indian restaurants in the United States, Jaffrey introduces the recipe with the following narrative:

> Until the advent of gas, most cooking in India was done on wood or coal, and one of the waste products of wood and coal is, of course, ash. Not wishing to waste even a waste product, we geared our cuisine so that while some foods were cooking on top of the flame, others were being roasted in the ashes. (Later, the ash was used like Comet to scour the pots and pans.) As a child, I remember begging

the cook to put some onions in the ashes, just for me. He would
pick out a tiny onion from the vegetable basket and bury it deep in
the ashes with his iron tongs. Then, about an hour later, he would
whisper to me that it was ready. I would pick off the burned outside,
scorching my hands as I did so, and gobble up the succulent inside.
(162)

A flavor of authenticity is added to Jaffrey's recipe for eggplant bharta because it is routed through a tale of childhood nostalgia for authentically
"Indian" dishes, steeped in tradition and prepared with love. Kathleen
Stewart argues that nostalgia rises to importance as a cultural practice,
and is structured more as "feelings": "the search for a past and a place
leads them to reconstitute their lives in narrative form, a story designed
to reassemble a broken history into a new whole" (261). The story encas-
ing the eggplant bharta recipe is one such reassembled story. For volun-
tary exiles and immigrants such as Jaffrey, culture—culinary culture—
is associated with "feelings" that take on monolithic and mythological
proportions. The actual, rather than affective, place of eggplant bharta
in Madhur Jaffrey's life may be of secondary importance. She tells a tale
about producing an authentic version of Indian cooking seductively
framed by a premodern tale of a simpler time, when eggplant bharta was
prepared over ashes, while remaining cognizant of the nostalgia for the
past driving her to seek creative strategies to fabricate authenticity:

Over the years, I discovered that the electric blender could do
much of what the grinding stone did, and much faster; that instead
of roasting eggplants in hot ashes as my mother recommended,
I could do it directly over a gas burner; that American meats just
couldn't be fried the Indian way because they contained too much
water and that it was often better to cook with canned tomatoes
than fresh ones because they had more taste and color. Slowly I began changing the recipes to suit the conditions. I managed to arrive
at the genuine taste of traditional dishes, but often had to take quite
a circuitous and unorthodox route to get there. (5)

Jaffrey's conscious attempts to fabricate authenticity are modulated by the
anxiety to reproduce authenticity, while trying to create a sense of home
and belonging in adopted homes and kitchens. This desire to feel at home
can elicit nostalgia for things that never were—nostalgia for a past blind
in some ways to the structural inequities and forms of difference that
might structure the past. Jaffrey's strategies to fabricate authenticity are

tempered by a logic that seeks to fix her own past in a particular moment free of care and worry, while simultaneously catering to a readership in search of the ever-elusive authentic Indian food. "Authentic" dishes exist in Jaffrey's repertoire, and by emphasizing creativity and innovation in the kitchen, she can re-create the conditions of an anterior original essence. At the same time, Jaffrey's palpable ambivalence about affirming a unified culinary national essence, one which faithfully reproduces an authentic Indianness, emerges in the autobiographical preface to her cookbook. She is reluctant to classify the varied cuisines of India under the homogenizing label "Indian," yet at other times the cookbook replicates the logic of hegemonic Indianness she seeks to complicate. Jaffrey is cognizant of the problems of purporting to cover all of Indian cuisine within the pages of one cookbook. She reminds her readers, "if you are looking for an encyclopedic tome encompassing all Indian food, you won't find it here," explaining that her book offers readers "the chance to understand and cook the food of one specific area—the region in and around Delhi, including the adjacent sections of Uttar Pradesh" (13).

Jaffrey, to be sure, is cognizant of the fine distinctions between the palatal preferences of Indians: "Indians can be divided into the rice-eaters and wheat-eaters. While most of South India and Bengal are considered rice-eating areas, Delhi, Punjab, Uttar Pradesh and Madhya Pradesh are generally considered to be the wheat-eating areas" (180). But to weave a coherent and compelling narrative, Jaffrey frequently alludes to what "we Indians" eat, evoking a secularist definition of national unity. Indianness, paradoxically, becomes defined broadly with attention to regional differences, but also reinscribes the hegemony of North Indian cuisine within Indian culinary repertoire by creating a cookbook in which the regional is conflated with the national.[1]

Yearning to nostalgically remember the simplicity of childhood and life back in the "homeland" while simultaneously being cognizant of the impossibility of this endeavor, Jaffrey's autobiographical musings and anecdotal stories bear traces of the classic immigrant story. Her reluctance to reify a monolithically defined Indian national identity is but one manifestation of having one's identity "minoritized." As cultural critic R. Radhakrishnan usefully reminds us, "we must keep in mind that in the United States the renaming of ethnic identity in national terms produces a preposterous effect. Take the case of the Indian immigrant. Her naturalization into American citizenship minoritizes her identity. She is now reborn as an ethnic minority American citizen. Is this empowerment or marginalization? This new American citizen must think of herself as an ethnic self that defers to her nationalized American status. The culturally and politically hegemonic Indian identity is now a mere qualifier: "ethnic" (205). Like the hypothetical Indian immigrant who figures in Radhakrishnan's formulations, Jaffrey's adopted persona in *Invitation* grapples with the minoritized status of Indian cuisine, marked in the minds of U.S. consumers as an ethnic cuisine. Jaffrey's text does not deny India's culinary diversity, but it also rejects the idea that Indian cuisine is always only an "ethnic" cuisine. Indian cuisine is strategically reified in her text to insist on its integrity as a "whole" and national entity.

In her text, the impossible task of the Indian in the United States is to make "Americans" aware of the cultural and culinary diversity and unity of India. Although she writes to an audience of "Americans" (presumably white), she also writes to Indian readers. This is most apparent in the introduction to the volume, where she describes the book as "a gradual maneuver in self-defense" (4), explaining, "there is no place in New York, or anywhere in America where top-quality Indian food can be found—except of course, in private Indian homes" (4). Explaining how this deflates her American friends fond of Indian food, she continues, "at this their faces fall and I begin to feel a familiar upsurge of guilt and patriotic responsibility . . . someone had to let Americans know what authentic Indian food was like and that I couldn't heartlessly ignore their curiosity and interest" (4). Placing patriotism squarely in the middle of her agenda, Jaffrey's words are also directed to an audience of responsible and "patriotic" Indians in the United States who care enough about their nation's culinary image to portray an "authentic" version of Indianness in the space of their homes and will then presumably turn to Jaffrey for guidance. Women—most frequently, though not unproblematically, associated with their positions within the domestic cultural economy—are often charged with maintaining the edifice of home life. As Partha Chatterjee has compellingly argued, "in the entire phase of the nationalist struggle, the crucial need was to protect, preserve and strengthen the inner core of the national culture. Its spiritual essence . . . The home was the principal site for expressing the spiritual quality of the national culture, and women must take the main responsibility of protecting and nurturing this quality. No matter what the changes in the external condition of life for women, they must not lose their essentially spiritual (i.e. feminine) virtues; they must not, in other words, become *essentially* westernized" (239). The home site becomes a space in which to produce a version of Indianness. As Sujata Bhatt's poem reminds us, nationalist discourse frequently casts the woman as a broker of cultural traditions. Diasporas produce their own version of this gendered logic, by repeatedly insisting it is the task of the female Indian immigrant subject in diaspora, or in this case, the cookbook author, to be vigilant about the faithful reproduction of Indianness.

While popular discourse insists on the clear recognizability of culinary "Indianness," cuisines are rarely structured by such uncomplicated and benign symmetries between food and nation.[2] Even while it is the implicit task of the Indian immigrant female subject to reproduce culinary Indianness with the help of cookbooks such as Jaffrey's *Invitation*, the historical circulation of commodities and spices between colonized spaces has sullied the bases of defining a "pure" Indian cuisine.[3] As historian Sucheta Mazumdar's careful reading of national origins within the context of the international trade in food and commodities suggests, "Indian" is not a clearly demarcated category within the world of food commodities. The argument that a particular dish is "Indian" because it combines "Indian" staples such as chili peppers, tomatoes, or cashews does not (and perhaps cannot) adequately take into account that "Indian" foods might come from somewhere else. Yet to brand this desire to view certain foodways as "essentially" Indian as an idiosyncratic conceit fails to grapple with the deep nostalgic investment in considering certain types of food to be authentically, and autochthonously, "Indian." Jaffrey's cookbooks chronicling the diverse array of Indian cuisines might, at least in part, be linked to the symbolic regional, or national sentimental significance attached to particular dishes. For the diasporic immigrant subject such as the Indian women in Sujata Bhatt's poem, mango chutney does not bear any independent intrinsic value as comestible; its value inheres in its symbolic connection to an articulation of national identity. In a vastly different context, that of the nostalgic-driven culinary preferences of Punjabis in contemporary India, as well as in diaspora, consumption of overtly ethnically coded food may well be about matters other than eating and palatal pleasure. As Mazumdar puts it, "eating *makkai ki roti* (corn flat breads) with *sarson ka sag* (mustard greens) in the spring is more of a symbolic statement of Punjabi regional identity today that nostalgically celebrates the rural roots of its sons of the soil rather than an accurate reflection of the levels of maize consumption in Punjabi history" (72).

"Meatless Days" and Culinary Nostalgia

Eating dishes such as *makkai ki roti* to affirm a Punjabi identity strongly resonates at a symbolic level, but as Pakistani American literary critic and author Sara Suleri points out in her memoirs, immigrants remain deeply invested in the ontological coherency of their culinary memories for reasons that exceed mere symbolism. Indeed, it is this nostalgia that drives immigrants, as Suleri puts it, to become "adamant, entirely passionate about such matters as the eating habits of the motherland" (22). *Meatless Days* is a self-reflexive memoir that provides snapshot glimpses into the life of Sara Suleri as she comes of age, both literally and intellectually, in postcolonial Pakistan. Food and culinariness are important thematic threads woven throughout the fabric of the text, but it is particularly in the second chapter, appropriately titled "Meatless Days," that Suleri provides the most substantial "food for thought." This chapter follows on the heels of the oft-discussed first chapter, "In the Company of Women," which ends with the (in)famous claim, "there are no women in the third world" (20), a phrase that has been debated at length within postcolonial, Asian American, and feminist literary studies. The chapter is an extended mediation on culinary memories spanning Sara's preemigration childhood, to her experiences as an adult in Connecticut and New York. It also draws attention to the mechanisms by which diasporic subjects grapple with the desire to fix memories and nostalgize the past. The last sentence of the previous chapter, "There are no women in the third world," invites a critique of categories. "Woman" and "third world" are denaturalized, configured instead as terms that fail to take account of the reality of those who might be considered to be "women" inhabiting this particular location in the "third world." This final sentence lends a symmetry to her deliberately polemical opening,

> the concept of woman was not really part of an available vocabulary: we were too busy for that, just living and conducting precise negotiations with what it meant to be a sister or a child or a wife or a mother or servant. (1)

But her list of other subject positions—child, sister, wife, mother, or servant—marks an implicit class bias. "Servants" are a subcategory of womanhood, but their only role is as servant; within Suleri's world, servants do not appear to exist as mothers, sisters, or wives. In Suleri's fiction, the culinary emerges as important counterdiscourse, destabilizing the mechanisms by which gendered national subjectivity is granted visibility and legitimacy in postcolonial spaces, at the same time that underlying class tensions complicate the potentially subversive aspects of the text. In the larger conversation from which this reflection is drawn, Suleri and friends debate over the accurate meaning of *kapura*. In the chapter titled, like her memoirs, "Meatless Days," Suleri tells a series of culinary tales in which Sara is repeatedly confounded by the ways in which food is never quite what it seems to be.[4] Narrating a tale about how she comes to equate sweetbreads with *kapura*, she marks her horror at receiving an "unequivocal response: *kapura*, as naked meat, equals a testicle" (21). She re-creates the scene of a conversation amid the "taut companionship of Pakistanis in New York" (21) when *kapura* becomes the topic of discussion:

> "But," and here I rummaged for the sweet realm of nomenclature, "couldn't *kapura* on a lazy occasion accommodate something like sweetbreads, which is just a nice way of saying that pancreas is not a pleasant word to eat?" No one, however, was interested in this finesse.
>
> "Balls, darling, balls," someone drawled, and I knew I had to let go of the subject. (19)

Sara wishes to think of *kapura* in more finessed and palatable terms under the misnomer "sweetbreads," but even as she admits to having to "let go of the subject," it continues to haunt her. Her desperate need for *kapura* to be sweetbreads is not merely about wanting to hold onto a childhood wish of thinking of *kapura* as a palatable item, or a "pleasant word to eat," it is also a symptom of Sara's desire to attach a primacy to her own (perhaps willful) distorted modes of naming foods.

While Suleri's attempts to be coy are undercut by an unequivocal affirmation that *kapura* are indeed male genitalia, Sara digests this revelation to mark her own uncertainty about the sanctity of epistemological, and ontological categories. She observes, "I was shocked. It was my mother after all, who had told me that sweetbreads are sweetbreads, and if she were wrong on that score, how many other simple equations had I now to doubt?" (23). Suleri's desire to know exactly what *kapura* is can be read as a symptom of her own location among a U.S.-based community of Pakistani expatriates. She nostalgically yearns for things to remain as she has remembered them, but she must confront a logic endorsed by cultural purists who refuse to accommodate alternative namings and culinary logic inconsistent with their memories and official renderings of history.

Later, she points out how in her childhood in Pakistan, "Our days and our newspapers were equally full of disquieting tales about adulterated foods and [the] preternaturally keen eye that the nation keeps on such promiscuous blendings" (29). She continues, "I can understand it, the fear that food will not stay discrete but will instead defy our categories of expectation in what can only be described as a manner of extreme belligerence. I like order to a plate, and know the great sense of failure that attends a moment when what is potato to the fork is turnip to the mouth. It's hard when such things happen" (29). Yet at the same time that she fears transmogrifications of potato into turnip, she also recognizes how a project that demands that food remain within neat borders might be doomed to fail. Even the "meatless days"— periods when meat would not be sold in local markets—are anything but "meatless." They are marked instead by the conspicuous consumption of all manner of carnivorous edibles by the wealthier families. As Suleri puts it, those "who could afford to buy meat, after all, were those who could afford refrigeration" (31). Commenting on the so-called meatless days, Suleri writes:

> the only thing the government accomplished was to make some people's Mondays very busy indeed. The Begums had to remember to give the cooks thrice as much money; the butchers had to produce thrice as much meat; the cooks had to buy enough flesh and fowl and other sundry organs to keep an averagely carnivorous household eating for three days . . . And so instead of creating an atmosphere of abstention in the city, the institution of meatless days rapidly came to signify the imperative behind the acquisition of all things fleshy. We thought about beef which is called "big meat," and we thought about mutton which is called "little meat," and then we collectively thought about chicken, the most coveted of them all. (33)

Her numerous tales of culinary transmogrification—hard-boiled eggs breaking out of their shells to form "gills and frills" (36); *kapura* that might be sweetbreads, testicles, or pancreas; potatoes that feel like turnips; meatless days during which the nation's elite voraciously consumed meat; and kidneys being associated with *kapura*—are more than mere nostalgic reversions to the past; these culinary transmogrifications are conscious attempts to repudiate master narratives proclaiming an authentic Pakistani subject. Suleri articulates her own uneasiness about presenting a complete and seamless narrative about her childhood memories of culinarity, admitting, "perhaps I should have been able to bring those bits together, but such a narrative was not available to me, not after what I knew of storytelling" (39):

my sisters and I would place ourselves in time by remembering and
naming cooks . . . there is something nourishing about the memory of all these shadow dynasties: we do not have to subsist only on
the litany that begins, "After General Ayub came General Yahya;
after the Bhutto years came General Zulu Haq," but can also add;
"Qayuum begat Shorty and his wife; and they begat the Punjabi
poet only called Khansama; he begat Ramzan and Karam Dad the
bearer; Ramzan begat Tassi-Passi, and he begat Allah Ditta, mean-
est of them all." (34)

Underlying the humor of using biblical language to describe the line of
cooks that passed through the Suleri household is an attempt to replace
the national(ist) hegemonic narrative with a consciously feminist script.
Sara's own tenuous connection with the past refuses to be circumscribed
by a patriarchal nationalist logic; rather, Sara strategically remembers
the past and commemorates the past on her own terms, rendering the
official face of Pakistan tangential to her own personal history, which
includes the domestic workers and cooks, or *khansamas* (Muslim cooks)
in her household. The Martinican theorist and poet Edouard Glissant
similarly comments on the political weight of alternatively rendered histories, a central feature of popular discourse in Caribbean cultural life.
Contaminations, politically and ideologically favorable in comparison
with the purported original, reject binary discourses of authenticity and
imitation:

The only traces of "genesis" identifiable in the Caribbean folktale
are satirical and mocking. God removed the White man [pale] too
soon from the oven of Creation; the Black man [burnt] too late;
this version would have us believe that the mulatto—with whom
the Caribbean would therefore wish to identify—is the only one to
be properly cooked. But another version of these three baked crea-
tures claims that the first was in fact not dark enough, the second
not sufficiently cooked [mulattoes], and the third just right [blacks].
The Martinican consciousness is always tormented by contradictory possibilities. These parodies of genesis do not seriously claim, in
any case, to offer an explanation for origins; they imply a satirical
attitude to any notion of a transcendental genesis. (141–42)

At the same time that Suleri's alternatively rendered history rejects hegemonic narratives of official historical doctrine, it is blind to the incommensurability of her class position and those of the very people she

claims are written out of the patriarchal national narrative. As literary critic Samir Dayal notes, "the problematic sign of class is raised only to be whisked away from under our noses by sleight of hand" (255). Suleri imagines herself linked to the cooks who are denied the agency to speak from their subject positions about their labor in the household. But with the exception of Qayuum, the cook who works in the Suleri household for a number of years, the voices of the cooks do not emerge in this chapter. The cooks serve, instead, as her personal yardstick, enabling Suleri to bask nostalgically in the memory of what the meatless days meant for her during her privileged days within the safe space of the Suleri household in Karachi, Pakistan. Suleri acknowledges that only the poor had to go without meat on the meatless days, but her nostalgic re-creation of eating meat during those days emerges at the expense of a discussion that might explore how and why those days became busy for the domestic workers who had to procure additional meat on the days preceding the meatless days of the week. She refers to what "we" used to eat during the meatless days, nostalgically recalling that elaborate meat dishes were prepared for them, but does not explore the role played by domestic workers in creating these sumptuous dishes or what they might have eaten. Their labors remain largely invisible to the nostalgic eye of Suleri, the writer, as well as Sara, the child. Suleri, the writer, seems to want to negotiate difficult issues and the problem of creating different categories to understand her historical and material positioning as a woman, but "servants" are not "women," and "cooks" are not part of her rhetorically constructed collective "we."

Following Michel Foucault, we must acknowledge the implicit epistemic violence involved in codifying discursive language. Linguistically, the categories we use to describe alterity create new hierarchies of difference. In the process of fashioning a language of inclusivity, new systems of classification, and hierarchical configurations are set into motion. Suleri's feminist-cosmopolitan project consciously rewrites the historical script, marking her affiliation with cooks rather than with the leaders of the nations in the service of a "feminine knowledge" (Carter 162) that "documents the perplexities of differences" (157), as Mia Carter argues, but Suleri's textual and political disruptions are indelibly bound to her class privilege, implicitly jettisoning other forms of knowledge. In producing an alternative discursive order, she creates new systems of classifications, arrangement, and distribution. Cooks, servants, and women are nonactors in Suleri's narrative, and are denied the pleasures of nostalgia, the very thing fuelling Suleri's desire to reimagine culinary practices, flouting conventional narratives of authenticity, and to render history otherwise.

"Kitchen Indians": Competing Notions of Indianness

And yet, the desire to imagine cuisines as authentic manifestations of national essences continues to haunt the psychic dimensions of immigrant nostalgia in South Asian American fiction. In Shani Mootoo's short story "Out on Main Street," two South Asian Americans, immigrants from Fiji and Trinidad, feud over who can claim ownership to a particular type of "Indian" dessert. Best known for her novel *Cereus Blooms at Night,* Shani Mootoo's fictional oeuvre inhabits interstitial diasporic spaces, unnamed and yet phantasmatically recognizable as diasporic contact zones. The scene of the title story of Shani Mootoo's collection *Out on Main Street* is an Indian eatery, Kush Valley Sweets, on Main Street, Toronto. The unnamed narrator and her girlfriend, Janet, both Indo-Trinidadians, frequent Main Street to, as the narrator puts it, to "see pretty pretty sari and bangle, and to eat we belly full a burfi and gulub jamoon" (45). Such visits may not be considered unusual; spaces like Devon Street in Chicago and Jackson Heights in Queens, New York, often attract Indian Americans and Indian immigrants seeking to connect with Indian cultural (and culinary) life. But the text refuses to be read as a simple narrative about a lesbian couple that visits a South Asian immigrant neighborhood merely to indulge and feed their nostalgia for "Indian" culture. The two main characters might frequent Main Street to eat *gulub jamoon* and *burfi,* two typical "Indian" sweets, and to look at pretty saris, clothing associated with India, but it is not to remind them of India. Critical of the forces that align the desire to consume with a longing to preserve the affective hegemony of "Indian" food, the couple's nostalgia for "Indian" food, rooted in their diasporic location, at once invested in consuming Indian food and distrustful of the hegemonic ideals of the Indian nation-state, is necessarily rhizomorpohic and anti-Manichean. Their nostalgia does not attach itself to a specific place but attaches itself instead to a more critical interrogation of how a set of cultural practices can allow subjects—queer or straight, man or woman—to attach meaning to culturally significant acts. Nostalgia, most frequently understood as cultural practice, can also be understood as critical praxis. As Sunaina Maira has argued, "desire, in the cultural politics of the diaspora, is closely intertwined with the collective yearning for an authentic tradition or pure place of origin" (194). Maira defines critical nostalgia as a more reflexive form of nostalgia attuned to the politics of consumption. To consume culture in all its varied forms, or to be nostalgic for cultural artifacts, is as much about imagining an inclusive future as it is about commemorating nostalgic memories of the past.

Because they enter the "Indian" neighborhood as a lesbian couple, Janet and her partner are already outside the traditional heterosexual framework of this particular cultural national space: their nostalgia is already coded as a form of critical praxis. The narrator explains, "mostly back home, we is kitchen Indians: some kind a Indian food every day, at least once a day, but we doh get cardamom and other fancy spice down dere so de food not spicy like Indian food I eat in restaurants up here" (45). Brilliantly naming herself a "kitchen Indian," the narrator marks her culinary kinship to Indianness without claiming the nation-state of "India" as her home. Lest we think that her version of Indianness is a spiced-down, or watered-down version of Indianness because the food where she is from is not as spicy as Indian food "here," she adds, "But it have one thing we doh make joke 'bout down dere: we like we meethai and sweetrice too much, and it remain overly authentic, like de day Naana and Naani step off de boat in Port of Spain harbor over a hundred and sixty years ago" (45). In establishing the historical conditions that brought her ancestors to the Caribbean, the narrator provides details to render her love for unnaturally sweet Indian desserts intelligible. She also describes the foods that give her palatal pleasure as "overly authentic," distorting the hierarchy between "home nation" and the diaspora. As I've argued elsewhere, early scholarship on diaspora, positions diaspora in a (hierarchically) subordinate relation to the nation-state. In such contexts, diaspora is typically presented as "the bastard child of the nation—disavowed, inauthentic, illegitimate, and impoverished imitation of the originary culture" (Gopinath, "Bombay" 317). But where diaspora and immigrants are often considered imitations of the "real" citizens in the home state, Mootoo's narrator imagines a way out of the trappings of this hierarchical construct of nation and diaspora, inverting the terms to figure the immigrant as authentic, and the "home nation" as the watered-down version not on par with the original found in diaspora.

At the same time that the narrator claims culinary kinship with Indianness, she is cognizant of the regulatory mechanisms of cultural citizenship, which exclude her because her performance of "Indianness" deviates from the normative coding of gendered performance. She admits, "Going for an outing with mih Janet on Main Street ain't easy! If only it weren't for burfi and gulub jamoon! If only I had a learned how to cook dem kind a thing before I leave home and come up here to live!" (48–49), both foregrounding her desire for sweets and voicing her discomfort at being in a space that views her as an outsider, because she does not speak Hindi, because she does not look Indian enough, and because she and Janet are a visibly lesbian couple. She derives pleasure from consuming sweets on Main Street but not from the looks that unequivocally position her as an uninvited intruder. After she musters up the strength to enter the eatery, she orders a *jilebi* and *burfi* for Janet and a piece of *meethai* for herself, setting in motion a debate between narrator and store owner about competing notions of ethnic authenticity and national legitimacy:

> He open his palms out and indicate de entire panorama a sweets and he say, "These are all meethai, Miss. Meethai is Sweets. Where are you from?"
>
> I ignore his question and to show him I undaunted, I point to a round pink ball and say, "I'll have one a dese sugarcakes too please." He start grinning broad broad like if he half-pitying, half-laughing at dis-Indian-in-skin-only, and den he tell me, "That is called chum-chum, Miss." I snap back at him, "yeh. well back home we does call dat sugarcake, Mr. Chum-Chum. (51)

Although she seems troubled by her inability to remember the correct term—after all, this is precisely the scenario she sought to avoid by preparing herself before entering the store—the narrator displays no outward signs of embarrassment for failing to have correctly remembered the term. Instead she subtly rejects his smugness without exhibiting signs of embarrassment for having "got it wrong." When she does use the term he insists is correct, "chum-chum," she does not equivocate on her own personal linguistic choices. Instead, she parodically reiterates his words, calling him "Mr. Chum-Chum," refusing to grant primacy to his logic of namings. In response to his loosely veiled, and all-too-familiar question, "Where are you from?" the narrator refuses to give him the satisfaction of acknowledging his underlying question, "What kind of an Indian are you?" by retorting that back home, a place she refuses to name, "we" call it sugarcake.

The refusal in "Out on Main Street" to locate any group as necessarily "original" undercuts notions of authentic, autochthonous citizenship. The storeowner who so vehemently polices the narrator's claims to culinary kinship with "Indian" foods is no more "authentically Indian" than the narrator and her girlfriend. He is not an "Indian" from India but a

Fijian immigrant of Indian descent. The Fijian store owner's inability to read the narrator as an "Indian," diasporic or otherwise, is cast as aberrant in the framework of this story. The cultural logic on which such suppositions are based often police the line between what can be deemed as authentic, cultural, and gendered citizenship and the performance of ethnicity. To be seen as "Indian" demands a particular set of performative behavior; if, and only if, the Indian-seeming subject speaks a certain way and recognizes the "correct" way of doing and saying things, can she be considered "Indian."

Gender roles continue to be implicated in the scripts of women's nationalisms and "cultural identities," particularly as they take root in the culinary realm. But Mr. Chum-Chum's insistence that the narrator learn the correct names ascribed to particular sweets is further complicated by its gendered implications. The narrator is doubly offensive to Mr. Chum-Chum not only because she refuses to adhere to the rigid linguistic rules, but also because she chooses to don queer butch attire. Mootoo's staunch refusal to follow the mandates of speaking and writing in standardized English can be understood as a gendered response to linguistic and political hegemony. Certainly, words could easily adhere to the dominant orthographic pattern. As Sharmila Sen suggests, "'baigan' or 'geera' could have easily been written as 'eggplant' or 'cumin' without sacrificing the meaning. But . . . the 'baigan' and 'geera' are far more evocative than 'eggplant' or 'cumin' because they are fossil sounds bearing the impression of a century-old Indo-Caribbean presence" (195). While both Janet and the narrator are lesbians, Janet's high heel shoes and long, flowing hair make her appear ultra "femme." In contrast, the narrator, who sports a crew cut and wears blue jeans tucked into her "jim-boots," is visibly "butch." Her refusal to perform traditional heterosexual femininity and her outwardly female masculine appearance do not correspond with the storekeeper's expectations that the narrator accept the "traditional" mode of being an "Indian" woman. While she might privately admonish herself for not having the "correct" word or phrase or knowledge of things Indian, she refuses to publicly affirm an exclusionary, chauvinistic version of citizenship that devalorizes and delegitimizes her experiences simply because she does not seem to fit into clearly demarcated categories of nation, gender, and sexuality.

"Out on Main Street" evocatively narrates a tale of how plural cultural contacts precipitate a rethinking of identity categories grounded on filiation. "Mr. Chum-Chum" and the narrator may be as much a product of a labor-driven diaspora as the narrator, but he identifies with a different version of national belonging—one that views diasporic histories and cultures as pale imitations of the "original." Within his framework, homosexuality and nonfemininity are also not legitimate modes of performative behavior. Unlike filial and rooted identities that map onto origin and filiation to acquire legitimacy, the narrator's relational identity is mapped in movement. She deploys a diasporic vocabulary and a nonconformist sartorial ethos. Rethinking these spaces and histories as points of relation and affiliation, rather than in terms of roots and filiation, creates spaces for interrogating the contradictory layering of lives mapped in multiple geographic spaces—racial, ethnic, and sexual.

The story repudiates a Manichean logic of belonging and not belonging in which Indians from India are rendered as more "authentic" (and therefore more knowledgeable or "correct") than diasporic Indians such as the narrator and her girlfriend. It is, however, worth noting the historical irony that binds the two characters insofar as both characters' lives revolve around sugar. The narrator, it is worth emphasizing, is the descendant of indentured laborers from India in Trinidad, and the store owners are Fijian Indians, descendants of another labor-driven diaspora that brought Indians to work in the sugar cane fields of Fiji in the nineteenth century. Patron and customer, then, have more in common than a mere appreciation for *meethai*. Both are descendants of diasporic workers, presumably descended from indentured labor brought to work in sugar cane fields, and now, both owner and customer feud over the "authenticity" of *meethai*—a food in which sugar is the primary ingredient. The animosity between the characters marks their palpable distaste for each other, but historical forces, colonization, and economic conditions that displaced their ancestors to disparate locales in the Caribbean Sea and the Pacific Ocean establish a nascent fraternity between the characters based on similar histories rather than on shared or acknowledged affinities.

Before concluding, I turn briefly to another short story in Shani Mootoo's collection titled "Sushila's Bakhti." This story, also set in a Canadian city, enters into the psychic and cultural life of its protagonist, Sushila, and unravels the rhizomorphic logic of culinary identifications within diasporic memories. Sushila, the narrator, is an Indo-Caribbean artist who continually battles the racialized implications of what it means to be read as an "Indian," "Paki," "Hindu"—everything but Trinidadian—by virtue of her brown skin, the "purest legacy left to Indians generations away from India" (63). Like the narrator of "Out on Main Street," Sushila's relationship to Indianness is mediated through a rhizomorphic relationship with food, and understanding the implicit rules governing consumptive practices and desires. Her feelings of rootlessness and disconnectedness from "Indianness" come to life when she finds herself using food in her art. When she chooses to give up painting her lucrative, but colorless depictions of "large temperate-zone fruit and immense cold-country vegetables" (60), opting instead to create art evoking the colors of her childhood, she covers a canvas made from a basmati rice burlap sack with clumps of metanil yellow food dye. Her decision to purchase the coloring agent at an "Indian" store sets into motion a brief debate over the "proper" use of things. The store owner from whom she purchases the food dye, an exile from Uganda of Ismaili origin, is suspicious of Sushila's desire to purchase the food coloring from the outset: "She explained that she was not using it for food, but as a pigment for painting. And he said, yes, she can use it as a dye, but not in food, he was obliged to make that clear. Actually, he said, people always come to buy it for food coloring and he fulfills his obligation to say that it is banned as food, but he knows what they are really doing with it" (65). The store owner assumes Sushila will use the metanil dye as comestible, rather than as coloring agent, powerfully speaking to a presumption about diasporic ignorance of homeland conventions. Sushila's thoughts return to food when she tries to understand her own inability to navigate the unwritten codes of diaspora. When, for instance, is the metanil food dye to be used as comestible, despite being deemed inedible, and when is it deemed acceptable to use it as a coloring agent? Her own dis-ease with navigating the terms of consumption, when to follow the rules, when to flout them, culminates in a yearning for "accurate details of Trinidad" and a concomitant recognition of the fallacious nature of her desires: "as [Sushila] tried to unblur details, to sort out which festival is which, the act of forgetting and remembering and inventing reminded her of her grandmother, who, like so many other Trinidadian Hindus and Muslims she knows, refused to eat either beef or pork because she couldn't remember which one it is that she, as a goodBrahminwoman wasn't supposed to eat" (66).

I end with this story by Mootoo to underscore how multiple, often-contradictory investments in consumptive practices make it necessary to reconceptualize nostalgia and its relationship to the desire to maintain cultural purity within spaces that we might think of, following Homi Bhabha, as the third spaces of diaspora. For Bhabha, the third space, unrepresentable in itself, nevertheless "constitutes the discursive conditions of enunciation that ensure that the meaning and symbols of culture have no primordial unity or fixity; that even the same signs can be appropriated, translated, rehistoricized and read anew" (37). Mootoo's nar-rators' distrust of narratives of "originality" and "purity" produces these third spaces where culinary signs are read anew and rehistoricized. For Bhabha, as well as for the characters in Mootoo's fictions, then:

> what is at issue is the performative nature of differential identities; the regulation and negotiation of those spaces that are continual-ly, *contingently*, "opening out," remaking the boundaries, exposing the limits of any claim to a singular or autonomous sign of differ-ence—be it class, gender or race. Such assignations of social differ-ences—where difference is neither One nor the Other but *something else besides*, in between—find their agency in a form of the "future" where the present is not simply transitory. It is, if I may stretch a point, an interstitial future, that emerges in-between the claims of the past and the needs of the present. (219)

Such interstitial spaces have been described by Smadar Lavie and Ted Swedenburg as "third time-spaces," analogous to Bhabha's notion of the third space, a terrain that "involves a guerilla warfare of the interstices, where minoritized subjects rupture categories of race, gender, sexuality, class, nation and empire in the center as well as on the margins" between the hyphens of identity (13). Sushila describes her grandmother as a reli-gious woman who takes it upon herself to instruct younger generations about Hindu cultural life. And yet, ironically, she "forgets" one of the cardinal rules that have distinguished orthodox Hindus and orthodox Muslims and passes on new histories and traditions to the generations below her. Because she cannot recall dietary rules that have traditionally separated Hindus and Muslims in the subcontinent, Sushila's grand-mother along with her community of Trinidadian Hindus and Muslims establish an alternative culinary logic implicitly disavowing pure geneal-ogies yoking food consumption with religious identity. The gastropoetic and gastropolitical logic that traditionally differentiates between Hindus as non–beef eaters and Muslims as non–pork eaters becomes submerged here, and a nascent fraternity organized around culinary practices emerges between "homeland" rivals because both Hindus and Muslims reject the consumption of pork or beef. However, the story does not read-ily answer whether Sushila's grandmother's forgetting is mediated by a desire to deliberately, and strategically, narrow the gap between Hindus and Muslims and the implications this has for understanding nation-hood from the vantage point of diaspora. As Ernest Renan reminds us, "the essence of a nation is that all individuals have many things in common, and also that they have forgotten many things" (11): nations and collectives are forged through collective acts of forgetting historical wounds. For diasporic communities, spatially and temporally distanced from the geographic parameters of the nation-state, a collective sense of nationhood and an affective longing for the home, and a fear of "losing" tradition morphs into a desire to vigilantly retain viability and visibility through a systematic attempt to ossify the fragments and shards of cultural practices deemed "authentic."

In the third spaces created through Mootoo's fiction, however, the future of diasporic communities is forged through creative acts of misrecognition and the deliberate blurring of ostensibly authentic details. But it is doubly significant that culinary practices, and sites of alimentary exchange become the sites upon which age-old anxieties about cultural purity are resurrected. Immigrants, as both Madhur Jaffrey and Sara Suleri point out, are deeply invested in the ontological purity of their cuisines. Suleri's narrative is one that casts doubt on the certitude with which expatriates adamantly and passionately defend the alimentary practices of the homeland. In its conception, *Meatless Days* is ambivalently situated between Suleri's desire to reject the official rendering of history, and the author's refusal to acknowledge the class-based implications of her own nostalgically rendered histories. Nostalgia for what was consumed in her pre-emigration home powerfully charges Suleri's narrative, but newer hierarchies, blind to class inequities, merely replace the gender hierarchies which Suleri flouts in order to render history otherwise. Read through and against Suleri's memoirs, Mootoo's stories complicate a simple logic of what we might think of as multiculturalist eating, a consumptive practice that commonly posits eating together as a way to overcome racial and ethnic differences. Mootoo's short fiction implicitly points to the bankruptcy of any idealized notion that diasporic existence necessarily produces fraternity between characters who share similar histories of migration and displacement. Such utopic desires imagine eating to be a solution to the fractious malaises of the world and are predicated on a sentimentalized and dehistoricized understanding of the power of consumption. The conditions of diaspora or becoming diasporic do not transcend differences of race, class, gender, and sexuality, "nor can diaspora stand alone as an epistemological or historical category of analysis separate and distinct from these interrelated categories" (Braziel and Mannur 5). In "Out on Main Street," patron and customer are not able to establish a form of what Svetlana Boym has described as diasporic intimacy simply because they have shared histories of dispersion and relocation. Indeed, if it is possible to be nostalgic for "Indian" food without being nostalgic for "India," the store owner's misogyny and homophobia stand in the way of establishing any sense of ethnic-based kinship among people in the diaspora simply because they might find pleasure and sustenance in consuming the same types of food. Culinary discourse is ambivalently coded and complexly situated; within the tradition of immigrant literature, culinary discourse sets in motion an extended discussion about the imbricate layering of food, nostalgia, and national identity. Through such discursive renderings of nostalgia, it becomes apparent that these homelands, both phantasmatic and contradictory, become spaces that are limiting or emancipatory, and typically both at once. Consuming ethnically coded food, in this context, is more than a cultural practice closely associated with kinship and ritual; it is also a long-standing material in global commerce and exchange. Culinary discourse therefore bears witness to the complicated historical processes that have occasioned international migration and diasporic dislocation, however ambivalent one might be about the actual process of dislocation.

2 / Feeding Desire: Food, Domesticity, and Challenges to Heteropatriarchy

Smack, gush, slobber—someone was enjoying a feast. Suddenly, I understood what was going on! Begum Jan has not eaten a thing all day and Rabbo, the witch, was a known glutton. They were polishing off some goodies under the quilt for sure.

—ISMAT CHUGHTAI, "THE QUILT"

I remember women by what we ate together, what they dug out of the freezer after we'd made love for hours. I've only had one lover who didn't want to eat at all. We didn't last long.

—DOROTHY ALLISON, "A LESBIAN APPETITE"

More than any of her other short stories, "A Lesbian Appetite" is one in which southern lesbian writer Dorothy Allison fashions a connection among food, sex, and love. In its evocation of memories of intimacy, shared foods and feelings, Allison's story unapologetically conceptualizes food preparation within the domestic sphere so as to accommodate a queer vision of kinship. Severing the seamless link between heterosexuality and food preparation, Allison tells a story of love and desire mediated through food that transgresses the gendered logic of the domestic space, fashioning a narrative in which food consumption and preparation in the domestic space are not circumscribed by compulsory heterosexuality. Instead, her story sutures food and sexuality, engendering affiliations that transgress the implicit heteronormative logic of the home.

The second epigraph is taken from Ismat Chughtai's 1941 short story "The Quilt," which has been lauded as an early expression of female-female intimacy within the Urdu literary tradition. Narrated from the perspective of a child, "The Quilt" tells a story about the relationship between the Begum, an upper-class Muslim woman and wife of the *nawab* (landowner), and her female servant Rabbo. The young girl who serves as the narrator is both troubled and fascinated by Rabbo and the Begum's intimate gestures under the quilt. Unable to fully comprehend what is happening, the child narrator interprets Rabbo and the Begum's intimate gestures as clandestine acts of consumption, but the reader recognizes that the sounds marking gustatory pleasure that emerge from under the quilt are actually the sounds of oral sexual pleasure; as Elspeth Probyn might phrase it, they are the sounds of "eating sex" (59). By isolating strategies to express their desire for one another without disrupting the logic of the home that calls for heterosexuality to be performed and upheld, Rabbo and the Begum do not reject the logic of the household, but rather work with its attendant fissures that render queerness invisible in order to articulate a form of same-sex desire, "unseen" and unmarked by standard ocular regimes. For cultural critic Gayatri Gopinath, the story is a site to examine alterior sexualities translated through and against the movements of diaspora; moreover, the story is a "useful site upon which to engage with the vexed question of how to read alterior sexuality across national and cultural locations" ("Homo-Economics" 102). But much remains strategically unanswered in the story. Who is pleasuring whom? And what does it mean that Rabbo is the Begum's servant, who has "no other household duties" save taking care of the Begum's bodily needs and desires? Not only is Rabbo the Begum's head servant, whose duties include serving and pleasuring her mistress, but these transgressions occur through Rabbo's privileged access to the *zenana*, a female-only space, off limits to the other servants. Thus, while the Begum and Rabbo's relationship develops within a heteronormative framework, it also works through a classed framework. These two moments in which food mediates gestures of female-female intimacy hint at an alternative reading of food—one that indicates an impoverished understanding of food as merely an edifice to buttress normatively coded expressions of sexual desire.

The home, never a neutral space divested of ideological constructions of gendered nationhood, is a site that produces gendered citizens of the nation. Homes as the familial domain, while not coterminous with nations, are sites that produce members of the nation in specifically sexualized terms. As Paul Gilroy notes, "families are not only the nation in microcosm, its key components, but act as the means to turn social processes into natural, instinctive ones" ("*There Ain't*" 43). The family and home become the primary socializing agents of the nation in microcosm. Postcolonial cultural critic Partha Chatterjee most presciently articulates the web of affiliation among domesticity, the "home," and the nation:

In the entire phase of the nationalist struggle, the crucial need was to protect, preserve and strengthen the inner core of the national culture . . . The home was the principal site for expressing the spiritual quality of the national culture, and women must take the main responsibility of protecting and nurturing this quality. No matter what the changes in the external condition of life for women, they must not lose their essentially spiritual (i.e. feminine) virtues; they must not, in other words, become *essentially* westernized. (239)

Preserving the domestic familial structure becomes the responsibility of women; but cooking and food preparation must be acknowledged for the central role they play in upholding the dynamics of domestic familiality. Preserving the sanctity of the domestic home space, creating a space where members of the household feel nurtured and protected, thus become important touchstones of women's labor. As Rosemary George notes, "the word 'home' immediately connotes the private sphere of patriarchal hierarchy, gendered self-identity, shelter, comfort, nurture and protection" (1). The home is part of the private sphere in which the values of patriarchy are reaffirmed, with women, paradoxically, located both at the center and at the periphery of the familial home space. Far from being neutral spaces, homes are contested sites "manifest on geographical, psychological and material levels. They are recognized as such by those within and those without" and thus become important sites for disciplining subjects to perform their given identity role (George 9).

But the home, as Allison's story illustrates, is also a sexualized space. It is a space that demands an isomorphic alignment between sex and gender within a heterosexual matrix; such logic holds male bodies to be necessarily heterosexual "men" and female bodies to be necessarily heterosexual "women." Within a rigidly patriarchal vision of nationhood, women are exhorted to maintain and uphold traditional domestic familial structures. The successful crossover hit film *Monsoon Wedding* is one such film to link food with queerness, even its nascent formations. Mira Nair's *Monsoon Wedding,*, self-billed as a film about the choices family members must make, is also framed as a film about possibilities: the female characters, though resolutely heterosexual, are lauded for their strength to stand up to patriarchy to protect their wishes and desires. As Jenny Sharpe notes, when tradition and modernity come into conflict, "*Monsoon Wedding* reveals that at the heart of the battle between tradition and modernity is not the question of a woman's sexual abstinence prior to marriage but her right to choose that is withheld through the double standards upheld for men and women" (71). In turn, the patriarchal figure, Lalit Verma, is lauded for his choice to side with his niece,

Ria, over his obligations to an elder family friend, Uncle Tej, when it is revealed that Tej molested Ria as a child.

In its articulation of choices, *Monsoon Wedding* also relays a tale about a subject who confronts what happens when he tries to avail himself of particular choices to follow his dreams and desires. In the film, the wedding between the daughter of a Delhi-based family and an Indian American from Houston, Texas, takes center stage. Amid this drama of heterosexual bliss and excess, however, is one apparently queer figure: the younger brother of Aditi, the bride-to-be, the corpulent, flamboyant, dance-loving and food-loving Varun. From his first on-screen appearance, Varun takes stage as a semicomic character whose desires interfere with the smooth and timely execution of the wedding festivities. When he makes his first appearance, Varun is watching culinary personality Sanjeev Kapoor prepare coconut chicken curry. Kapoor, recognizable to the diasporic viewership of *Monsoon Wedding* as the host of the popular cooking show *Khana Khazana*, makes only a brief appearance via the television set in the Verma household. But this brief moment punctures the narrative, hinting that Varun's sexuality cannot be circumscribed by simple heteronormative logic. As Varun voices his desire to continue watching the show so that he may figure out the last step of preparing coconut chicken, he is wrenched away from the television set by his mother, Pimmi (Lilette Dubey), and asked to get dressed for prewedding festivities instead of wasting time watching a cooking show.

Such hints toward Varun's nascent queerness are addressed later in the film when the patriarch, Lalit Verma (Naseruddin Shah), enters into a heated debate with his wife, Pimmi, about their son's future, asking whether Varun should be sent to boarding school to discipline him into being more "masculine." Consider the following exchange between Lalit and Pimmi:

LALIT: He's going to boarding school and that final. He's wasting his life staying here, watching TV the whole day. There's no one here's to discipline him. *He doesn't listen. I give up.*

PIMMI: He also needs love and affection. He's such a sensitive boy, Lalit. And he's so wonderful with all these creative things.

LALIT: Creative things like singing and dancing. Cooking sesame chicken. *Let's find him a nice boy.*

PIMMI: Don't say that. Why do you always look at everything like that?

LALIT: You know what I heard him telling Tej Bhaisahib? What he wants to be when grows up?

PIMMI: What?

LALIT: He said he wants to be a chef (*laughs*). *Our son will be a cook!* Tej Bhaisahib nearly fainted with surprise! *A cook?*

PIMMI (*laughing*): *He's just a kid.* Doesn't mean anything.

LALIT: He's a fool. Our son will be a man when he grows up, understand? He'll be educated properly. He won't be singing and dancing at people's *shaadis*[1]

Lalit rehearses an age-old critique that squarely places the responsibility for "proper" child rearing on the wife-mother's shoulders. Pimmi is derided for "spoiling" their son and for not disciplining him into performing his masculinity within the home. Lalit's homophobia is palpable as he asks Pimmi what will become of their son, with his love for cooking and cooking shows like *Khana Khazana*. He asks Pimmi, will he become a *khansama* (cook), the next Sanjeev Kapoor to take middle-class India by storm? Should they try to find a "nice boy" for him to marry? Varun's comfort in spaces of female homosociality, as well as his dedicated interest in choreographing and performing a dance at his sister's wedding, cast him as queer. For Lalit, a lack of interest in cricket coupled with an excessive interest in cooking and dancing marks Varun as queer.

But while Varun's character has popularly been read within a queer framework, the film refuses to provide a simple answer to the question of his sexuality. Is he straight? Is he gay? Varun's queerness, marked by his interest in cooking and dancing, emerges against the backdrop of the celebration of heterosexual Hindu familial life. In this film full of disidentifying subjects, Varun is the only character who is allowed the possibility of queer desire. As Gayatri Gopinath notes, queerness in *Monsoon Wedding* is shifted "away from the bodies of adult women . . . and onto that of the adolescent boy. *Monsoon Wedding* relegates queerness to the realm of immaturity and couches it merely as a stage that precedes the responsibilities and requirements of proper adulthood" (*Impossible Desires* 123–24). Although the film locates queerness within the immature male body and while Varun's dancing and cooking may be viewed with suspicion, marking the emergence of queerness within the Verma home in Delhi, the film complicates the notion that queerness is a "Western" phenomenon with no roots in South Asian domestic structures. Despite the father's exhortation to raise Varun as a "man," Varun cannot be disciplined into heterosexuality. Instead, the attendant fissures within the domestic space become productive spaces from which to recalibrate how desire manifests in the home space.

Implicit in *Monsoon Wedding's* use of Sanjeev Kapoor's television show *Khana Khazana* is the notion that the show (which aims to teach Indian women how to cook with ease) also has a particular resonance for a preteen gay-identified boy. Varun is interpellated by the logic of cooking, but for him, cooking is not about maintaining the edifice of home life. And yet cooking shows and cookbooks carry a particular currency, operating as ideological guarantors of gendered normativity. Cookbooks may interpellate women within the household economy as "wife," "mother," "daughter," but food preparation enables queer desire to find a mode of expression to articulate alternative visions of kinship. Like their predecessor, the cookbook, cooking shows are malleable social artifacts, capable of producing gendered national subjects. Prior to the advent of the cooking show, a genre I later examine in more detail, the primary tool utilized to connect cooking with national formation is the domestic manual or cookbook.

In South Asian contexts, domestic manuals and cookbooks discipline women into performing wifeliness. As Arjun Appadurai notes, cookbooks

> combine the sturdy pragmatic virtues of all manuals with the vicarious pleasures of the literature of the senses. They reflect shifts in the boundaries of edibility, the proprieties of the culinary process, the logic of meals, the exigencies of the household budget, the vagaries of the market, and the structure of domestic ideologies. The existence of cookbooks presupposes not only some degree of literacy, but often an effort on the part of some variety of specialist to standardize the regime of the kitchen, to transmit culinary lore, and to publicize particular traditions guiding the journey of food from marketplace to kitchen to table. ("National Cuisine" 6)

Linking national identity with the task of housekeeping, Kala Primlani's *Indian Cooking: With Useful Hints of Good Housekeeping* instructs its readers that to be a good Indian "housekeeper" one must be equipped with a thorough knowledge of Indian cooking, broadly defined. First published in 1968, the text was serialized in recipe columns in *Hindvasi*, a Sindhi-language daily in India; before being translated into English, it was compiled into a Sindhi-language cookbook and continued to circulate into the 1980s and 1990s (Appadurai, "National Cuisine," 3–14). Primlani's cookbook argues that in order to maintain the integrity and structure of the familial home space, it is crucial to know one's way around a kitchen. Primlani speaks to an audience of married women seeking advice on how to run a household. Her female readers are always named as "wives"; they can never be "women" who might need to learn how to manage a home outside of the strictures of heterosexuality or matrimony. Female subjectivity is wholly predicated on their position within the household as the wife, or, more accurately, housewife.

Rather than suggesting that Primlani's book is a quaint collection of obsolete gestures, intent on reproducing "good" Indian wives, I want to suggest that *Indian Cooking: With Useful Hints on Good Housekeeping* is part of a larger tradition of cookbooks that are as much about cooking as they are about domestic management.[2] In addition to recipes for "classic" Indian dishes such as *do piaaza* gravy (onion gravy) and *palak* (Indian spinach), *Indian Cooking* also includes extensive household hints. These hints include step-by-step recipes for removing stains from clothing and simple recipes designed to create shining floors and sparkling mirrors (21). Primlani informs her female readers that "the home, where the housewife spends so much of her time and where the master of the house returns for rest after a tiring day's work, must, as a matter of duty, be kept clean. Just as a change from soiled clothes into clean clothes gives comfort, so too, a neat house makes him relaxed" (21–22). At the same time, a wife's apparent success at having produced a clean and orderly home is marked by the invisibility of her labor. A veiled threat of violence, hostility, or disturbance to the peace of the household inheres in the suggestion that the patriarch is entitled to return to a clean home (how will he respond if the house is not clean?), thereby producing expectations about gendered roles within the household. The patriarch does not have to say anything about what he needs or wants as this should be self-evident. Women's work, then, emerges as that which is indispensable but that which must remain invisible.

Primlani's handy hints dispense essential advice but obviate the need to have to search for answers to common problems, allowing the housewife to circumvent the potentially embarrassing situation of having to ask for help in activities deemed "common sense." In a section titled "Six Golden Rules," Primlani promises, "if you keep in mind the following six rules, most of your difficulties in cooking will disappear and a desire will develop in you to prepare new kinds of food," thereby offering comfort to the reader who perhaps does not navigate the home with ease (41). In her list of suggestions, she explains why the housewife must take care not to relegate tasks to other persons. As she notes, "very few housewives attach importance to cooking with their own hands. Either they put the kitchen in charge of servants or do the cooking in a stereotyped manner. They will cook in the same monotonous way with the result that the master of the house does not find the food tasty and the children do not feel happy either" (41). Primlani's stance embodies two apparent contradictions: on one hand, she instructs her readers to perfect the art of performing a few tasks well, rather than acquiring superficial knowledge of many tasks. On the other hand, she instructs her readers to be on the guard against monotony. Inherent in the contradictions is a hint of ambivalence; it might be the role of the new Indian woman to build the home, but at the same time, she must readily identify as a homebuilder and consistently reinvent that script in order to nurture happy families living together in the domestic sphere.

But as the title suggests, it is not enough for the housewife to whom such cookbooks are targeted to know how to cook or to manage her time efficiently; she must know how to reproduce Indian food. Indianness as such is never defined, but it becomes apparent that to be Indian is to necessarily embrace a particular cosmopolitanism. Her recipe book includes "basic recipes" for "Indian" dishes such as garlic and fenugreek leaves and Indian spinach, as well as "Western" recipes such as English spinach, mashed and creamed potatoes, and white sauce. More than an attempt to espouse a more inclusive definition of "Indianness" that bridges the "East" with the "West, this gesture insists on a qualitative definition of Indianness mediated by class. The recipes themselves may not be Indian in a narrowly defined sense, but more conventionally fit under the rubric of "Continental cuisine," a category that includes all manner of "Western," American, and European food. With its roots in an Anglo-Indian tradition, "Continental cuisine" references the European mainland but is commonly understood in opposition to "Indian" cuisine. [3] To be Indian, one must be equally conversant in preparing "Indian" and "Continental" culinary specialties. The versatile and resourceful housewife prepares *kormas* and *kassaundies* as easily as she creams potatoes and boils eggs.

Unlike cookbooks commonly encountered in diasporic settings such as Madhur Jaffrey's *Invitation to Indian Cooking*, Primlani's efforts are not intended to provide tantalizing recipes that represent the diversity and delectability of Indian culinary practices. Many of the recipes catalogued in the book for basic curries abound in cookbooks, and there is nothing particularly unique about Primlani's recipes, nor do they make for a more diverse or varied Indian cuisine. Instead, the book derives its popularity as well as its utility from its practical approach to the basics of household management. It bills itself as a straightforward attempt to catalogue activities, ranging from cooking "Indian" and "Continental" dishes to cleaning windows, that are deemed necessary for the efficient management of the private realm of the domestic sphere. By virtue of the author's presumed experience, she is in a unique position to help Indian women run efficient households on their own and can thus be relied upon to help her readers become "good Indian women." Reproducing the nation within the domestic space becomes aligned with more than producing Indian cuisine; it is equally about preserving the structure of the home, keeping it clean and always respecting the patriarchal structure of the home. The power of patriarchy is such that men ought to partake in the pleasure of returning to the domestic space without having to acknowledge that their wives have labored to create a comfortable space for them. An important power/labor differential emerges here: just as women's labor must be rendered invisible, so too must masculine power, which has the privilege of being unnamed.

Domestic manuals such as Kala Primlani's *Indian Cooking* script national identity formation through culinary practices within the home as necessarily gendered processes. Food and kinship are undergirded by a compulsory heterosexuality that has the privilege of being considered the norm within the home. And yet homes are deeply sexualized spaces, even when queer-identified subjects find the home to be hostile spaces. They experience deep ambivalence toward the notion of home, experiencing it both as a safe space of refuge or shelter that nurtures their desire for a person of the same sex, and as a space that is implicitly heteronormative. But, to ask a simple question with far-reaching political consequences, what happens when food catalyzes a queer relationship that works both with and against the regulatory heteronormative logic of the home site? Compelling attempts to grapple with the complexities of this question emerge from a range of cultural forms in which intimate bonds of queer kinship are established through the act of food preparation within the heteronormative home space. The novel *Reef* (1994) by Sri Lankan British author Romesh Gunesekera, the controversial film *Fire* (1998) directed by the Indian Canadian filmmaker Deepa Mehta, and Shani Mootoo's novel *Cereus Blooms at Night* (1996) are works that deploy culinary practices as a possible script to articulate queer kinship.

Feeding Desire in *Reef*

In Sri Lanka, the *Ceylon Daily News Cookery Book*, edited by Hilda Deutrom (1964), has come to represent an attempt to chronicle the nation's history through its culinary offerings. In the front matter for that volume, first published in 1929, an unnamed reviewer notes, "good cooks thrive best in the wholesome atmosphere of good homes" (i). The book, subsequently reprinted nine times in five different editions, catalogues the nation's history, and the impact of Arab, Malay, Moorish, Portuguese, Dutch, and British occupation on the native Sinhala and Tamil cuisines. The *Ceylon Daily News Cookery Book* contains a "representative list of the recipes handed from generation to generation of Ceylon's housewives, reflect[ing] the march of the Island's history" (ii). It responds to the dual need of building an archive of national (culinary) history and reminding women of their "duties" to nurture happy families who are clean, well fed and well nourished in the "wholesome atmosphere of good homes" (i). The *Daily News Cookery Book* is an important artifact in Sri Lanka's cultural history, particularly in its diasporic reaches. *A Change of Skies*, by the Australian-based Sri Lankan Yasmine Gooneratne, is one novel to bear the culinary freight of Deutrom's cookbook. Published in 1991, Gooneratne's *Change of Skies* is one of the better-known South Asian Australian novels. Oscillating between the perspectives of Jean and Barry Mundy, a Sri Lankan couple who immigrate to Australia, the novel can be read as a meditation on the process of writing oneself into an Australian literary tradition as much as it is about the processes of forcible assimilation immigrants undergo in their attempts to forge a home in a new space. Once in Australia, both undergo a series of changes, not least of which are name changes. Bharat and Navaranjini Mangala-Davasinha become Barry and Jean Mundy. Barry, a linguistics professor at Southern Cross University in New South Wales, is intent on two writing endeavors. The first is to collect and edit the writings of his grandfather Edward, who sailed from Colombo to Queensland in 1882, in a volume titled *Lifeline: The Journal of an Asian Grandee in Australia, 1882–1887*. The second is to produce a guide for new immigrants.

The seemingly quieter Jean possesses a kind of candor and strength that is easy to overlook. Early in the narrative we learn of Jean's desire to be a writer. Barry's gentle chidings, reminding her about the fine distinction between fact and fiction, do not deter her from her desire to write; in the end, she learns to hide her writings from her husband. At the same time, Navaranjini, before she becomes Jean, is a woman wholly in touch with the significance of culinary practices. Her ambivalence about leaving Sri Lanka for a completely unknown Australia first takes shape in her observation about what little she knows of the country. While glancing through a magazine, she stumbles across a promotional advertisement for Australian dried fruit. She then takes note of how her knowledge of the country to which she is about to immigrate is almost entirely about its foodways: "The pears and peaches out of large tins labeled IXL throughout my childhood, I thought, must have been Australian . . . [A]t Christmas time . . . there had been red and green apples for sale at Cargill's and Miller's, sitting in boxes marked 'Tasmania' or 'New South Wales', each apple wrapped in a square of green tissue paper. Beside the apple boxes, decorated with plastic holly and mistletoe, there had been trays of walnuts and raisins from Australia, and crystallized pineapple" (17).

Navaranjini's cognizance of how Australian foods are already part of her world in Sri Lanka, thanks in no small part to the workings of transnational commodity economics, signals her readiness to negotiate the gendered contexts of immigration. Her relationship to the domestic space facilitates her understanding of what she needs to do in Australia to negotiate her sense of loss. As she notes, "I do a lot of cooking, now that we live in Australia and have no servants in the house, so my thoughts about living here do tend to get a bit mixed up, sometimes with my herbs and spices" (119). For Jean, the kitchen becomes a space to negotiate her in-betweenness; it is a "brown" space in the terms Richard Rodriguez has used—a space of admixtures, new creations, and fusions This culinary knowledge better equips Jean to survive amid new surroundings. Jean becomes the type of immigrant who does not assimilate to a mainstream culture in the way immigrants are so often exhorted to fall into line with the national culture; rather, she makes Australianness adapt to her lifestyle.

By the middle of the narrative, Jean writes to her sister in Sri Lanka, revealing that she is writing a book, or, as she calls it, "my little cookery book" (207). Most interesting in this process, however, is the narrative she provides explaining the place of her intended cookbook. In constructing a genealogy for Jean's cooking, Gooneratne evokes both factual and fictional sources: *The Ceylon Daily News Cookery Book* edited by Hilda Deutrom and an unnamed cookbook by a fictionalized author, Mrs. Juliet Fernando, serve as inspiration for Jean. And yet it is the fictionalized cookbook that educates Jean far more effectively. As Jean observes, "before she left Grandmother gave me a present, a cookery book by a Mrs. Juliet Fernando. I have been reading through it carefully, and have learned from Mrs. J. F. some interesting facts. Vera, did you know that Sinhalese husbands have been known, on encountering a grain of sand in their plate of rice, to fling the entire dish on the floor? So Mrs. J. F. says. She also warns wives that a household in which a husband begins to talk rapturously about food he has eaten in hotels, restaurants or other people's houses is headed for disaster" (207). In the best (or worst) tradition of women's cookbooks, Juliet Fernando's cookbook does more than share recipes: it teaches women how to be good housewives. But for Jean, being a housewife does not carry the same resonance as it did before she left Sri Lanka. Without an extended family to buttress her everyday life, Jean becomes the type of pioneer who has to forge meaning out of her new surroundings. For Jean that process of education occurs through cooking. In her letter to Vera, she notes, "I am now collecting recipes, and especially recipes which combine Oriental and Western ingredients and methods of preparation" (208). In producing a cookbook as her first real public act as an immigrant, Jean establishes a kinship with the earlier waves of immigrants. In so doing, she recognizes the politics and labor around food by placing herself alongside waves of Chinese, Turkish, and Lebanese immigrants from contemporary times reaching back to the Gold Rush era, who work with food in order to gain any kind of economic foothold in Australia.

The gendered nature of her situation positions her ideally to broker advice about how to inhabit the space of Australia while being Sri Lankan; Jean becomes what Madhur Jaffrey has been to Indian immigrants to the United States and Britain, and what Charmaine Solomon has been for the Asian community in Australia—a guide able to lead her community in their quest to reproduce ethnicity within the home for those particularly plagued by the anxiety of authentically reproducing national essences in diasporic culinary contexts. The fact that Jean does not adhere stubbornly to a pure Sri Lankan essence also speaks to her willingness to engage a more hybrid understanding of identity. So for Jean, food is more than an affirmation of her cultural identity. It also represents a way for her to write herself into an Australian and a diasporic tradition. Her husband devotes his life in Australia to producing a comprehensive guide to immigrant life, but the guide never materializes. Where Barry fails, Jean is able to flourish. While there remains something powerful about Jean's agency, Barry is unable to find a voice because his words are framed through a different register. While both wish to find a particular mode of writing to serve as a guide for new immigrants as they negotiate the complexities of displacement and movement, Jean's cookbook becomes more successful in the end partly because the immigrant's voice is rendered most palatable when charged with gastronomic power. Food, as Tseen Khoo notes, is the acceptable face of multiculturalism: "hunger for the cosmopolitan face means that Australian civic acceptance is often conditional upon repeated and acceptable versions of that difference" (21). Food is one of those forms of acceptable cosmopolitan difference intimating what it means for Jean to use the culinary to guide immigrants to life in Australia. Her cookbook exceeds the culinary; it succeeds where Barry fails in providing immigrants with strategies for survival. In fact, there is something deliciously subversive about Jean's gesture; her cookbook fits into a tradition of women's writing where women transact advice among each other. Cookbooks in diasporic settings are rarely just about food. They are also a cultural form of exchange to indicate how one might face the challenges of leaving home, how to negotiate the pull of nostalgia while also battling the implications of trying to assimilate.

For Jean Mundy, Hilda Deutrom's cookbook offers a script to articulate her diasporic Sri Lankan identity. But in *Reef*, the first novel by Romesh Gunesekera, Deutrom's cookbook is recontextualized for a queer narrative of kinship with playful, even subversive undertones. Like *Monsoon Wedding* and "The Quilt," *Reef* tells a tale of queerness born in the South Asian domestic space. Set in the 1960s against the backdrop of escalating interethnic conflict between Sinhalas and Tamils in Sri Lanka, *Reef* is a coming-of-age story pivoting around the central character, eleven-year-old Triton. The novel begins with Triton in London in the 1980s. A chance encounter with a fellow Sri Lankan at a gas station prompts Triton, the narrator, to recall his childhood and his twenty-year affiliation with his employer Ranjan Salgado, an unmarried Sri Lankan man with a penchant for marine ecology. In Triton's words, it "begins in 1962: the year of the bungled coup" (15). While the political upheaval brought on by ethnic conflicts between the Sinhala and Tamil populations in Sri Lanka resulting in the mass dispersal of Sri Lankans to Australia, Britain, Canada, and the United States is a constant presence, the political unrest in Sri Lanka never enters the foreground of the story; instead, it serves as a yardstick marking the passage of time as Triton passes from childhood to adolescence and finally into adulthood, as well as his passage from household servant to business entrepreneur who owns a restaurant. Through the course of the narrative, we see how Triton forms a bond with Salgado that culminates in their eventual emigration from Sri Lanka to England.

As the always-present-yet-invisible servant, Triton is privy to private conversations and intimate encounters between persons in the house. While the text continually alludes to the world "out there," Triton is wholly immersed in his new world within the walls of Salgado's home. For Triton, "Mister Salgado's house was the center of the universe, and everything else in the world took place within its enclosure" (27). Trion devotes himself to Salgado, preparing intricate and sumptuous feasts to earn a few good words from his employer and the object of his affection.

Initially he is not accorded much importance in the house, but following the dismissal of Joseph, another servant in Salgado's house, Triton is given more responsibility within the household domestic hierarchy. Triton's ascent from general household help to central household figure and cook is cast in hyperbolic terms. He downplays the importance of global upheaval in light of the monumental shifts in his own life within the Salgado home: "All over the globe, revolutions erupted, dominoes tottered and guerilla war came of age; the world's first woman prime minister—Mrs. Bandaranaike—lost her spectacular premiership on our island, and I learned the art of good housekeeping" (55). Although Triton's lessons in good housekeeping are relegated to the edge of his mental and emotional grammar, positioned as an afterthought at the end of the sentence, it is clear that this is the most important global shift in his universe. Even as the world is in a state of flux, what matters is that he is one step closer to having reign over the household.

Gunesekera directly calls attention to Deutrom's cookbook in naming the chapter focusing on Triton's coming-of-age "Cook's Joy." This chapter, which places Triton squarely at the center of narratival development, also references the Cook's Joy brand of cooking oil produced by the British Ceylon Corporation during the 1960s. Noted for "improv[ing] the flavor of food," Cook's Joy is prominently advertised in the *Ceylon Daily News Cookery Book* along with other household foods.

The advertisement for Cook's Joy cooking oil is an important interlocutor to this chapter, showing how Gunesekera's novel reimagines the terms under which Triton fits into a domestic structure. As one advertisement boasts, "clever cooks choose Cook's Joy because it makes all the difference to a meal . . . It is pleasant to use and economical." Pictured in the advertisement is a blown-up image of a bottle of Cook's Joy oil. Standing behind the bottle are three sari-clad women. The right portion of the image pictures an apron-wearing woman looking at fish frying in a life-size frying pan. Because it appears within the pages of a cookbook intended for "housewives," the joy of cooking is marked as a female activity. It is the female cook or the housewife who can and should relish being able to prepare foods. Triton, as a male servant, is not the intended audience of the advertisement. Nor, for that matter, is he burdened with upholding Sri Lanka's culinary traditions. To thus name the chapter after the popular brand of cooking oil is to reimagine the terms of culinary national discourse. The chapter named "Cook's Joy" is not concerned with maintaining the fabric of Sri Lankan culinary home life; rather, the term "cook's joy" comes to stand in for the affective pleasure Triton derives from cooking for Salgado. While it is not transgressive to think of a male in the role of household domestic servant, it is significant that Triton is named a "housekeeper." Triton toils for his master, but for the housewives who read Deutrom's cookbook, it is the wife who works for the "master." Triton's presence as the flamboyant household domestic servant, by contrast, disrupts the gendered and sexualized structure of household management.

Gunesekera's novel is not traditionally queer in the sense that it does not foreground gay sexual practices between the male characters, but the term "queer" is useful in naming Triton's presence as a disidentificatory one that disrupts the home space resulting in a queering of that space. As David L. Eng suggests, queer is not limited to subjects who "readily self-define as queer, gay or lesbian." Instead, a historically disavowed status renders them "queer as such" (*Racial Castration* 18). *Reef*'s espousal of a politics of non-normativity enables desire that can be labeled homosocial or homophilic marks how a nonconsummated form of same-sex desire can emerge within the heterosexual structure of domestic space.

Despite the emergence of a nascent homophilia, the relationship between Triton and Salgado is not egalitarian; Triton is, after all, under the employ of Mr. Salgado, a mere cook in his home. Salgado is highly educated, while Triton has only completed schooling up to the fifth standard (about fifth grade); Salgado is a propertied subject who owns the house, while Triton is employed as a cook in the house. Several class-based distinctions differentiate the two, but an affinity develops between Salgado and Triton that endures longer than any of Salgado's relationships. Friends come and go, but as long as they live within the domestic space, Triton remains the constant presence in his life, providing alimentary and emotional nurturance. Triton's desire for Salgado, however, is not predicated on the promise of sexual satisfaction. In part, the master-servant dynamic between Salgado and Triton render sexual relations between Salgado and Triton taboo. While the text remains resolutely ambiguous about naming the nature of Triton's desire, it articulates Salgado's appreciation of Triton's culinary prowess.

And yet the text is rife with moments in which Triton articulates a queer desire. The lead-up to a dinner party allows Triton to overhear a conversation between Salgado and his girlfriend, Nili, in which the latter inquires where Salgado obtained the love cake, Triton's confectionery creation of eggs, cream, and *cadju* (cashews):

> "Where did you get this, this cake?"
>
> "Triton made it," my Mister Salgado said. *Triton made it.* It was the one phrase he would say with my name again and again like a refrain through those months, giving me such happiness. *Triton made it.* Clear, pure and unstinting. His voice at those moments would be a channel cut from heaven to earth right through the petrified morass of all our lives, releasing a blessing like waters springing from a river-head, from a god's head. It was bliss. My coming of age.
>
> "Your cook?"
>
> *"Your life, your everything,"* I wanted to sing pinned up on the rafters, heaven between my legs. (74–75)

Salgado and Nili's flirtation is routed through the exchange of love cake, but Triton also participates in this wooing game. When Salgado praises the love cake, Triton becomes sexually aroused. Thus while Triton plays a part in helping Salgado woo Nili by baking love cake, the act of sharing cake cannot be understood solely in terms of desire between Salgado and Nili. Rather, Triton emerges as a vital actor in this love triangle. He cares less whether Nili enjoys the cake. What matters is how Salgado speaks about *him.* Triton's joy is heightened by Salgado's praise, climaxing at the moment that he imagines Salgado proclaiming Triton to be his "everything."

While Nili continues to be a presence in Salgado's life, eventually moving into the house, her presence cannot be read as an affirmation of compulsory heterosexuality. Whenever Nili visits Salgado, Triton prepares ever more complex and elaborate dishes designed to satisfy her voracious appetite. At the same time that he derives satisfaction from seeing Nili's appreciation for his food, he is equally attuned to how the reticent Salgado seems invigorated by Nili's appetite. Triton's observation that "he seemed so radiant when she was there with him that I wished she would come more often and lift the monkishness from our monastic house"

(79) acknowledges Salgado's desire for Nili, but also allows for the possibility that Triton comes alive when Nili is present because she enlivens
Salgado in a way that makes him more attentive to and appreciative of
Triton. While it is never made clear whether Triton's feelings are recip-
rocated, a triangulated form of desire emerges among Triton, Nili, and
Salgado. He can receive much-coveted praise from Salgado only through
his interactions with Nili; in this sense, Triton and Salgado's relationship
queers the text insofar as Triton's ability to effect gustatory pleasure in
Nili—ironically—nourishes and nurtures his relationship with Salgado.

Despite the obvious specular pleasure that Salgado derives from
watching Nili eat, he rarely eats in front of her. Nili's remark to Triton,
"your Mister Salgado never seems to eat . . . What is it about this house
that makes it hard for you to eat?" (108), is met with an uncomfortable
silence. Triton's inner thoughts, unheard by Nili, explain why Salgado
can eat only in Triton's company: "He needed his privacy to feel comfortable . . . there was no security in eating in the company of a lot of people;
attention always got divided. Only the intimate could eat together and
be happy. It was like making love. It revealed too much. Food was the
ultimate seducer. But I could not tell that to Miss Nili. I had not even
thought it through at the time" (108). This passage reveals an intimacy
between the two men that cannot exist between Nili and Salgado. While
Triton is sexually aroused by Salgado's praise for his cooking, it never
translates into a sexual act. But when it comes to eating, an activity
deemed intensely personal and sexual, Salgado can only eat alone, or
in Triton's presence, thereby altering the traditional hierarchy between
master and servant, where the two will generally eat separately and in
different spaces.

But is eating together or the shared communion of food with a lover
a substitute for sex? Triton describes food as the "ultimate seducer," suggesting that his culinary skills allow him to seduce Salgado. Further, Salgado can establish an intimate kinship with food only when he eats with
Triton. As the narrative unfolds, it becomes clear that Triton continues
to serve as Salgado's cook, feeding and nurturing him long after Nili and
Salgado part. Through a complex relationship with food, then, Salgado
and Triton develop a powerfully affective bond. Triton may never consummate his desire, but the seductive potential of food suggests that Triton can route his desire for Salgado in nonphysical terms, transgressing
traditional borders between persons of different class statuses within the
same household. Eating together becomes a partial substitute for sexual
gratification. By preparing food with an eye toward pleasing and seduc-

ing Salgado, Triton gives voice to a desire that can escape detection, even by Nili. In effect it is through his culinarily disidentificatory acts within the household that Triton is ultimately able to let his affection for Salgado develop into a form of love that brings him pleasure within the domestic space.

Same-Sex Desire and Food in *Fire*

Deepa Mehta's successful and controversial film *Fire* offers a somewhat different example of same-sex desire emerging within a domestic household, one in which the shared communion of food gradually paves the way for an articulation of same-sex desire. Following its release in 1998, *Fire* has become an important example of how "non-Western" queer sexualities attain legibility. My reading of *Fire* builds on this existing criticism to suggest that food has been overlooked and needs to be reintegrated into analyses of this film. Though the absence of critical attention on the place of food in this film may be explained by the fact that food is by no means the primary axis along which the narrative of the film develops, it would be an oversight to ignore how and where food figures into the film's narrative. At its most progressive, the film articulates how practices of everyday life are re-signified, allowing for a form of female homoeroticism to emerge at the interstices of heterosexuality and homosociality in the Kapur household. As Gopinath notes, "the articulation of female same-sex desire within the space of the domestic directly confronts and disrupts contemporary nationalist constructions of the bourgeois Hindu home as the reservoir of essential national cultural values, embodied in the figure of the Hindu woman as chaste, demure, and self-sacrificing" ("Nostalgia, Desire" 480–81). In *Fire*, various homosocial rites occur within the parameters of daily life for Radha and Sita. As acts of disidentification, the interactions with food allow for the articulation of desire between the two lead female characters, providing another point of engagement, one that considers the role of class privilege in according choices to the middle-class female protagonists.

Set in the middle-class neighborhood of Lajpat Nagar in New Delhi, India, *Fire* tells the story of two women, Radha (Shabana Azmi) and Sita (Nandita Das) who are trapped in emotionally and sexually unfulfilling relationships with a pair of brothers, Ashok (Khulbushan Kharbandha) and Jatin Kapur (Jaaved Jaafri). As the narrative develops, the bond between the two female lead characters deepens under the watchful eye of the household domestic, Mundu, and the mute biji, mother-in-law to Radha and Sita. The film culminates when Radha and Sita leave the Kapur family home after Radha undergoes a symbolic and literal trial by fire. In their everyday lives, Radha and Sita are part of the home but must negotiate the contours of being stuck in unfulfilling marriages. Jatin, Sita's husband, divides his time between his lover, Julie, and his video rental store. Ashok, Radha's husband, devotes his time to Swamiji, a holy man who has been instrumental in teaching Ashok how to control bodily and sexual desire.

Initially the two female leads bond out of necessity more than desire; Radha's husband, Ashok, has chosen a life of monkish celibacy over sexual fulfillment because, as the doctor tells Radha, she has "no eggs in ovaries" and is therefore unable to bear children. Once she ceases to be useful in a reproductive sense, Ashok no longer needs her. Only when Sita enters Radha's life does this change. Working in the family business alongside Sita provides Radha with the means and desire to exit the fraught home space. Radha spends her time working in the kitchen of the family business, a take-out food establishment, and eventually Sita begins working alongside Radha. As the relationship between Radha and Sita develops, the kitchen subtly transforms into a space where the women can spend time together under the watchful eye of the men of the house. At the same time, the mundane nature of their work in the kitchen makes it possible for their affections to go unnoticed.

As they further their bonds of intimacy, they use food to mark their deepening feelings for one another. While preparing food in the kitchen, Radha mentions to Sita, "Certain spices are good for some occasions and some for others. Did you know that black pepper gives you energy which is why it is given in such abundance to newly-wed husbands. For better or for worse!" When Sita inquires which spices are given to brides, Radha responds, "Green cardamoms, to make the breath fragrant." As she speaks, she also places a green cardamom pod in Sita's mouth. Sita provocatively exhales, asking Radha if her breath is fragrant. Through this suggestive exchange of a cardamom pod, the women engage in a playful ritual of coquetry. This exchange renegotiates the "traditional" exchange that might take place between a bride and a groom, allowing same-sex desire to be articulated under the auspices of culinary exchanges within the realm of heterosexual privilege.

Radha and Sita later transform another ritual of heterosexual marriage to mark their desire for one another. On Karva Chauth, the women ritually fast to ensure their husbands long lives, but the rest of the day is spent in each other's company. The transformation of Karva Chauth into a ritual marking female same-sex desire can also be read in conjunction with Kirin Narayan's argument that "in Hindu traditions, it is important to think of multiple, perhaps even contradictory versions rather than [emphasizing] a single correct and authoritative one" (30). Sita's willingness to reinterpret Karva Chauth in more queer terms is also evidenced by her recognition of the hypocrisies that govern the ritual fasting. As she and Radha begin the rituals of the annual fast, she references Ashok's devotion to Swamiji, "I think Ashok bhaiya should keep this fast for Swamiji," emphasizing that Ashok is more devoted to this holy man than his own wife, Radha. Though Karva Chauth seems to limit the range of subject positions available to women, this narrative, incommensurable with its fantasies, ruptures the annual ritual such that it falls away from the cultural jurisdiction of heterosexual Hindu culture. Instead, it is part of a Hindu tradition that A. K. Ramanujan describes as "indissolubly plural and often conflicting with texts often acting in dynamic interplay as 'contexts, pretexts and subtexts' to other texts" (qtd. in K. Narayan 38). Mehta productively calls into question the typical rendering of Karva Chauth as depicted in mainstream Bollywood. Where blockbuster Hindi films about the rites of marriage and its associated rituals like *Kabhi Khushi Kabhi Gham* (Sometimes Happy, Sometimes Sad) and *Hum Aapke Hain Koun?* (Who Am I to You?) position Karva Chauth as an indisputably heterosexual ritual of female self-abnegation, Mehta reinserts a narrative of homosociality to the ritual, imagining the possibility of female-female intimacy through a shared experience of deprivation and hunger.

And yet scholar and activist Madhur Kishwar critiques the film precisely for its willingness to reinterpret female-female homosocial intimacy as a pretext for queer desire. Kishwar notes that massaging an older sister-in-law's feet or oiling one another's hair are acts of female intimacy that are "totally accepted among Indians" and therefore not homoerotic, or homosexual. Where one might identify the potential for homoeroticism to emerge through homosocial rituals, Kishwar is quick to foreclose the possibility of homosociality dovetailing into an expression of homosexuality. As Monica Bachmann conjectures, "Kishwar sees the open expression of female homoeroticism as a threat to Indian women's ability freely to express physical affection" (236).

Such moments of homosocial intimacy in the film are not limited to rituals of grooming the body. When Radha and Sita find themselves outside of the kitchen and outside the home, food allows them to fashion a language to express mutual desire. As they meander through the local market purchasing vegetables for the evening meal, they exchange stories passed on to them from their mothers. In response to Radha's comment, "my mother used to say that the way to a man's heart is through his stomach. Apparently it's a great English saying," Sita mentions, "my mother says that a woman without a husband is like boiled rice. Bland and unappetizing—useless. This must be an Indian saying!" Each aphoristic thought passed on from mother to daughter places food squarely within a heterosexual framework, establishing a continuum between English colonial and Indian postcolonial patriarchies. For Radha's mother, cooking is a tool to woo men; for Sita's mother, a woman has no depth or interest value without a husband; not only is she unappetizing, but she is also useless. Through this exchange of food stories, or what Meredith Abarca dubs "charlas culinarias," Radha transforms the latent meaning of the "Indian" aphorism by observing, "I like plain boiled rice." Meredith Abarca suggests: "The language of food serves different needs; it is spoken in public kitchens and in private ones; it is a language spoken by many women . . . who speak the language of everyday cooking to express artistic creation, manifestations of love, self-assurance and economic survival" (120–21). For Radha, this double-edged gesture marks more than an affinity for "plain boiled rice"; embedded within her words is an articulation of desire and gendered agency. Using the language of food, Radha expresses desire for Sita while undermining the logic of compulsory heterosexuality which would deem a woman metaphorically described as plain boiled rice to be boring and unappetizing.

These culinary scenes complicate a queer reading of the text that would cast the relationship within a butch/femme, seducer/seduced dyad. In the scenes involving food, Radha is the seducer. She places the cardamom pod in Sita's mouth, and she subtly flirts with Sita by telling her that she finds "plain boiled rice" more interesting. Read against the other scenes in which Sita is seen to be the "seducer" who initiates physical lovemaking as well as the pivotal first kiss, these two scenes involving food disrupt a simple seducer/seduced dynamic. Both women seduce one another, creatively marking their desire for one another in slightly different ways. Radha, the woman who has been a paragon of wifely devotion in the film, begins to chart an alternative path for herself using food as her means of expression. Up until this point in the narrative she dutifully feeds her mother-in-law, indulges her husband's "need" to be celibate, prepares meals for the family, and works in the family business. Eventually, she refuses to feed her mother-in-law, asking Ashok to feed her instead, at the same time that she gradually begins to use food to give voice to her desire for Sita. Where same-sex desire might be frowned on if it were to be expressed overtly, the film captures how everyday activities associated with food preparation are imbued with subversive potential to further the bonds of intimacy between Radha and Sita.

Throughout the film, culinary practices are transformed in order to speak of and to non-normative forms of desire; such moments are underwritten by a logic of playful subversion. But the weightiest and most horrific transformation of culinary space takes place at the film's end. When Ashok learns of Radha's "betrayal," he pushes her away from him and into the kitchen's gas burner, at the moment the women are about to turn their backs on the trappings of heterosexual domesticity. That the fire originates from the gas burner, a household appliance used to cook food in the home kitchen, rather than in the "take-out" kitchen, is a harsh indictment of the intractability of domestic space. The gas burner ignites Radha's sari, ejecting her from the home space. This final gesture hints at the latent danger in articulating queer desire. The image of domestic harmony disturbed through the attempt to set Radha on fire using the kitchen stove is laced with palpable horror. To punish Radha for transgressing the implicit heteronormativity of the home, Ashok literally seeks to immolate his wife. It is at this moment of allowing oneself to be immolated that Mehta refines the narrative of wifely devotion so central to the Hindu epic *Ramayana*. Within Hindu mythology, Sita is best known as the self-sacrificing and loyal wife of Rama. In the epic, Rama is sent into exile for fourteen years accompanied by his devoted wife, Sita, and brother Lakshmana. When left alone at their cottage, she is protected by the "Lakshman Rekha," a line drawn by her brother-in-law Lakshmana to "protect" her. Yet Sita is lured into crossing the line and is kidnapped by the demon Ravana, disguised as an elderly sage. After she is rescued by Rama, Sita's tribulations are not over. She must undergo *agni pariksha*, a "trial by fire," testing her purity and devotion. By coming out of the fire unscathed, Sita proves to society that she is a paragon of wifely devotion.[4]

Mehta's narrative refines the dominant Hindu narrative, imbuing Radha Kapur's character with Sita-like qualities.[5] Radha Kapur is a loyal wife by most estimations, and her devotion to her husband and family is rendered legible through the similarities to the epic tale. In her own way, Radha Kapur follows her husband into a version of exile, one that refuses the possibility of sexual intimacy. Confronted with a life of exclusions and regulations, Radha Kapur crosses the invisible borders laid out by society by seeking to chart her own path with Sita. But most ominous of all is Radha's "trial by fire," when Ashok watches with detached indifference as his wife's sari burns. The burning here takes place at the moment Radha's inner strength is being tested to the core. That she survives the fiery flames emanating from a domestic household appliance is eventually an act of purification for Radha that frees her to be herself. To burn, and allow one's body to burn, is to seek a rebirth, the kind that finally allows Radha to free herself from the shackles of domestic wedlock.

Home and Away: Take-Aways and Restaurants

For Radha and Sita, the world beyond the domestic space will free them from the drudgery of their lives. Key to this utopic vision is the notion that material realities can be transformed by imagining new possibilities within the existing structures of inequity. The film intersperses the present with scenes of Radha as a child sitting with her parents in a field of mustard-yellow flowers. Throughout the film, Radha speaks about wanting to see the ocean, and her mother advises her not to look so hard, but to close her eyes and imagine the ocean. At the moment when Radha finally leaves her husband of fourteen years, the film flashes back to the moment when Radha the child looks at the field of flowers and declares, "I can see the ocean! I can see it." The ocean is not tangibly present in the fields of rural northern India; instead, she allows her imagination to guide what she sees so that she can imagine the horizon capture the essence of her desires.

As the film cuts from the scene of Radha's burning sari to the flashback of Radha's childhood, it transitions into the final shot of the film, a darkened rain-soaked scene in which Sita and Radha are reunited at the Nizamuddin Shrine. The film's melancholic but utopic ending suggests that Sita and Radha's relationship to food allows them to imagine a way out of their past realities and into a future where culinary knowledge becomes a means to securing economic survival. Sita's famous tag line in the film, "we can find choices," is symbolically important but also forecloses the possibility of an engaged class critique that might engage how their status as middle-class women facilitates their departure from and survival outside of the protective yet repressive shell of the Kapur household. If Radha and Sita can survive together in a world that Jatin describes as "hell for a divorced woman," it is not solely because they possess the kind of culinary knowledge to "find choices"; access to the means of production within a capitalist economy also allows them to "find choices" and to find their ocean amid a field of yellow flowers. At the moment when Sita and Radha are planning to embark on a new life together, Sita surmises: "I wish we could be together forever. I'm serious. Let's leave. Jatin has Julie, Ashok Bhaiya has Swamiji and Biji has Mundu. They won't even miss us!" When Radha's voice of reason intervenes to ask, "And how will we survive?" Sita assertively responds, "we'll start our own take-away, *of course*," emphasizing the vital role that the women have played in the Kapur family business.

Sita's logic, the inevitability of opening a "take-away" after quitting the domestic space, invites comparison with *Reef*. Now in his adult phase, Triton has relocated to England with Salgado and has successfully opened a restaurant. Eliding questions about how the migration takes place, and only briefly suggesting that the political unrest of the 1960s precipitates their departure, the narrative remains silent about the intervening years between Triton's departure from Sri Lanka and his arrival in England. However, it evocatively narrates how the two men find comfort in one another's company. Triton continues to cook for Salgado, who reciprocally introduces Triton to his world of ocean ecology and literature. Imagining a fusion of their two passions, Salgado recalls: "I used to plan it in my head: how I'd build a jetty, a safe marina for little blue glass-bottomed boats, some outriggers with red sails and then a sort of floating restaurant at one end. You could have produced your finest chilli crab there, you know and the best stuffed sea-cucumbers. Just think of it: a row of silver tureens with red crab-claws in black bean sauce, yellow rice and squid in red wine, a roasted red snapper as big as your arm, shark fin and fried seaweed. It would have been a temple to your gastronomic god, no?" (187). But when Triton suggests opening a restaurant together, Salgado insists that Triton needs to accomplish this on his own, for himself, and eventually resolves to leave England to join Nili, or Tippy, as he calls her, thus forcing Triton to live on his own for the first time in twenty years.

In the closing pages of the novel, Triton muses: "I knew he was going to leave me and he would never come back. I would remain and finally have to live on my own . . . I would learn to talk and joke and entertain, to perfect the swagger of one who has found his vocation, and, at last, a place to call his own. It was the only way I could succeed: without a past, without a name, without Ranjan Salgado standing by my side" (190). While it is troubling that Triton's entry into adulthood, as well as his ability to imagine himself on an even footing with Salgado, coincide with the end of the queer narrative, it would be a gross oversimplification to negate the importance of Salgado or to suggest that the text's apparent return to compulsory heterosexuality invalidates a queer reading of the entire text. By not framing departure as a precondition for sexual liberation, the text demands a rethinking of the connection between queer desire and the home site. In the typical queer bildungsroman, the outside world looms large as the site of liberation and freedom. The outside world holds a certain promise for Radha and Sita's dream of opening a take-away, and Triton's dream of opening a restaurant, but it is the domestic space that gives birth to queer desire. Both of these narratives usefully intervene in discussions that position the South Asian domestic space as a repressive site hostile to antinormative relationships.

At the same time, *Reef* polices the possibility of adult queer desire. For Salgado, Triton's love can only safely exist when the latter is a child. Once he reaches adulthood, his desire becomes dangerous. Like Varun, Triton's queer sexuality is nonthreatening because it is located within the body of a child. But Gunesekera's novel goes one step further (or backward) than *Monsoon Wedding*. It positions queerness as a childhood aberration that will not only be corrected but vehemently denied with the passage to adulthood. Just when it becomes possible for Triton to emerge as a viable partner, the novel forecloses that possibility and returns Salgado to Nili.

Cooking as Resistance in Paradise, Lantanacamara

While *Fire* and *Reef* do much to further the notion that queer desire might emerge within the home space, they do little to suggest how edifices of queer desire might be maintained by domesticity, and how a queer relationship might thrive after the initial articulation of same-sex desire. *Cereus Blooms at Night*, a novel by Shani Mootoo, on the other hand, is much more deliberate in its exploration of how culinary knowledge can sustain the subject who does not have the means of existing outside the home space. For Mala Ramachandin, the mute protagonist of *Cereus Blooms at Night*, culinary knowledge is one of the primary modes of survival at her disposal. Set in the ironically named town Paradise on the fictional island of Lantanacamara in the Caribbean, *Cereus Blooms at Night* is a hauntingly tragic novel about a family that must come to terms with the consequences of numerous betrayals. The novel is narrated from the perspective of Tyler, a gay male nurse who befriends Mala Ramachandin, an elderly resident at the Paradise Alms House, a nursing home for the elderly. Positioned on the periphery of society, Tyler and Mala have "a shared queerness" (48) that takes shape in the act of storytelling. For Mala Ramachandin, the elder of the Ramachandin daughters, cooking becomes the antidote to her deeply embedded trauma. From a young age, she learns to live through and against the pain of betrayal. When a plot to flee her abusive husband, Chandin, with her children and lover, Lavina Thoroughly, goes wrong, Mala's mother, Sarah, leaves her children behind with their father. Life takes a tragic turn for the Ramachandin daughters, and, to protect her sister, Asha, from their father's wrath, Mala bears the brunt of the abuse and is subject to nightly raping such that the townsfolk of Lantanacamara look on with pity at Mala as a woman "whose father had obviously mistaken her for his wife" (169). Despite efforts to dull her pain and to forget the trauma of being left behind, the anniversary of her mother's departure is overlaid with grief and a strong desire to both commemorate the loss and forget its effects. As the anniversary of her mother's departure approaches, Mala "strategizes against" the pain of its memories, undergoing a complex ritual of self-immolation to tear at the fabric of her insides. She prepares a chili pickle for weeks in advance and at the appointed hour consumes the bottle so that she is burning inside. Her physical pain on most days does not match her emotional pain, but on that date, at that appointed, traumatic hour, she needs to take an extra step to negotiate the pain and to feel such an intense level of bodily pain that she literally does not have to think.

> She thrust her finger into the bottle, scooped out a heavy clump of raw pepper and shoved the finger into her mouth. She scooped up more and then more . . . she didn't swallow, keeping the fire on her tongue by then so blistered that parts of the top layer had already disintegrated . . . she pressed her tongue against the roof of her mouth, dispersing the slush to the tender pink flesh on the sides and under her tongue . . . Pepper mush oozed past her clenched gums and spilled into the sides of her cheeks . . . She heaved, trying to find cooling air but the air entering her mouth sent her lacerated flesh into further agony. A tide of peppery saliva cascaded over her lips. She ran to the balcony and spat, salivating and expelling sauce and pepper flesh and seeds. . . . Her flesh had come undone. But every tingling blister and eruption in her mouth and lips was a welcome sign that she had survived. She was alive. (133–34)

This metaphoric self-immolation is the only way Mala can survive the cyclical trauma of her life, the only way she knows how to work through the pain of her emotional scars. The deep and tragic irony of Mala's life is that after the women of the Ramachandin household leave her behind, she is unwittingly thrust into a system of domestic indentureship where her every move must be dedicated to running a smooth household for Chandin, a man who, like Ashok, demands the women of the house to fall in line with his needs and desires—physical, psychic, and sexual. For someone like Mala, culinary knowledge can never be exclusively about pleasure and intimacy; rather, it is tied up with her ability to survive within a home space governed by Chandin Ramachandin, a patriarchal figure hostile to female bodies and queer bodies.

In his desire to maintain the illusion of being the head of a normative household, complete with a wife to ensure the smooth running of the domestic space, Chandin becomes the kind of patriarch who demands that Mala deny herself any possibility of autonomy and personhood. As the implicit "wife" of the household, Mala's culinary knowledge extends to being expected to prepare a hot meal of Chandin's choice on a daily basis. He only need utter, "curry a brown fowl," and it is "understood the meal must also include rice, split pea dhal, curried channa or aloo and one sadha roti" (201). When Mala, unable to procure chicken for the evening's meal, presents fish instead, Chandin is so incensed at this apparent flouting of his authority that he rams the fish stew into Mala's face, causing a different kind of burning. Mala is forced to feel the acridness of the chilies sting her eyes. Amid this scene of violence, Mala mobilizes her culinary strengths to block out the pain of his blows: "she slipped her tongue out of her mouth and licked the stew on her face. The taste of garlic and anise erased his smell. The stew was indeed well seasoned, perhaps the best she had ever cooked" (205). When he demands she prepare his desired meal of fowl, Mala strategizes to placate Chandin, preserve her self-dignity, and exact revenge. For the fresh chicken in the fowl curry, she substitutes a dead pigeon, rancid and disease-ridden. Here, Mala succeeds in serving "fowl," but the drunken Chandin is unable to detect that his curry dish is more foul than fowl. As Mala observes, "he tasted curry spices and that was enough to appease him" (207). In exercising his control over Mala, Chandin refuses to eat fish (inedible to his tastes), and yet Mala "cooks back," serving him something that is both inedible and foul, thus marking how her own culinary knowledge becomes essential for her survival. As a character who feels betrayed by same-sex desire, Chandin becomes the repository of a violent patriarchal culture. "Cooking back" is one of the only weapons in Mala's arsenal within a home more like a battlefield, almost always shrouded with the veil of violence. As such it is unsurprising that when Mala can no longer tolerate her father's abuse, when he has raped and humiliated her one time too many, she calls on her culinary knowledge to end his life. She first knocks him out using a weapon from her kitchen, a meat cleaver. But the real poetic justice of her action comes from the fact that she locks Chandin in a room and allows him to slowly die of starvation. Her recuperation of her body and self, then, is effected through her reappropriation of the same tools and space that marked her domestic indentureship in the Ramachandin household.

"A Shared Queerness"

The deliberate juxtaposition of these different narratives lends itself to an interpretive strategy which frames cooking as a queer epistemology. Queerness by definition resists and refuses to serve the needs of domestic heteropatriarchy. A system of disidentification, queerness recognizes the implicit privilege and power of heteronormativity but also refuses to engage its effects and expressions without also transforming that logic. Further, queer diasporic cultural production creates sites to "contest traditional family and kinship structures—of reorganizing national and transnational communities based not on origin, filiation and genetics but on destination, affiliation, and the assumption of a common set of social practices or political commitments" (Eng et al. 7). Where domestic manuals and cookbooks discipline women into performing wifeliness, there remain spaces for repudiating this master narrative that would seamlessly suture cooking and heteronormativity within traditional familial and kinship formations. Food offers Triton the language to express love and affection. He lovingly prepares for his boss without having to fear the repercussions of actually articulating that pained and overdetermined utterance, "I love you." For the characters in *Fire*, women who have to negotiate the dangers of articulating love, food becomes a way to articulate without speaking. Mala, denied the ability to express her love for Ambrose, uses food to channel her feelings for Ambrose. At the same time, food is also the weapon she uses to repudiate Chandin's claims on her. Food is her way to assert control and to ultimately extricate herself from the shackles of Chandin's incestuous love. Lest we think of cooking solely as a weapon to punish Mala's abusive father, Mootoo introduces another vector to cooking. Cooking retains no intrinsic immutable value for Mala. It becomes meaningful only when the intended consumer is someone she cares about. To cook for her father, Chandin, is "a chore she performed without much thought or caring" (202). But when cooking for Ambrose Mohanty, her childhood friend and nascent lover, "cooking had become a delightful production" (202). For Mala, as with Triton and Radha and Sita, cooking becomes a vibrant act of sharing love.

Through relationships with culinary practices and food, queer subjects produce antinormative, nonreproductive relations between men, and between women in the domestic space, a space that is typically configured to be hostile to queer desire. The worlds created by these works highlight the powerfully affective potential of food and its ability to engender antinormative forms of desire that challenge the notion that the home is a necessarily heterosexual formation designed to reproduce citizens who will uphold tradition and its concomitant values. In the process, each work fashions a narrative open to the possibility of exploring how food becomes a language through which to also queer the domestic space, unstitching the seams of heterosexuality to weave an alternative narrative that exhorts us to imagine an alternative world, however utopic and unrealizable those worlds might seem to be. In their resolute optimism about the possibility of other worlds, these works nudge us to imagine an alternate worldview, an alternate form of culinary epistemology where to cook and to prepare food might be but one way to chip away at the edifice of heteronormativity and to imagine a world where culinary practices might serve to bind people less on structures based around filiation and grounded identities, but through a commitment to a shared vision of the world and, as Mootoo so appropriately phrases it, "a shared queerness" (48).

PART TWO

Palatable Multiculturalisms and Class Critique

3 / Sugar and Spice: Sweetening the Taste of Alterity

Undoubtedly, one can write while eating more easily than one can speak while eating, but writing goes further in transforming words into things capable of competing with food.
—GILLES DELEUZE AND FELIX GUATTARI,
"WHAT IS A MINOR LITERATURE?"

Life without candy is unfathomable for Americans today.
—JANE DUSSELIER, "BONBONS, LEMON DROPS
AND OH HENRY! BARS"

Despite the eventual failure of Triton and Ranjan's relationship in *Reef*, the earliest gestures toward intimacy are marked through the sharing of love cake. Charmaine Solomon's classic tome on Asian cooking suggests that love cake might well be the most coveted and contentious of confections because it reigns supreme as the confectionery choice of many as well as the confection with the most variations known to cooks in the Sri Lankan diaspora. For Mala in *Cereus Blooms at Night*, baking a cake for Ambrose allows her to express her desire for him. Establishing networks of intimacy enabled through shared consumption becomes an overt marker of desire. But sweets and confections buttress more complex and heterogeneous narratives than ones that simply mark desire. In a more politically charged sense, sweetness signifies much more than mere desire. Sidney Mintz's wonderful exploration of the relationship between sweetness and power began the important work of understanding sugar and sweetness to be inextricably linked to relations of colonial power. Indo-Trinidadian author Ramabai Espinet notes that the desire for sweetness was a major force compelling the flow of labor from the Indian subcontinent to Trinidad. In her novel *The Swinging Bridge*, the nation-state is translated playfully but with powerful political resonance as "Chinidad, land of sugar" (3–4). The West's pursuit of sugar and spices has subjugated populations of laborers—first through African slavery and later through policies of indentureship of Indians and Chinese populations. This history of inequity demands a thorough examination of how the politics of production buttresses the aesthetics of food writing. With its moorings within a matrix of colonial power and production, sugar is inextricably linked to consumptive practices. Indeed, it was the high demand for sugar in the West that set in motion the wheels of colonialism, which systematically garnered strength from shackling the bodies of colonized subjects into the exploitative world of sugar plantation labor. "Sweetness," however, is not restricted to palatal matters but often extends into epistemologies about constructing modes of reality. As such, what might be the literal or discursive strategies available to authors to address the politics of consumption?

In Asian American literary studies, the concept of food pornography has most frequently spoken to processes of cultural consumption and the commodification of ethnicity. Food pornography names the ethical project of writers who commodify and exoticize minoritized cultures for mainstream readers using an Orientalist understanding of food as a signifier of difference. Originating from *The Year of the Dragon*, a play by the well-known Chinese American playwright Frank Chin, the term "food pornography" can be defined as an exploitative form of self-Orientalism in which Asian American subjects highlight the "exotic" nature of their foodways by exaggerating the terms of their otherness. It is considered a form of cultural self-commodification through which Asian Americans earn a living by capitalizing on the so-called exoticism embedded in one's foodways. As Sau-Ling Wong notes, food pornography superficially appears to promote rather than devalue one's ethnic heritage, but "what [it does] in fact do is to wrench cultural practices out of their context and display them for gain to the curious gaze of outsiders" (56). To write about food, then, is to enable a form of cultural consumption with Asian Americanness taking on the role of commodity-comestible.

But as books acquire the status of commodities subject to consumption, it becomes imperative to consider other models of consumption. Following Jean Baudrillard, we might conceptualize an alternative mode of consuming difference, a type of consumptive practice in which actual eating is jettisoned in favor of alternative forms of consumption— visual, olfactory, and psychic. "Hyperreal eating" becomes a useful form of critical scaffolding in that it names the consumer as a necessary part of the exchange between commodity, consumer, and cultural broker. It speaks to the desire of the consumer who subscribes to a politics of multiculturalist eating—the notion that eating widely can overcome racial difference—as well as to the practice of simulating eating without physically ingesting food. This process also names the author and publishing house as actors within the process of hyperreal eating. Through the literary idiom they create, as well as the marketing strategies deployed by publishers, a new generation of Asian American popular writing has emerged. Traditionally overlooked by critics, this genre counters the conventional practice of positioning Asian American authors as writers who must unquestioningly pander to the demands of mainstream readers hungry to consume palatable narratives about racial and ethnic difference. Within the framework of popular multiculturalism, ethnic-themed novels became the flavor du jour, satiating America's appetite to consume difference often in what we might conceive of as "sugar-coated" realism wherein a culinary idiom deliberately and strategically produces palatable narratives of otherness. Such forms of novelistic discourse modulate the North American public's propensity to consume alterity and are rooted in and routed through a desire to sublimate eating into a nonphysical activity, allowing for a guilt-free consumption of otherness.

But how, we might ask, can one consume food without eating? Such evidence for these possibilities is found within the affectively charged culinary landscape of American commodity culture, an arena that best describes what I conceive of here as "hyperreal eating." Quite distinct and apart from the world of Asian American cultural production, hyperreal eating has strong resonances within the bath and body market. In the years since the advent of low-carbohydrate dieting, an upsurge has occurred in dessert-inspired bath and body products marketed to young women. In a world where "Atkins" is no longer just a surname, where "South Beach" is not just a vacation spot in Florida, and where foods deemed rich, sugary, and calorie- and carbohydrate-laden have become the most latent threat to the foodie's desire to consume novelty, a range of alternatives to food have emerged in consumer markets which capitalize on America's interest in conspicuous consumption. Similar moves to create culinary-inspired treats can be found in other commodities that circulate widely in North American malls and shopping centers. Philosophy, a company specializing in bath and body products, offers up a line to tantalize taste buds without the guilt of calories. As part of Philosophy's line of shampoos and shower gels called "The Cookbook," one can "indulge one's sweet tooth" by lathering up with flavors of shower gel named café au lait, chocolate crème coffee, and white chocolate hazelnut cake. The popularity of commodifed culinary-inspired treats for the face and body such as The Cookbook line and several other brands on the market signals a cognitive rupture in understanding the relationship between food and consumption; it becomes not just permissible, but preferable to engage in a form of consumption that renders "eating" obsolete or, at the very least, unnecessary. In an era when women are limiting carbohydrate intake, such products make it possible to nourish one's visceral appetite for sugar without actually eating. Companies marketing such products engage in the business of selling commodities that masquerade as "snack[s] for the skin, an external form of nourishment that offers the sensual experience of food without the sugar, fat, and shame so commonly associated with real-life eating" (Tringali 35–37).

The consumption of crème brûlée sugar scrubs instead of crème brûlée tarts sets in motion a commodifed exchange whereby one sublimates the appetite to eat. Consumption itself becomes "hyperreal" wherein the consumer consumes the hyperreal product, preferring "signs of the real for the real itself" (Baudrillard 166). Limiting consumption to an epidermal level, these products play on the fear of the socially constructed fat body, typically the "taboo *verboten* site around which other commodities proliferate" (Braziel and LeBesco 6). Bodily excesses and the fear of corpulence become containable through the mere power of suggestion. Through hyperreal rather than actual eating, that which is forbidden can be gluttonously consumed without the fear of embodying a culturally constructed notion of corporeal excess.

Hyperreal eating reminds us that consumption of food does not necessarily involve eating, while gesturing to ways in which culinary desire can morph into other types of desire, equally visceral. So what does it mean to eat without eating? What happens to the desire to consume delectable treats within a cultural economy that so closely polices excess at the same time that it hungers for palatable treats and difference? One arena in which there has been a sustained interest in forms of consumption that don't involve eating is in the literary world. Food writing has always enjoyed a certain level of popularity, but in the early twenty-first century, culinary narratives and their concomitant imaginings of otherness have become far more prevalent within the literary marketplace. The burgeoning popularity of the culinary-themed novel discloses the acute presence of hyperreal eating as a viable strategy to market the ethnic-themed novel. The culinary-themed novel becomes positioned as a more palatable and acceptable mode of representing difference precisely because it is anchored in a culinary idiom, but also because it functions as a commodity, thus furthering the notion that literature by and about minoritized subjects is necessarily enjoined to a consumptive understanding of racial and ethnic difference.

While the world of fashion has seen an upsurge of interest in India-inspired fashion, or "Indo-Chic," there are clear analogues in an interest in Indian-marked commodities in other cultural spheres. With its roots in the critical success of writers like Salman Rushdie, Arundathi Roy, Rohinton Mistry, Monica Ali, and Jhumpa Lahiri, the rapid rise in popularity of South Asian literature has led to the flowering of a cottage industry of writings about the South Asian diaspora. The multiplicity of these narratives is matched by their heterogeneity; while many writers have earned a degree of critical acclaim, several others including Chitra Bannerjee Divakaruni, Nisha Minhas, Bharati Kirchner, and Kavita Daswami have enjoyed greater popular appeal akin to that which Amy Tan has held in the market for Chinese American writing in the United States. In such a climate, readers turn to a wide range of South Asian American fiction to encounter realistic and palatable depictions of desi life.

Within this genre of popular literature is the subgenre of "food writing." While being among the more popular texts among mainstream readers, they are rarely brought into the fold of critical South Asian diasporic studies. This invisibility is linked to the perceived palatability of the genre. Popularity often translates to the notion of this literature "selling out" by pandering to Western tastes. Like Frank Chin, who disparages the culinary-themed novel, denigrating it as a form of "food pornography" wherein the terms of ethnic and racial difference are so exaggerated so as to make difference palatable, the food novel comes under fire from critics. Indeed, one might go so far as to critique Asian American food writing for being spiced with the flavor of exoticism or excessively sugarcoated. But the tendency to write "palatably" might also be interpreted as a response to the implicit mandates of publishing houses. As Ketu Katrak suggests, minority writers must contend with a literary marketplace "eager to consume marginal cultural products, and when the game of inclusion and exclusion is played without the players always knowing the rules" (195). While there can be little to refute Katrak's contention that the literary marketplace is eager to consume difference, the multiculturalist publishing boom has not turned writers of color into unwitting pawns of the system, unaware of the rules of the game. Certain types of writing continue to struggle to find a sustained public voice, but more popular works have easily found their way into different sectors of the literary marketplace.

A literary subgenre that allows authors to work within the rules of the system is food writing. Because culinary narratives affectively simulate hyperreal eating, food writing falls within the range of "acceptable" literary interventions—safely ethnic, and apparently nonpolitical because they figuratively serve marginalia up on a platter, deploying a "frame of reference accessible and acceptable to 'mainstream' Americans." [1] Culinary-themed novels such as *Pastries: A Novel of Desserts and Discoveries* and *Mistress of Spices* uphold the notion that novels about food are the latest commodity in the niche market for ethnicity catering to the notion that desi cultural practices are consonant with culinary practices. In such novels, often denigrated for being "overly spiced" or "sugarcoated," eating plays second fiddle to the guiltless consumption of difference. But while the "acceptable," even palatable, narrative is one that enjoys popularity, such writing is not—contrary to what Chin might suggest—automatically apolitical. Recalling Gilles Deleuze and Felix Guattari's now classic statement about the task of minor literature, writings that "a minority constructs within a major language" (17), the ethnic-themed food novel is always already political; its language and discursive strategies contravene into majoritarian discourse, deterritorializing major ("American") literature by providing an alternative cognitive map to deconstruct the notion of an immanent understanding of American personhood. It is in this sense that culinary writing is a form of minor literature, not merely a reductive form of food pornography, naively pandering to the tastes and desires of mainstream readers wishing to consume delectable narratives of alterity.

Pastries, a relatively recent installment within the fictive worlds of South Asian America, is a novel which plays into the interest in hyperreal eating. Briefly, it is about an Indian American with a passion for baking who struggles to find a place for her business in an increasingly corporate climate. When the protagonist's business starts to fail, she turns to spirituality to help her heal. Thus, the challenge to literary critics stems from negotiating how the novel mobilizes an Orientalist idiom to render intelligible the protagonist's psychic angst and existential dilemmas prompted by the looming failure of the protagonist's small business. Orientalism emerges in this novel as a response to the incurable injuries inflicted on the individual and collective spirit by the insidious operations of late capitalist machinery. In mimicking the conventions of an Orientalist parable to fashion a narrative sensitive to the exigencies of capitalism, *Pastries* is not a simple Orientalist novel, which literary critics can lambast for formulaically rehearsing age-old stereotypes about the languid East. Rather, it deploys the language of hyperreal eating in conjunction with discursive strategies that might be understood as ambivalently Orientalist to levy its critique of matters deemed unpalatable.

In a similar vein, *Mistress of Spices* has come under fierce attack for its apparent deployment of a vulgarly Orientalist frame. Framed by the seductive appeal of the ethnic immigrant food enclave, the novel generates images of a haptically overloaded India lodged amid sacks of rice and fragrant spices, thus reifying Orientalist images of otherness. Furthermore, *Mistress of Spices* has been voraciously consumed by the North American mainstream reading public, perhaps because as a multicultural commodity, it transforms the dusty immigrant enclave of the spice store into a mythically alluring terrain where so-called exotic spices can magically resolve interpersonal problems.

But Orientalist narratives do not emerge solely from writings by those who can unequivocally position themselves beyond the purview of the so-called "Orient." As Edward Said has persuasively argued, Orientalism wields discursive authority only when leveled by those who have power. By extension, those bodies occupying "Orientalist" spaces, phantasmatic or real, are capable of producing narratives laced with Orientalist gestures, if they are in a position of discursive power. As Lisa Heldke notes, the Orientalist is a "professional who interprets the Orient for his reader, and in the process, quite literally makes the Orient (as object of the West) come into existence. The Orientalist helps to make the Oriental available to Westerners by explaining and interpreting the Orient for them" (89). Indian Americans who serve as powerful cultural brokers in the literary arena cannot simply be viewed as passive objects subject to penetrating Orientalizing gazes. Rather, their cultural power has given Indian American writers considerable cultural capital within the world of literary publishing to interpret the impenetrable East for willing readers. In sum, both novels fashion a narrative that is vexed with the materiality of race and class for South Asian Americans and at the same time is shrouded with an appetizing veneer of palatability. What could be more appealing to the lay reader than a novel about spices or one about pastries and desserts? This chapter suggests that *Pastries* and *Mistress of Spices* mobilize an ambivalently Orientalist discursive structure in which to contain the racialized worlds of South Asian America. Foregrounding the ambivalence of the Orientalist rhetoric in each novel thus allows for an interrogation of how texts that mimic the conventions of the Orientalist parable might deploy a culinary frame in order to render critiques of late capitalism and racism palatable.

Spicy Enclaves and Curanderas

Imagine yourself in the bustling activity of a bazaar in Delhi, Dhaka or Karachi, a kaleidoscope of dazzling colors and fragrances swirling about you—mounds of spices, piles of nuts, and wafting smells of ripe fruit, curry and coconut oil. Not so far from this fantasy is the little Indian market where I shop. You pull open the door and a string of brass bells jangle, ushering you into another land. The heady aromas of cardamom, black pepper, perfumed incense, and rose-scented sweets fill the air. You are surrounded by exotic provisions with colorful wrappers and labels. The strains of a sitar resonate from a far corner. There is the rustle of a saree as the storeowner's wife emerges from an aisle to greet you. "Namaste! Welcome!"—LINDA BLADHOLM, THE INDIAN GROCERY STORE DEMYSTIFIED

With these words, Linda Bladholm begins her description of a "typical" Indian grocery store in the United States. Her painstaking description of the interior of the grocery store serves the singular purpose of demystifying the space of the Indian grocery store. As the narrative progresses, she introduces readers to the actors in her staged version of everyday Indianness within the space of the Indian grocery store— "the tall, graceful Mrs. Raja with "henna-streaked, oiled hair coiled at the nape of her neck" (15), her husband and their children, fifteen-year-old Meena and twelve-year-old Yasmin. But without doubt, the most formidable character is the store itself. Bladholm vivifies this space, providing detailed explanations about the layout of this imagined store, complete with a labeled map and verbose descriptions about the colors, spices, and aromas of this fantasy landscape. *The Indian Grocery Demystified* underscores how Orientalist notions about India as an exotic and mystical space continue to pervade popular American discourse about Indian foodways and Indian immigrant culinary practices. While Bladholm only wishes for everyone to share in her love of India, the opening pages of the guide drive home the point that Indianness can be penetrable if one has the patience to unravel all of its mysterious ciphers and codes. Curiously enough, Bladholm's rendering of the spice store falls in line with *Mistress of Spices,* a film directed by Paul Mayeda Berges with Gurinder Chadha serving as the screenwriter. Based on Chitra Bannerjee Divakaruni's novel of the same name, *Mistress of Spices* features the Indian starlet Aishwarya Rai and Indian American cooking show host Padma Lakshmi. Spice Bazaar, the setting of the film, is an Indian grocery store in a racially diverse and economically depressed neighborhood in Oakland, California. Spice Bazaar is transformed on-screen into an Orientalist den of difference peppered with scenes of delectable spices. Through the penetrating gaze of the film, spices are presented in their natural habitat as well as in the space of the store. The apprentice mistresses of spice learn how to recognize spices in their natural habitat. From lush scenes of green cardamom growing on vines to cinnamon bark delicately peeled from a tree and turmeric root unearthed from the ground amid a field of verdant nature, to gnarly ginger dangling provocatively from tree branches, the scene cuts to another setting of delectable spices in Spice Bazaar. Bunches of dry red chilies hang decorously in a corner, dishes of red chili powder are arranged appealingly in the store window, cinnamon sticks lie in wicker baskets, and rice- and lentil-filled gunny sacks border the walls of the store. In this way, the film presents the Indian grocery store along the lines depicted by Linda Bladholm. The store is a space of excess, replete with a reified Indianness that comes alive through color and haptic overload.

But how does either version of the grocery store match up to the actuality of this important cornerstone of immigrant cultural life? Both Bladholm's description of the Indian store and the version rendered on-screen by Berges and Chadha's film differ markedly from Purnima Mankekar's ethnography of grocery stores in the Bay Area of California. Mankekar identifies Indian grocery stores as important cultural sites for the production of Indian culture, noting that the commodities the stores sell are "deeply enmeshed in the social lives and identities of Indians in the Bay Area" (211). For Mankekar, the commodities sold in Indian grocery stores are not significant simply because they feed immigrant nostalgia for the fabled homeland. They matter because they enact a form of "polyvocality"—engendering complex emotions among its consumers: pleasure, ambivalence, and, in some cases, hostility (210). Central to the drama of the grocery store—if one can label the everyday goings-on as "dramatic"—are the dynamic forms of exchange and community constructed around the commodities within the space of the store. With this in mind, I turn to *Mistress of Spices* to examine how the "everyday" intersects with the "dramatic" in the Indian spice store.

Published in 1997, Chitra Bannerjee Divakaruni's *Mistress of Spices* emerges against the backdrop of mainstream America's Orientalist fascination and revulsion with the "authentically" ethnic. Because its overtly self-exoticizing terms routed through the culinary imaginary approximates the style of food pornography, the novel is frequently omitted in Asian American literary studies and discussions of Indian American literature. My aim in exploring the nuances of this text is not to serve as an apologist for the novel; rather, it is to attend to the incommensurability of the novel's critical and popular reception. It has been lambasted by literary critics at the same time that it has been voraciously consumed by the mainstream. My reading of the novel recognizes that it is laced—or, perhaps more appropriately, peppered—with problems. But by offering a few close readings of selected chapters, I hope to peel away some of the decorous language and imagery that envelop the novel in order to examine some of the stories of the Indian American community lodged under Divakaruni's sacks of fenugreek, peppercorn, and black cumin. Unlike many other works, including more highly visible works by Indian American authors Abraham Varghese, Bharati Mukherjee, and Jhumpa Lahiri, Divakaruni's novel addresses the demise of the multiculturalist project, and the attendant failure of assimilationist strategies within the U.S. racial and ethnic landscape. And, in large measure, this comes about because non– English speakers, immigrant laborers, victims of racial violence, and youth gang members are among the cast of characters found within the pages of the novel.

Mistress of Spices tells the tale of Tilo, an Indian American immigrant and curandera who owns an Indian grocery store named Spice Bazaar located in Oakland, California. Much of the novel focuses on Tilo's interactions with an array of characters, mostly varied individuals from the South Asian community in Oakland who meander in and out of the store as part of their everyday, routine lives as immigrants in the United States. Along the way, Tilo meets and falls in love with a young Native American named Raven. It is this romance that ultimately tilts the novel away from its critical freight, sacrificing a nuanced exploration of the varied vagaries of immigrant life to produce a more palatable narrative complete with narrative closure effected through the promise of romance and heterosexual union.

In the novel, the lead-up to the eventual realization of heterosexual romance is populated by a raw exposure of everyday immigrant life. Michel de Certeau suggests that the invisibility of everyday life renders history important; in *Mistress of Spices*, the novel's architecture is built around the invisibility of everyday life for South Asian immigrants. Indeed, the space of invisibility and the site of the everyday that powerfully produces relevant histories and narratives of diasporic melancholy is Spice Bazaar, the domain of Tilo, the curandera. But within this space of the everyday brought to life within the pages of the novel is a latent Orientalism that would shroud the stuff of everydayness in diasporic Indian life with palpable exoticism. It quickly becomes clear that the novel is coated with the markers of Orientalism: each chapter is named for a particular spice—turmeric, cumin, and asafetida. As a *New Yorker* review notes, this renders Divakaruni's prose "so pungent that it stains the page" (164).

Within the corpus of South Asian American writing, *Mistress of Spices* is second only to Bharati Mukherjee's *Jasmine* in being considered the bête noire of South Asian American literature. Like Mukherjee, who, as Debjani Bannerjee notes, "caters to a First World audience while still mining the Third World for fictional material" (173), Divakaruni has come under fire from literary critics both in the United States as well as on the subcontinent for creating a novel which packages ethnicity within a palpably "exotic ethnic" framework. One of the most stinging critiques emerges from one of India's preeminent literary critics, Meenakshi Mukherjee. Mukherjee lambasts the text for using food as an intuitive index to contain Indianness: "in this tale of a mysterious eastern woman the distinctly 'Indian' flavour of the title is intensified by naming the sections 'Turmeric,' 'Red Chili', 'Peppercorn,' 'Lotus Root' and ending, for good measure, with a climactic chapter called 'Maya' in case the seasonings have not been sufficiently cooked. For those in India, spices are taken-for-granted ingredients of daily cooking and do not carry any cultural connotation. They assume a symbolic value only when dislodged from their normal context" (200–201).

While Mukherjee is not wrong to cast aspersions upon the uncritical use of food to contain Indianness, diasporized settings are not the only spaces where food becomes yoked to a sense of cultural identity. Often regional identities bear stronger ideological weight than the category of the "national." Chitrita Banerji's rich account of the foodways delves into the stereotypes and preferences of regional communities in India. Her book's title, *Eating India: An Odyssey into the Food and Culture of the Land of Spices*, calls to mind the deep connections between food and region in India. To suggest the power of stereotype within the Indian context, she notes: "food, like race and ethnicity, can be all too easily stereotyped. The dismissive clichés about southern cuisines that I had grown up with—always vegetarian, swimming in coconut oil, having little to offer beyond bland idlis, dosas, uthappams and curds-rice— have thankfully crumbled away" (56). For many communities in India, geographic landscapes have produced certain foodways which, in turn, produce an emotional investment in certain foods, marking a deep connection between food and place. For the coastal communities of Kerala and Bengal, seafood reigns supreme. In the desertscapes of Rajasthan, where fresh vegetables and produce are in scarce supply, cooks make the most of, "nonperishable items like sugar and ghee and buttermilk" (174) to produce distinctively Rajasthani fare. Ideological investments in food, then, are not created merely by the conditions of transnationalism, even as the experience of diaspora and dislocation might intensify the cultural connotations of food. Moreover, the notion that spices occupying the status of "taken-for-granted" is also what lends Indianness within the parameters of the nation-state of India its claims to normativity. In Mukherjee's formulation, unlike Mootoo's rendering of diaspora in "Out on Main Street," the homeland is granted the status of original, and diaspora is the imitative category that imbues food with symbolic cultural capital. Implicit in Mukherjee's critique is the notion that the use of spices alone contributes to what she derisively terms "local colour" narratives. To assume that the mere cartography of Divakaruni's text, the naming of chapters by spice, is cause for concern is to significantly overlook how food might contain meanings that exceed the merely descriptive. The problematic nature of the text's cartography, instead, arises from the seemingly uncritical use of food to buttress rather than jettison exoticism as a frame to apprehend difference.

A radically different approach to using food as an organizing thematic emerges from the pages of Joanna Kadi's politically affective collection *Food for Our Grandmothers: Writings by Arab-American and Arab-Canadian Feminists*. In stark contrast to Divakaruni's use of spices in *Mistress of Spices*, *Food for Our Grandmothers* refuses the dichotomy between food as pleasurable commodity for apolitical consumption and food as a mode for indexing social and political change. The collection emerges self-consciously in the footsteps of radical writings by U.S. women of color such as *This Bridge Called My Back: Writings by Radical Women of Color* to articulate a radicalized feminist sensibility for Arab American and Arab Canadian feminists. In the introduction to the volume, Kadi explains how food is more than an emotional anchor for the text and the stories contained in its pages. Food, in its essence, is vitally and constitutively an organizing principle for the work and for the lives chronicled therein. As Kadi explains, "the book is an offering back to our grandmothers/our community . . . it offers appropriate food for our grandmothers—the Arabic food that many of them made daily . . . A common Arabic food is used to embody the themes connecting each section, and a recipe using that common food accompanies each section" (xx).

Each section of *Food for Our Grandmothers* is classified under the rubric of olives, bread, laban (yogurt), grape leaves, or mint. The section titled "Olives" carries the subtitle "Our Roots Go Deep: Where We Came From" and makes clear why olives are a fitting intellectual rubric to understand Arab American history: "Trees in various parts of the Arab world date back thousands of years and many still bear fruit. This is a fitting image for a discussion of our history. Olive trees represent our long connection to our land and culture. Thus, one of the violations committed by the Israeli army/ government upon the Palestinian people, the uprooting of centuries-old olive trees, is horrific. Those trees represent Palestinian connection to the land as well as their livelihood and culture" (3). Following each narrative, Kadi provides a recipe using that ingredient. The narrative and recipe serve as a prelude to what follows: a selection of essays tracing the entangled web of affiliation between land, sovereignty, nationalism, and feminism. The culinary titles, then, are not self-evident categories of inclusion, mere descriptors of a codified signifier of Arab difference within the North American imaginary. Rather, olives, bread, laban grape leaves, and mint become intellectual rubrics through which to unsettle their very assignations as tantalizing ingredients of Middle Eastern cooking.

Within the political and imaginative borders of India, but also crossing over into the imaginative realm of diasporic boundaries, is Esther David's novel *The Book of Rachel*, which also uses a culinary rubric. Published in 2006, it is the third novel by David, a Bene Israel writer based in Ahmedabad, India, and is one of the few literary works to narrativize the Jewish diaspora within India. In *The Book of Rachel*, David fashions a narrative about an elderly Bene Israel Jew, Rachel Dandekar, the last remaining Bene Israel Jew in the coastal community Alibaug. Rachel's family members are twice-migrants. Descended from the Bene Israel Jews who migrated to the Malabar coast of India, Rachel's family has since left India and migrated to Israel. The novel is a moving chronicle about how Dandekar works against the efforts of real estate developers to protect the last remaining synagogue in Alibaug, one of the few visible markers of a Bene Israel Jewish culture along the Malabar coast. In her efforts to save this edifice of Jewish life in India, she mobilizes the help of diasporic Bene Israel Jews who have ironically turned away from India to find a home in Israel, what Rachel Dandekar glibly dubs the Promised Land. In rendering this feminist parable of one woman who battles sexism to literally protect sacred ground, the novel deploys a culinary frame not unlike that used by Divakaruni. Each of the chapters in

David's novel is named after a signature dish within the Bene Israel Jewish culinary repertoire such as chik cha halwa, mince cutlets, or puranpoli. Each chapter introduces the Bene Israel dish via a recipe. David establishes each recipe's significance to the Bene Israel context before moving into the narrative proper, in which the significance of the dish unfolds against the backdrop of the novel's narrative trajectory. In this way, food is a cultural idiom that indexes the importance of food within the Bene Israel community while marking the distinctiveness of that ethno-religious group so invisible within the Indian bifurcated imagination of Hindu-Muslim. At the same time, the novel uses food to mark a feminist rendering of community. Each recipe, after all, is not designed merely to replicate cultural norms but to marks the ways in which Rachel Dandekar firmly resolves to protect the last remaining vestiges of her diasporic Bene Israel roots.

Chitra Divakaruni's novel unsettles critics and readers alike *because* of the absence of a discernible critical rationale for its use of food as an organizing problematic. Rather than using food as a means to dismantle categories of racism and sexism, her text yokes food to a descriptive, rather than critical, Indianness: food is rendered so one-dimensionally that it appears unable to extend its field of signification beyond that of mystical Orientalism. Developing this mystical-Orientalist thread, Tilo's appearance in the spice store is almost magical. From her location in India, she is transported by First Mother, also known as the Old One, a mystical maternal figure who governs a community of young women, secret healers, and curanderas, teaching them the curative power of spices. The maternal center of this community of women, First Mother is the center of a diasporic map. As Rajayshree Khushu-Lahiri and Shweta Rao point out, the Old One's pedagogy is based on the traditional Hindu gurukul, the hallowed ancient Indian school where primarily male pupils and teachers (gurus) lived and worked together in the pursuit of knowledge. Like the male-dominated gurukul of pre-colonial India, the Old One's version of the Hindu Gurukul upholds orality as part of a sacred tradition. But within the novel's imaginary, Khushu-Lahiri and Rao suggest, the hierarchy of the Hindu gurukul is transformed because all the students in this sacrosanct learning community are women (9). Once the Old One is satisfied that she has successfully transmitted knowledge to her young curanderas, she sends them out to serve as mystical guides to communities of Indians scattered throughout the nodes of diasporic South Asia. From the beginning, Orientalism collides with a sense of historical reality in Tilo's self-posturing as an "architect of the immigrant dream" (28). She is someone who carefully dispenses spices imbued with curative powers to those who meander into her Oakland store, which serves as a microcosm of "India." A single woman for most of her life, Tilo is the consummate diasporic helpmate, partner to all needy South Asians. exhorted to aid only her own kind—the South Asian community. The Old One, spiritual guide to Tilo, reminds her : " 'remember why you are going,' the Old One said. 'To help your own kind and them only.' The others, they must go elsewhere for their need" (68).

The novel comes to life via Tilo's interactions with the individual characters, primarily South Asian diasporics who, unbeknownst to themselves, come to Tilo's store not just to purchase spices, but to receive her guidance. As these individuals meander in and out of her store to feed their nostalgia for the immigrant homeland, Tilo learns about their psychic and racial traumas as Indians in the United States and dispenses spices to help her customers negotiate their problems. Each spice is a kind of salve charged with particular curative powers able to effect a kind of racial and ethnic healing specific to the particular dilemmas faced by immigrants from the South Asian subcontinent. Fenugreek, to be dispensed to women ,"renders the body sweet again, ready for loving" (47); cinnamon is named the "destroyer of enemies to give . . . strength, strength which grows in your legs and arms and mostly mouth till one day you shout *no* loud enough to make them, shocked, stop" (40); chandan (sandalwood) "relieves the pain of remembering" (27). But each spice, she explains, "should be taken only under the supervision of a qualified Mistress." Thus the novel effects an immediate shuttling between reality and Orientalism to position spices, not as commodities within circuits of colonial exchange and exploitation, but as magical palliatives that counter the effects of racism and social inequity.

Like other popular food novels that borrow from the magical realist tradition, notably Laura Esquivel's *Like Water for Chocolate,* and Joanne Harris's *Chocolat, Mistress of Spices* presents food as a magical palliative able to dispel the slightest hint of discomfort. Like the magical chocolates in Harris's novel, spices have the ability to engender love and to help characters overcome personal difficulties. But, unlike in Esquivel's or Harris's novels, the problems that Divakaruni's characters face are a direct consequence of their position as racial, classed, and ethnic minorities within the United States. This is doubly significant because Divakaruni's characters are not the model minority doctors, lawyers, and recently arrived university students who yearn for the "homeland," ubiquitous in Indian American fiction, nor are they the parodic, often stereotypically depicted,

Indian Americans prevalent in celluloid culture. Instead, the characters evoke a complex, heterogeneous South Asian immigrant community in the United States: Haroun, a Kashmiri Muslim cab driver, is a victim of a racially motivated attack; Lalitha Ahuja is a battered wife seeking to escape an abusive husband, but is constrained by her legal status as an immigrant dependent on her husband, who is equally frustrated with his life in the United States; Jagjit is an alienated teenager who turns to a life of gang violence as a way to lessen the dangers of the xenophobia he faces from his racist classmates; Ramu is an elderly Gujarati immigrant who struggles to understand his granddaughter Geeta's choice of a Chicano partner instead of an arranged marriage; and the Bougainvillea girls are a group of young women who rub up against Tilo's nerves in their inability to see nuance in Indianness. The problems they bring to Tilo are varied and diverse and expose the profoundly melancholic, and often violent, effects globalization, migration, and movement might have on the lives of immigrants and exiles.

Despite this rendering of a heterogeneous South Asian community, the novel's culinary Orientalism is difficult to overlook. With its focus on how spices can remedy the injuries of racism, sexism, and homophobia, the novel journeys through a form of what Vijay Prashad calls "New Age Orientalism." The novel is premised on the notion that Indian Americans are besieged with problems because they are unwilling and unable to allow positive "spiritual" energy to enter into and change their lives for the better. As spiritual guide to the desi community, Tilo exhorts characters to chart their own journey toward a better life, dispensing spices that aid the individual to find the strength from within, as if ingesting turmeric in the correct doses can disinfect the visceral and psychic wounds inflicted by racism and sexism. In this capacity alone, Tilo bears a striking resemblance to Deepak Chopra, the highly visible Indian American demi-god of self-help whom Vijay Prashad dubs a "New Age Sly Guru" (47).

In his influential work on the racial position of South Asian Americans, *The Karma of Brown Folk,* Prashad examines the Orientalist bases of Chopra's burgeoning New Age enterprise that purports to cast India's ancient ayurvedic heritage into contemporary terms for troubled American subjects. Vijay Prashad understands the problem with Deepak Chopra's philosophy to be thus: "if there are problems in the United States, Chopra tells us, they are to be located within the deep structures of an essentialized human personality, and not in the institutions and social structures of our world" (48). In his self-help guide *The Seven Spiritual*

Laws of Success, Chopra evokes the importance of "personal responsibility." "I know that taking responsibility" Chopra writes, "means not blaming myself or anything for my situation." Individuals are exhorted to accept situations instead of seeking change. In Chopra's pop Hinduism, principles of karma can be evoked at will to advance a regressive understanding of class- and race-based inequities. Institutions, social organizations, and state apparatuses are absolved of their culpability in creating the conditions of inequality and discrimination that permeate many levels of classed immigrant realities. Chopra notes, "everything that is happening at the moment is a result of the choices you've made in the past" (40). Experiences with racism, classism, and sexism become privatized, shifting the burden of inequity to individuals. Applying such a logic to the "real-life" problems that Divakaruni's characters encounter, an immigrant like Jagjit in *Mistress of Spices* who is profoundly alienated from school life and turns to a life of gang violence because of the ever-present threat of racist violence directed against him would, in Chopra's estimation, be motivated by a spiritual imbalance that can be corrected only if he takes "personal responsibility" for allowing himself to feel angered by the racial slurs he has to endure such as "nigger wetback asshole" (39).

The thrust of Chopra's message is to impress upon consumers the importance of maintaining the status quo: don't work to change the world; don't educate others. Consumers are exhorted to seek a path of nonconfrontation, or, more accurately, nonaction. Chopra's suggestions dovetails with a plan of action which refuses to acknowledge how a path of social justice and collective action might yield greater equity for disenfranchised individuals and community. Consumption thus becomes the source of redemption within Chopra's framework. [2]

Divakaruni's solutions to race- and class-based discrimination, though decidedly less pernicious than what Chopra suggests, are not far removed from Chopra's solutions. The individuals who frequent Tilo's store to buy spices, along the way receiving advice about how to make their way through immigrant life in the United States, must take charge of their life and not blame others if they are to see improvement in their everyday racial lives. And yet if this particular strategy of imbuing strength in the power of inner resilience seems to be at the center of the novel's fault lines, it is intriguing that Divakaruni seems to undercut this message at the same time. Tilo's abilities to ameliorate the lives of her customers are not entirely due to the magical power of spices. Lalitha, a woman whose everyday existence is one of violent abuse—she is beaten and raped by her husband on a daily basis—turns to Tilo's curandera abilities to help her through her troubles. Initially Tilo tries to help Lalitha resolve her problems by slipping a handful of turmeric wrapped in an old newspaper into her grocery bag. Tilo tells Lalitha that turmeric has the power to counter the physical and psychic burn of being raped nightly. But when the turmeric fails to bring an end Lalitha's pain, Tilo turns to another spice. Fennel, she tells Lalitha, is a "wondrous spice. Take a pinch of it raw and whole after every meal to freshen the breath and aid digestion to give you mental strength for what must be done" (104). But for Lalitha, who needs more than a temporary salve to stave off the intense pain and horror that modulate her daily life, Tilo's words are cheap, offering her little by way of a concrete strategy to extricate herself from a cycle of abuse. Faced with Lalitha's increased skepticism, Tilo searches for another solution to help Lalitha: "I reach for the small bag of fennel to press into her palm, but it is not there. But here is the packet on top of this stack of *India Currents* magazine, where surely I did not place it. Spices, is this a game or is it something you are telling me? There is no time to ponder. I pick up the packet and a copy of the magazine. Give her both" (105). Shortly thereafter, Tilo receives a letter from Lalitha, writing to her from an undisclosed location that is later revealed to be a battered women's shelter:

> you know that magazine you gave me? In the back were notic-
> es. One said, if you are a battered woman, call this number for
> help . . . the woman on the line was very kind. She was Indian
> like me, she understood a lot without my telling. She said I was
> right to call, they would help me if I was sure of what I wanted to
> do . . . Two women picked me up at the bus stop. They tell me if
> I want to file a police case they'll help me. Also they can help me
> set up a small tailoring business if I like. But they warn me things
> won't be easy. (269–70)

As critical race scholars and analysts of domestic abuse in immigrant communities have argued, there is a racialized dimension to domestic violence. Contrary to the apparent mysticism of the novel, Lalitha's trauma is not resolved by her ingesting a magical potion of spices and wishing for the best, but by taking a concrete step to extricate herself from an abusive situation. Lalitha ultimately takes that step, but there is the necessary structural scaffolding in place to enable her to make this "choice."[3] Without the shelter, Lalitha's life would not so easily take a turn for the better. Amid the options provided by the shelter is the possibility of opening a tailoring business. When Lalitha first enters the space of the store to share her troubles with Tilo, the latter remarks on Lalitha's graceful embroidery skills where "every cloth she touches with her needle blooms" (14). Tilo goes so far as to imagine Lalitha as an independent agent, capable of using her labor to open her own shop, "Lalitha Tailor Works." While this moment suggests that Tilo may have visionary qualities, it also hints at her cognizance of what it will take for Lalitha to articulate agency. Tilo is aware of the limitations of her own worldview: spices alone cannot challenge patriarchy, abuse, or racism. Rather, an engaged praxis of labor, collective action and solidarity are the essential ingredients necessary to create new recipes for survival. Indeed, for all of the characters in *Mistress of Spices*, the mere consumption of spices and careful love and attention from family does not help to lessen the trauma of their experiences with racism. They cannot simply wish away the experience of pain and suffering by letting it go. Lalitha's story illustrates the paradoxes that run central to the narrative. The novel works to fashion a narrative attuned to the racialized encounters particular to Indian American immigrant women, less conversant in English and wholly dependent upon the lives and worlds of their husbands. Part of the narrative's trajectory is to address the attendant failures such disenfranchised subjects experience in trying to fashion lives in the United States. As such, the lives they lead run counter to a narrative of easily fetishizable ethnic identity.

In a reading of contemporary South Asian diasporic literature, the critic Sheetal Majithia notes that fictional installments like *Mistress of Spices* "fetishize the experience of immigration, so as to perpetuate easy translation and dubious interpretation, processes that uncannily resemble Orientalist and imperial projects of literary and critical representation" (52). Majithia classifies Divakaruni's fiction as part of a larger corpus of fiction insensitive to racially complex and nuanced "realities" of South Asian American life. In Majithia's words, "instead of fiction that confronts the contradictions produced by the racist violence of the Dotbusters in New Jersey in the mid 1980s, or that perpetrated against Rishi Maharaj in 1998, the systematic exploitation of South Asian domestic labor, or anti-immigration legislation; we are instead provided recurrent narratives of romance that imagine a stable or unified South Asian American identity" (53). More than one critic has admonished *Mistress of Spices* for framing heterosexual romance as a solution to the fractious malaises of the world. But the novel is hardly free of the kind of vexing questions Majithia identifies as absent from the writings of authors such as Divakaruni. At a purely narrative level, Divakaruni's novel presents a spectrum of characters who confront the very contradictions of racist violence Majithia describes. *Mistress of Spices* includes fictional versions of the Rishi Maharajs of South Asian America and engages narratives about racist hate crimes. But where Divakaruni's novel fails is in providing a sustained counternarrative to an imagining of South Asian American identity as stable and unified. Majithia accurately identifies the way in which romance contravenes into narratives of South Asian American life to fetishize the very traumas and realities of immigrant existence. Romance frames this narrative to resolve the interpersonal traumas and travails that plague Tilo, the mistress of spices. When her curandera abilities fail to provide a script that might ameliorate the traumatic conditions plaguing her customers' lives, she leaves behind a life that is dedicated to bettering people's lives. Instead of remaining committed to provide a space of healing for her community, she uses romance as a way to opt out of the system.

But despite the use of romance as a sugary gloss coated over an otherwise unpalatable narrative, the nature of that romance and its nuances bear further scrutiny. Romance, heterosexual union, and marriage between an Asian American woman and a white American male become fetishized as tools for social advancement and assimilation into the United States. But might the terms of romance contain other, more challenging, possibilities when the romance creates a web of affiliation between persons of color? Tilo's romantic affiliation with Raven destabilizes the trope of social mobility, forging instead an unlikely affiliation between two "Indians"—one of South Asian origin, the other Native American.[4]

While the romance with Raven is instructive in understanding how Divakaruni fashions a politics of solidarity with communities of color, the weightier counternarrative to framing romance emerges less from Tilo's choice of Raven as a romantic partner, and more from her choice to free her body from the sexual shackles placed around it by the Old One. At the center of the text's latent Orientalism, where spices take on a magically curative role, is an aggressive nationalism predicated on the careful policing of female bodies and female sexual autonomy. At the behest of the mythically rendered Old One, a repository of the national state, Tilo is denied sexual or gendered autonomy. Among her specific tasks, she is strictly forbidden from forming interpersonal relationships in which she might exercise sexual agency. By virtue of her position as a mystic emissary from the "homeland," she must be a diasporic helpmate to all and partner to none. To express sexual autonomy or desire is constructed as an ethical betrayal of her filial responsibility to protect the "children" of the nation—scattered around the world. The spice mistresses including Tilo are reminded: "you are not important. No mistress is" (5). The Old One's worldview insists that mistresses function as caretakers to South Asian diasporic communities. In a climate where female bodies are aggressively policed and denied the possibility of sexual pleasure, Tilo's romance with Raven becomes an act of political disavowal against a gendered system that castigates women for allowing their bodies to function as more than repositories of tradition. Her choice to love Raven is a reaction against what is willed for her body thus becoming an act of defiance and reclamation of gendered personhood. It is an articulation of desire that, to follow bell hooks, "disrupts, subverts, and makes resistance possible" (200). This final act of romantic union between Raven and Tilo refuses to foreclose the possible of female desire; moreover, it is a gesture that does not grant primacy to the edicts handed down from the "homeland." Beginning as but one member of the complex diasporic network of spice mistresses, Tilo eventually becomes a sole agent whose relationship to food and spices extends beyond a logic of national filial piety, thus leaving the doors open to imagine the possibilities of women exercising sexual autonomy from what is mandated for them.

Economic Citizens and the World of *Pastries*

If *Mistress of Spices* is framed by the triumph of romance over the everyday inequities of life in racialized America, *Pastries* is marked by the ways in which the failure of romance paves the way to struggle against the inequities created by corporate America. In the wake of a failed relationship, Indian American baker Sunya Malhotra struggles to protect her once-thriving cake shop from being driven out of business by the predatory actions of larger corporate conglomerates. A young Indian American who comes of age against the backdrop of social activism, Sunya Malhotra is defined by her efforts to affirm the place of locally owned establishments against the backdrop of ever-deepening threats from the impersonal forces of globalization.

Not unlike *Mistress of Spices*, *Pastries* uses the visual register of gustatory pleasure to create an enticing veneer for a story about a lone South Asian American woman struggling to make her living as the owner of a pastry shop. When *Pastries* was first released in the United States, the book's cover bore an image of a woman's face from the nose down; all that is visible is a female mouth lined with red lipstick nibbling on a chocolate-covered pastry. Superimposed on the image of the pastry is the title of the novel. Adorning the edge of the cover is a rendition of the lace-edge of a doily, over which appear the subtitle, *A Novel of Desserts and Discoveries*, and the author's name. Savvy to what will entice readers to enter into the world of Sunya Malhotra—a second-generation Indian American baker and café owner raised in Seattle and the Pacific Northwest by a single mother—the novel's cover mines the appeal of confections, inviting the reader to enter into a hyperreal world of consumption made all the more enticing by the image of a racially ambiguous woman's lipsticked mouth seductively biting into a pastry. This easy conflation of sensuality and consumption is not accidental; but more pointedly, the novel is a near-perfect example of hyperreal eating in its production of the notion that we turn to commodities—cultural, cosmetic, inflected by the culinary to consume difference and to sublimate the very desire to eat.

But in this novel it becomes clear that there is more to sweets and pastries than meets the eye. Set in Seattle, the novel's social canvas includes a new round of global trade talks slated to take place during the Third World Trade Conference, a loosely veiled version of the World Trade Organization summit which took place in Seattle in 1999. As Seattleites and liberal progressives from around the world converge to protest the reshaping of business practices and the protection of the interests of global capital, Kirchner introduces her protagonist, Sunya Malhotra, a self-defined baker and owner of Pastries Café, a "trendy bakery" in the bohemian, alternative neighborhood of Wallingford. The Third World Trade Conference provides a strong backdrop to the novel and its cognizance of where local and global capitalist practices have a devastating impact upon local cultures and businesses. As larger national structures battle the implications of global capitalism, Sunya finds herself the unwitting participant in her own battle against global capitalist structures closer to home. Sunya is immediately thrust into what the local food columnist for the *Seattle News* dubs the "Bakery War" as local food writer Donald Smith informs Sunya of the imminent arrival of a large chain franchise named Cakes Plus in her neighborhood. As it enters the bohemian neighborhood of Wallingford, Cakes Plus begins to strategically undermine the independent bakeries and coffee shops which have been the mainstay of the neighborhood, including Pastries Café, Sunya's pastry shop. Sunya is slow to accept that Cakes Plus may steal her customers, noting "my café, though it barely ekes a profit, has become an informal social center, a pied-a-terre to the patrons. Surely they wouldn't desert their second home for some franchise" (7). But Donald Smith is quick to remind her of Cakes Plus's reputation as a "steamroller" of small businesses, known to cannibalize recipes made popular by the smaller establishments only to then sell them at half the price. Sunya's response, "how as a small business owner will I compete with a long-established bakery financed by the region's preeminent bread company that has enough money to buy a full-page advertisement in the *News*?" (8) carries the freight of a business owner who suddenly has to reconcile her craft as a baker with her new role as vigilant protector of her much smaller business.

And yet Sunya is a reluctant partner in the warlike dance between Pastries Café and Cakes Plus. Unlike her soon-to-be ex-boyfriend, Roger, Sunya does not consider herself a social activist. So deep is Roger's commitment to the plight of farmers in less-developed countries that one of his major feats during the round of protests is to enlist Indian environmental activist Vandana Shiva to speak about a "bleak future of absolute control where even seeds were monopolized by greedy international biotech corporations" (29). While Roger considers his involvement against what he dubs "Transnational corporations—'world elites,' 'parasite' or 'Mafia families' taking over the planet" (11), Sunya considers his rhetoric to be "standard radical boilerplate" (12). This disjuncture between their political positions vis-à-vis the role of transnational corporations scripts Sunya's actions as born less out of a politicized progressive sensibility and more out of a sense of ethical responsibility to herself and her employees.

As the novel progresses, it becomes apparent that such distinctions, which might binarize the work of activism against transnationalism and the work of protecting local businesses, are, at best, tenuous. Embroiled full-scale within the "Bakery War," Sunya becomes interpellated into this maneuvering between Pastries Café and Cakes Plus as an agent of change whose actions begin to implicitly espouse an ethics of survival. Paula Mathieu's compelling analysis of economic citizenship and her discussion of Starbucks' deliberate and concerted efforts to "build a Starbucks nation" refine Saskia Sassen's definition of economic citizenship to suggest that globalization redefines "citizenship in economic terms." For Sassen, "economic citizenship means accepting the definition of political agency around the roles each of us plays in the cycle of global production and consumption." To this, Mathieu adds, "economic citizens act by critically examining and questioning the dominant narratives that are circulated in and about the economic system" (113). Compelled to examine her changing role within the economic system that is slanted against her, Sunya becomes an economic citizen who must confront the system intent on writing her out of the dominant narrative of global capital in Cakes Plus's ever more aggressive effort to dominate the market.

As Sunya's ambivalent induction into a dissenting economic citizenship begins, she is made aware of how the economic system is built around exclusions designed to undermine the edifice of her personal and economic autonomy. As Cakes Plus begins to acquire a lion's share of the market, her reputation as a baker is called into question by the well-placed columns penned by Donald Smith. To add fuel to the fires that threaten the very basis of her livelihood, Sunya has entered a phase where she has lost her touch in the kitchen, a point that Donald Smith announces to his readers with seeming glee. As she struggles with her decreasing facility as a baker, she must contend with a series of forces that simultaneously close in on her autonomy as a business owner. Regular vendors opt to cancel long-standing contracts with Pastries Café; her star baker, Pierre Talon, is hired away by Cakes Plus, and his apple pies, perfected at Pastries Café, as Smith notes, become "standard fare at every Cakes Plus Store" (189); and the health department plans surprise visits to Pastries Café. As Sunya's life begins to unravel, it becomes apparent that a small business owner like Sunya cannot survive in a climate where the larger business has a firmer foothold on the situation. To add insult to injury, Sunya learns that Donald J. Smith, the reporter and author of the weekly "Bakery War" column, is on the payroll of Northwest Bread, the parent company of Cakes Plus. Aware that this dual loyalty works against Smith's business interests to "make a single negative remark about Cakes Plus in his column" (77), Sunya comes to the depressing realization that her business is facing imminent failure.

Faced with this unholy alliance between the "objective" food reviewer and the CEO of her competitor, Sunya affirms her decision "to stay and fight" (78) to protect Pastries Café. Sunya's commitment to work against Smith and Northwest Bread exposes the ethical issues implicit in the food reviewing business. Certainly, part of the flagging interest in Pastries Café emanates from the perceived loss in quality of Sunya's baked goods, or the fact that Cakes Plus seizes upon her recipes, reproducing and repackaging them for the mass consumer market at a fraction of the cost. But equally significant in this changing dynamic is the role played by Donald Smith. Quite clearly, Cakes Plus uses Smith's reviews as part of a deliberate economic strategy to systematically drive Sunya out of business; the company is unforgivingly portrayed as one that will pull out every known trick to destroy her business and reputation as a much-loved and trusted baker within the local community. Not surprisingly, even before Cakes Plus opens its Wallingford branch, Sunya is urged by venture capitalist Dushan Bashich, Sunya's mother's fiancé, to sell her bakery to the Cakes Plus conglomerate. In his words, "it is a war you are most unlikely to win" (75). Sunya fights to keep her bakery from being devoured by the machineries of capital but is ultimately unable to win this battle.

Perhaps the final straw for Sunya arises from a conflict with an unlikely player, Jim Paradise, the real estate baron from whom Sunya rents space to run Pastries Café. His refusal to renew her lease is a direct result of his decision to lease property to Willy Cartdale, the proprietor of Cakes Plus. In Sunya's mind, Paradise's collusion with Cartdale runs counter to his second career as a volunteer for "Lettuce Link, a local nonprofit organization growing organic vegetables for low-income families" (263). She reminds him of his ethical commitment to the "common good," pointing out how he has made "a second career out of feeding disadvantaged families [his] organic vegetables" (263). But so tenuous is the separation of his two realms of economic activity as real estate baron and organic farmer, that in order for Paradise to pledge commitment to Lettuce Link, he needs the capital he would earn from evicting Sunya from her premises, and in turn, entering into a business partnership with Willy Cartdale.

Kirchner's novel exposes the capitalist machineries that converge against the interest of locally owned businesses; in so doing, her novel carves a space to think through the deleterious effects of global capitalism, where talent and good intentions alone are not able to sustain young persons of color or young entrepreneurs seeking to provide viable economic alternatives to the machinery of industrialized capitalism and global franchises. In its raw and painful exposure of the psychological damage wreaked upon Sunya's life as a result of the colluding efforts of real estate owner Willy Cartdale, newspaper reviewer Donald Smith, and Dushan Bashich, Kirchner's novel provides a scathing but thoughtful critique of the plight of a woman of color aiming to sustain a small business for her local community. Sunya's heart-wrenching struggle to keep her cherished business alive is starkly portrayed; Kirchner's ethical choices in the novel to convey the systematic challenges to Sunya's autonomy as an economic citizen do not sugarcoat any aspect of her imminent failure.

One of the hallmarks of global capitalism's unrelenting power is its ability to redefine communities, stripping everyday citizens such as Sunya of their agency and their ability to act as independent actors within their local communities (Mathieu 112). But it is precisely at the moment when the novel stands poised to levy its ethical critique of global capitalism that it retreats into a palatability that is simultaneously self-defeating and laced with Orientalism. When Sunya can no longer face the personal and economic effects of being the owner of a popular, but failing business, she begins to lose her bearings—both personally and economically. But her road to recovery is remarkably short. In lieu of adhering to her initial ethics of fighting back to secure her own financial independence, she turns inward for spiritual guidance. When she first learns of a bakery in Kyoto, Japan, run by a Buddhist master baker, Mori Matsumoto, she writes him off as a "quack," marking her skepticism at the notion that "people can heal themselves by baking" (240). Despite a personal invitation from Matsumoto to enroll in his baking school, she notes that she "can't afford to take that many days off for some dubious 'feel good' enterprise" (243) centered on baking. But soon thereafter it becomes apparent that the road to saving her business is cluttered with seemingly insurmountable obstacles, and she eventually decides to travel to Japan to become Matsumoto's apprentice. The Japan that she turns to is a spiritual nexus that teaches her to "relinquish her ego while in the kitchen" and to "put aside emphasis on daily realties and to practice compassion" (301). Sunya's excursion into Japanese-inspired spirituality teaches her to let go of the small matters and to forgive those very individuals who have so calculatingly conspired to run her out of business. Sunya's personal redemption thus resides in her ability to make the kinds of ethical choices that compel her to forgive those very structures and individuals who have so invidiously ridden her of a livelihood. Within the novel's denouement, then, Sunya's character undergoes a dramatic reversal. Gone is the resilient figure who promisingly asserted, "my privately owned business, my sense of community, my desire to see individuals retain control over their destiny are at odds with mainstream society's growth-oriented philosophy" (249). All that is left is someone who has internalized her own marginalization and learned to forgive the structures which have conspired to marginalize her success such that, by the end of her apprenticeship with Matsumoto, Sunya concludes, "I can be contented and peaceful regardless of how my bakery is doing financially" (309). Sunya thus begins to redefine her sense of personhood from one where she is solely an economic citizen to one where she becomes defined by her craft. At the same time, this shift unsettles the ethical bent of the novel because it offers personalized and apolitical solutions to problems created by the deliberate and strategic efforts to undermine local businesses like Pastries Café. Rather than take up the challenge of exploring how and where collective action might help keep Sunya's failing business from drowning amid a sea of predators, the novel neatly packages the unsettling narrative of Sunya's economic destruction into a palatable frame by suggesting that she, as an agent of change, can overcome her own troubles merely by seeking inner peace and reprioritizing her goals. The novel promisingly sets out to flout the conventions of food pornography by offering a trenchant critique of what it means to try to keep a failing business alive and to resist the incursion of global capital; but it sugarcoats the very real difficulties she faces as a businesswoman who has to contend with big business penetration by presenting her problems as being resolvable through her search for psychic realignment. By the end of her apprenticeship with Matsumoto, she notes, "Cakes Plus is competition, an obstacle in my path, only if I believe it to be so. Rather than anguish about how it may take business away from me, I'll just concentrate on running my small bakery. I may have to cut down the hours of operation and the volume of baked goods I produce daily, but as long as I can, I'll hold on to my shop. I am different from Cakes Plus, and in the difference resides my strength. Cakes Plus has actually given me an opportunity to awaken" (309).

Thus, the novel that begins by connecting the protests against the Third World Trade Conference with Sunya's plight to save her local business ultimately suggests that Asian-inspired philosophies hold the answer to her problems. At the heart of Sunya's journey is an implicit repudiation of the novel's political trajectory. Cakes Plus and other economic conglomerates are absolved of any guilt, and, in the process, the novel undercuts itself by rendering palatable the bitterness of its critiques. By the close of the novel, Sunya's acquiescence to unfair business practices eventually allows the enticing aroma of baking pastries to overwhelm the stench of Kirchner's stinging indictments of big business.

Beginnings, Middles, and Endings

If there is one sure thing about food, it is that it is never just food—it is endlessly interpretable—materialised emotion.—TERRY EAGLETON, "EDIBLE ECRITURE"

In using a culinary frame that adheres to the tenets of food pornography, *Mistress of Spices* dilutes the stench of the unsavory stories with the affective overflow of the aromas and passions of Indian spices, creating

one of the biggest paradoxes in the novel. The novel compellingly addresses hate crimes, the trials faced by immigrants who toil for hours in
7–11s and gas stations, domestic violence, and the difficulties that cab
drivers face—precisely the kinds of issues Majithia laments that South
Asian American fiction fails to undertake. But at the moment where
the narrative stands positioned to productively consider what enables a
critical articulation of food, the narrative turns to a version of magical realism inspired by Deepak Chopra's pop ayurvedic philosophy and
romance, commodifying a fictional conceit about Indian mysticism. In
its reliance on an Orientalist frame where the novel repeatedly echoes its
refrain of spices having an ameliorative effect on people's lives, the text
enacts a version of "palatable multiculturalism": those narratives that are
messy and complicated, those narratives that signal to the ways in which
Indian American characters are troubled by matters of class and racial
inequities become submerged beneath the heterosexual romance that
ultimately becomes the novel's resounding cry to privilege palatability,
even as that romance works to articulate female sexual autonomy.

In so doing, *Mistress of Spices* charts a path around thorny terrain
rather than postulating an aesthetics that would work through and
against impediments in its path, while being ever-mindful of the very
real threats these obstruction pose. Indeed, it is all too easy to overlook
the pains and difficulties the characters face; instead, what remains is the
lingering smell of spices wafting through the store, magically releasing
characters from their starkly real traumas. This is reminiscent of Sau-
Ling Wong's reading of "stone bread" in *Obasan*, Joy Kogawa's novel
about the Japanese Canadian internment. In Kogawa's novel, the image
of processing and digesting the dense bread allegorizes the intellectual
journey readers must undertake in order to "get through the narrative
complexities" (21). For Wong, the stone bread represents moments which
bear witness to the violent racism, injustices, and traumas intrinsic to
the internment experience. *Obasan*'s writerly strategy is to disclose those
stony moments, which in turn compel readers to consider and be troubled by the challenges of digesting such forms of political unpalatability.
The stone bread becomes an aesthetic response to political unpalatability
and social injustice. *Pastries* and *Mistress of Spices*, one might rightly
conclude, are unable to fully overcome the need to offer up tasty mor-
sels for hungry readers that can be easily digested. Sunya's moment of
epiphany while apprenticing as a baker in Kyoto led her to articulate,
"Cakes Plus is a competition, an obstacle in my path, only if I believe it
to be so" (309). And yet there is something foolhardy about suggesting

that a realignment of one's belief mechanisms alone can chip away at the edifice of economic inequality. To be sure, *Pastries* garners interest because it plays on the seductive appeal of confections. The novel, replete with enticing descriptions of pastries, sweetens the reader's palate, but at the same time these gastro-pornographic moments are punctured by the "stonier" moments in the narrative. Unlike the decidedly unpalatable narrative Kogawa offers, it is no accident that the comestibles of choice in Kirchner's and Divakaruni's novels are sweets and spice. Both Kirchner's and Divakaruni's novels mimic the Orientalist parable to provide a narrative that, though easily consumable, also contains narratives rife with complexity, contrary to the conventions of popular food novels typically unable or unwilling to engage complexities about race, class, and gender.[5]

For works of South Asian American or Asian American literature, where an ethics of social justice becomes an important index of aesthetic quality, the deep vexations that emanate from these novels are often undercut by the overtly easy solutions proffered by the novels' denouement. As works of popular literature, *Pastries* and *Mistress of Spices* privilege the kind of palatable beginnings and endings that frustrate and thwart the political and narratival complexities which drive the novel forward. Majithia's distrust of romance and Mukherjee's distrust of food, to be sure, acquire greatest legibility when we consider the final gestures of unmitigated sweetness at the end of the novel as a repudiation of each novel's treatment of race and class. To be ambivalent about *Pastries* or *Mistress of Spices*, thus, is necessarily multidimensional. Just as *Pastries* provides strong critiques of what it means to own an independent bakery in an era where global capitalism and downsizing has meant that chain stores are taking the place of corner shops, *Mistress of Spices* punctures its own narrative about magically curative spices by suggesting that ingesting spices without a praxis of collective action is not a viable palliative against racism. By the novel's end, Tilo turns her back on the store. On one hand, the text blatantly peddles exoticism, but on the other hand, the stories are not so easily digested and made palatable. Lalitha's story, for instance, is not so malleable as to allow spices to magically solve her problems. Divakaruni evocatively narrates Lalitha's suffering without casting her as a hapless victim. Similarly, despite her own efforts to let go of all that has happened, Sunya's narrative of personal fulfillment is incomplete if we do not also take stock of what turned her into an economic citizen who worked to save her flailing business. These are the "stony" moments impeding the smooth flow of the narrative. And yet each novel, subject to the processes of commodification, enters into a cultural field in which American consumers turn to popular narratives in order to keep the Asian American subject as epistemologically fixed, thus undercutting the ethics of each novel. The politically and socially valent critiques of the structures of racism and classism are jettisoned in favor of palatable endings. Ultimately spices are not able to heal subjects, but it is the overpowering aroma of spices wafting through Divakaruni's novel masking the malodorousness of the troubling stories that has led critics, perhaps hastily, to overlook the novel's well-intentioned attempt to negotiate complexities.

In their failure (or refusal?) to conclusively provide a viable alternative to food pornography, these novels have come to be read within an ethics of betrayal, suggesting, as does the South Asian American cultural politics blog site *Sepia Mutiny*, that they are the kind of South Asian–themed works that come packaged with prefabricated recipes that will lure readers into a web of Orientalist renderings of difference. Deconstructing the cover and front matter of *The Mango Season*, a novel by Amulya Malladi, the authors of this blog post satirically comment on how the cover art formulaically reproduces standard norms to contain difference. Among the details they discuss from the book's cover are references to curry, foreign boyfriends, and arranged marriages; misspelled ethnic words; images of hennaed hands, tropical fruit, and sari borders; and the use of Samarkan type (Romanized English rendered as a faux Devanagiri Hindi script). The posting then moves on to identify common culinary tropes lodged on the contents page. I don't fault the posting for its sharp-witted and humorous deconstruction of the novel's cover, but it does fail to acknowledge how the novel advances a radical critique of racialized assumptions. In its parodic critique, the *Sepia Mutiny* posting isolates the following statement as an example of the "Phoren Boyfriend" trope: "Priya Rao left India when she was twenty to study in the United States and she's never been back. Now, seven years later, she's out of excuses. She has to return to give her family the news. She's engaged to Nick Collins, a kind loving American man. Marrying a foreigner is going to break their hearts." While the novel rehearses an all-too familiar scenario of East and West coming to a head as the Indian daughter seeks to marry the American man of her choice only to rub up against orthodox Indian parents who frown on interracial relationships, it also refuses to disclose Priya's fiancé's racial identity. It is only at the novel's end, when the traditional parents and progressive daughter end their dance around cultural restrictive norms that the protagonist lets it slip that Nick, the American fiancé, is actually Black. Priya comments: "'And at least,' Ammamma said with a broad shrug, 'he is white, not some kallu.' I froze. Damn it! Had I forgotten to mention Nick was Black?" (22).

This ending offers a number of possible interpretive possibilities. On one hand. the novel might be critiqued for only introducing this overt racial narrative on the penultimate page of the novel. Few South Asian diasporic works, after all, seriously undertake the task of examining the highly charged valences of framing heterosexual romance within a Black-Asian rather than White-Asian matrix. On the other hand, the introduction of Blackness at this juncture calls attention to how readers always already assign race to characters. The presumption of Nick's whiteness disturbs and disrupts the narrative, thus casting aspersions on the novel as a formulaic reiteration of the oppressive arranged marriage trope. Malladi's novel thus offers what we might conceive of as narrative thickness. While it works through and against the conventions of an all-too-familiar Orientalism, it also demands that we read the narrative closely, through and against our expectations of the subgenre of food and immigrant writing. Alongside the numerous recipes included in the novel, this final narrative provides a tentative recipe to reexamine food novels. Culinary-themed novels, commodity-comestibles with marked crossover appeal, enjoy far greater visibility than novels which render explicit an engagement with an ethics of social justice.

But in the interest of grappling with the narrative complexities running through the novels, we cannot simply dismiss these forms of popular writing because they are framed through Orientalism with neatly and palatably packaged beginnings and sweet endings. It becomes imperative to take stock of the "stones" impeding the smooth flow of the sweetened narrative. This form of sugarcoating might be understood as a writerly strategy: an attempt to render palatable narratives about the exigencies of race, class, and capital. As such, a praxis of reading whereby we don't necessarily fetishize only endings and beginnings emerges as a strategy to work within an ethics of social justice while creating a palatable exterior.

This strategy resonates strongly with a kind of feminist politics of writing. One way to read this narrative strategy is to follow the lead of feminist literary critic Rachel DuPlessis in considering the novel as one that "writes beyond the romantic ending" (4). DuPlessis's study of the female romance asks why the genre frequently ends in marriage or death. Arguing against the notion that these outcomes are necessarily disempowering, thus rendering such novels orthodoxically misogynist and unfeminist, DuPlessis calls for closer scrutiny of the "relations of narrative middles to resolutions" (4) as a step toward understanding the politics of "writing beyond the ending." This strategy accords greater agency to the actions of the female protagonist before her narrative culminates in the kind of erasure of personhood precipitated by marriage or death. For South Asian American studies, it becomes crucial to provide the kinds of politically valent readings that also accommodate the possibility that those novels which fashion narratives to be consumed by mainstream publics might exhibit signs of hyperreal consumptive practices, while at the same time producing narratives resistant to those structures of containment. In this way, it becomes possible to identify texts like *Pastries* and *Mistress of Spices* as being politically savvy, rather than simply as tales that espouse an acritical ethics of Oriental mysticism.

It is perhaps telling that a model for readerly practice closely resembling DuPlessis's generative reading—leaving open the room for alternative possibilities beyond what might be containable within the pages of a novel—is also present in Salman Rushdie's Booker Prize–winning novel *Midnight's Children*. Perhaps Rushdie's postfatwa location in New York might invite us to rethink his position vis-à-vis Indian America. But I allude to him here not to give Rushdie the last word, or to carelessly dub him Indian American because he is now on the North American side of the Atlantic, but because the novel anticipates some of the concerns eventually given shape by Indian American writers in the 1990s and beyond. It is evident in *Midnight's Children* that food is a powerfully affective political and social metaphor. The narrator, Saleem Sinai, spends his days pickling. His nights are spent creating another type of preservative, his narrative about Indian postcolonial political life. He explains: "my chutneys and kassundies are, after all, connected to my nocturnal scribblings—by day amongst the pickle vats, by night within these sheets, I spend my time at the great work of preserving. Memory, as well as fruit, is being saved from the corruption of the clocks" (38). As the narrative draws to a close, the novel hints at how preservation of history must always acknowledge its incompleteness and partialities. To more completely account for these contingencies and partialities, Saleem Sinai creates thirty pickle jars, one for each year he has lived; one for each of the thirty intervening years between the narrator's present and India's independence in 1947; and one for each chapter of the novel. To these jars, he adds an empty one for what is to come, accommodating that which cannot be contained and pickled, that which cannot be explained because the narrative itself cannot be fully contained. The inclusion of an extra pickle bottle situates the novel's project as one that is necessary nontotalizing, cognizant of its location at the point of becoming rather than the point of being. Through Rushdie's metaphor, it is possible to suggest that endings, veneers, and beginnings should not be naively fetishized. Read in context of the image of stone bread from Joy Kogawa's *Obasan*, we realize that the dense inner core is where critical South Asian diasporic studies must wrestle the most. It is here rather than on the sugarcoated exterior that we find the most food for thought *in Pastries* and *Mistress of Spices*. In those spaces "beyond the ending," we must continue to think through the layers of meaning. Through such a reading of culinary-inspired fiction, it becomes that much more feasible to consider the sweet and spicy culinary narrative as a viable aesthetic response to matters of everyday political significance.

4 /   Red Hot Chili Peppers: Visualizing Class
          Critique and Female Labor

Entrust the selection of materials and the whole management of affairs
to a commercial company, like for instance, the East India Company.
Allow them to make use of as much corruption as they please. Throw in
various green things, such as incompetent judges, cruel tax-gatherers,
and overbearing military officers. Stir up the above with a large Spoon of
the Ellenborough pattern. Mix the above with native superstitions, and
by no means spare the official sauce. Allow the above quietly to ferment
for several years without taking any notice of how matters are going on.
When you come to look into the state of things, you will find that you
have as fine an Indian pickle as you could wish. You need not trouble
yourself about the jars, for they will be supplied to you afterwards, gratis.
For further particulars, inquire of the great Indian Pickle Warehouse in
Leadenham Street. N.B. No pickle is genuine unless there is the mark of
"John Company" plainly visible on the face of it.
                —ANONYMOUS, "HOW TO MAKE AN INDIAN PICKLE," 1857

Moving from narratives about culinary Orientalism to contemporary
narratives attuned to the exigencies of class, capitalism, and labor, I
want to indulge in an anachronistic detour, delving back into the pages
of history to the moment of the Indian Uprising, or Sepoy Mutiny of
1857 (hereafter Uprising). Putting forth an analysis of this moment is
appropriate for this chapter, not because of the deep-seated connection
between culinary beliefs and the Uprising, but because it offers a singular instance of when action and resistance coalesced around the mutable
significance of food. For most historians of India's colonial period, the
winter of 1856–57 is most closely aligned with nationalist agitation and
anticolonialist fervor in the northern states of India, a historical moment that would culminate in the Indian Uprising of 1857. A particularly
telling anonymous prose poem published that year in *Punch*, "How to
Make an Indian Pickle," satirizes the perceived state of chaos and corruption within the East India Company (here referred to as John Company). Scripted in the form of a recipe, the poem identifies the East India
Company's policies as the root cause of the Uprising, here referred to as
"the pickle." While the sympathies of the poem's anonymous author are
not made explicit, the words paint an unsympathetic portrait of the Brit-

ish East India Company. The pickle—a preservative designed to contain and preserve—becomes symbolically linked with the purported failure of John Company to contain the Uprising, and by extension the very real threat to the edifice of the British Empire in India. The insurgency of the Indian soldiers is what lands the forces of British imperialism in a "pickle." The undisciplined bodies of the Indian soldiers become a potent threat because they epitomize the troubles to empire: the refusal of Indian bodies to be contained by the demands of imperialist enterprise.

At around the same time that the anonymous poem appeared in the pages of *Punch,* another type of culinary message was making its way across portions of northwest India, the area of British India that would soon become associated with the Indian Uprising of 1857. In *The Glass Palace,* a multigenerational novel about an Indo-Burmese family set in India, Burma, and Malaysia, Amitav Ghosh imagines this historic moment: "Well before the firing of the first shot, signs of trouble had appeared on the north Indian plains. Chapatis—those most unremarkable of everyday foods—had begun to circulate from village to village, as though in warning. No one knew where they came from or who had put them in motion—but somehow people had known a great convulsion was on its way" (246). Here, the convulsions parallel events in the *Glass Palace.* In the wake of an imperial coup, a series of rumors circulate among insurgents and supporters of the new leader via informal channels in a manner reminiscent of the 1857 "circulating chapatti incident."[1] This historical incident has generated a great deal of speculation, most of which hones in on the fact that a series of seditious messages, apparently encoded within chapattis, circulated rapidly through a number of villages in northwest India. One of the earliest historical accounts of the episode suggests that a local villager would deliver chapattis to the adjoining village with an injunction to make six others—to be then delivered to people in the adjacent villages, with instructions to act in a similar manner: in this way, the chapattis were passed on rapidly from village to village (Carey qtd. in Guha 239). The "circulating chapatti incident" has become linked with the anticolonial resistance of the Uprising of 1857: some accounts suggest there were messages enclosed within the structure of the chapatti itself; others suggest that the chapatti had symbolic meaning known to the anticolonial organizers.

I begin with this brief exploration of the "circulating chapatti incident" because it is an important rejoinder to the place of food in historical and cultural life. As Homi Bhabha has so persuasively argued, the incident "represent[s] the emergence of a form of social temporality that is iterative and indeterminate" (200). The incident also represents the iterative impossibility of understanding culinary gestures: yoked as they are to cultural practices, any act of food preparation can scarcely be seen to accurately and unproblematically reproduce intractable cultural norms. The very difficulty in yielding any kind of iterative fixity about the meaning of the chapatti incident speaks less to our poverty of understand "what really happened" than it does to the impossibility of establishing epistemological boundaries around the gesture itself. The chapatti incident underscores the mutable significance of food: more importantly, it also exposes the limits of complete epistemological certainty. Yet amid a larger cultural field that signals to the very limitations of what might be deemed knowable, we must also confront the traveling and continued symbolic application of this historical fable. For if nothing else, what this gesture firmly states is that food at this particular historical moment became a source of anxiety for the colonial powers because it became linked to struggles for freedom, national identity, and self-determination. Food becomes an agent of change, not an *a priori* fixed comestible, but something whose essence eludes complete mastery and understanding. We might thus consider food a vehicle of protest or an agent of change, not merely a passive vessel to reflect cultural norms.

One cannot ignore the fact that the history alluded to in the poem above, which lands the British imperialist forces in a pickle, also has recourse to another history of comestibles. The trigger for this mutiny also revolved around culinary matters. As Indian cultural history including Ketan Mehta's tribute to Mangal Pandey, legendary hero of the Uprising, attests, the most salient feature of the Uprising has to do with food. Introduced within the closing years of the 1850s, the then brand-new Enfield rifles to be used by the Indian troops included a paper cartridge that contained both ball and powder charge. To use the cartridge, it was necessary to bite the end off and push it down the muzzle of the rifle. To facilitate this, the cartridges were rumored to be heavily greased with a mixture of cow and pig fat. The conundrum facing the largely Muslim and Hindu soldiers within the British army had everything to do with dietary requirements: the Muslims would have to allow pig fat— a proscribed dietary item—to pass their lips, and Hindus would have to come into contact with fat from the sacred cow. While the British purportedly realized their mistake, replacing the animal fat grease with vegetable oils, the visceral disrespect exhibited by the East India Company had not failed to remind the Hindu and Muslim soldiers of the East India Company's refusal to respect culinary choices rooted in political and religious beliefs. While countless cultural narratives have emerged around the Uprising of 1857—narratives about nationalism, patriotism, and anticolonialism—the one I am most interested in here concerns itself with the affront to religious foodways encapsulated in the attempt to forcibly impose the use of Enfield rifles among the Indian ranks.

Collectively these histories yield two radically important interpretive possibilities; first, the notion that food can metaphorically speak to political unrest, and second, that the narrative is not about securing a knowledge base about what people eat, but how food is used to determine how people act. While food studies has paid scant attention to this second narrative, there is ample evidence to suggest that food cannot always be located within a simple and codifiable cultural field that merely tells us how people have acted culturally and socially. Rather, food also contains narratives about political resistance and insurgency.

Quite apart from the political tensions of mid-nineteenth-century Indian anticolonialist agitation are instances of culinary-related activism in other historical moments and geographical spaces. In the context of twentieth-century Asian American history, Jane Dusselier points out how food functioned as a form of protest within the Japanese American internment camps of the 1940s. Her study focuses on how Japanese American communities reinvented culinary rituals within the internment camps. Certainly, no other Asian American group in the United States in the twentieth century has had to fight against being deterritorialized as much as the West Coast Japanese Americans. Nonetheless, with more invigorating alliances between Asian and Arab American studies, one can find parallels in the ways Arab Americans are being displaced from homes and communities.[2] Against government-sanctioned measures to deterritorialize the Japanese Americans, Dusselier unearths a startling and compelling narrative about how the "Japanese Americans reterritorialized the camps by using the space of food to expand their realm of political activity" (137). Dusselier understands how food satisfies more than mere alimentary gratification: food in the Japanese American internment camps becomes powerfully resignified as a space through which to dissent, critique, and rupture the existing structures of institutionalized racism. Like the circulating chapatti incident of 1857, the use of food as protest creates a cognitive frisson. Up against other interpretive strategies, such moments show the radical potential of food: more than a palliative for dislocation, more than a chronicle of nostalgia, more than a placeholder to cement cultural exceptionalism, food can also push forward a radical critique of race, class, and labor. On the heels of the previous chapter, I thus offer an alternative reading that asks us to look more closely at how food is presented and to read the conditions of its representability in fiction, film, and poetry inspired to undertake a class critique.

The particular constellation of works I examine triangulate in fascinating and important ways, enabling an invaluable critique of race and labor, a type of inquiry that has been slow to transform food studies. The cornerstone piece is Ketan Mehta's 1986 film *Mirch Masala*. A film about gendered hierarchies and food production in pre-Independence India, *Mirch Masala* (released in the United States under the title *Spices*) interlocutes with two radically different South Asian American cultural texts: Chitra Divakaruni's poem "The Makers of Chili Paste," and the experimental short video by Deb Ellis and Prajna Parasher about restaurant workers in Chicago, *Unbidden Voices*. At stake in this chapter is understanding how and why *Mirch Masala* might be considered to be an antifood film that through its complex interweavings with Divakaruni's poem and Ellis and Parasher's films pushes forward a radical critique of food production and the gendering of the bodies involved in bringing food to the table. Adding Divakaruni's poem to this conversation is essential, if for no other reason than to examine how her lyricism allow us to undertake a more nuanced view of the scope of her work, which Asian American studies has all too easily dismissed for its exoticizing narratives of palatable difference. And yet few of the critics who are quick to dismiss her work have engaged in any significant way with her more politically articulated poetry. *Unbidden Voices* is perhaps even better positioned to advance a class critique because it draws inspiration from Mehta's film in order to unearth narratives about working conditions in Chicago-area Indian restaurants. At the same time, *Unbidden Voices* examines the place of food within visual registers through its very rendering on-screen.

Central to my analysis will be an exploration of how these three works reshape the terrain of the food film. When we consider the place of food in film and literature, food is often most saliently constructed as what propels the narrative forward. As film studies scholar Laura Lindenfeld notes, "food, meal preparation and eating provide the central driving force for the film's narrative structure and thus provide excellent barometers to measure social hierarchies and relationships" (7). Anne Bower presents a taxonomy for understanding what counts as a food film:

> Food has to play a star role, whether the leading characters are
> cooks (professional or domestic) or not. This means that often the

camera will focus in on food preparation and presentation so that in close-ups or panning shots, food fills the screen. The restaurant kitchen, the dining room and/or kitchen of a home, tables within a restaurant, a shop in which food is made and or sold, will usually be central settings. And the film's narrative line will consistently depict characters negotiating questions of identity power, class, spirituality, or relationship through food. (6)

I deliberately turn away from what Lindenfeld and others have identified as a "food film" while remaining vigilant about thinking how the terms offered might compel us to rethink what we typically understand to be a food film. The social documentary on food, with its emphasis on charting a history of resistance and rendering visible the conditions of labor and exclusion and sexism, would not typically be considered a "food film." My aim is not to posit a logic of inclusions to argue that documentaries are food films but to reterritorialize the space occupied by the food film to provide a more engaged class critique of food and its contexts in a South Asian transnational frame. To examine what we might conceive of as alternative turning points and barometers for measuring social relationships, I look at how the social documentary deterritorializes the genre of the food film, wresting its necessary connection to consumption, delectability, and palatability to produce an antipornographic narrative more concerned with the values of production.

Collective Action: Food as Protest.

After creating matter, man and mind,
God was bored,
So he sprinkled some chilies and spices,
and made the world more colorful.
—FROM MIRCH MASALA

Anne Bower suggests that the hallmark of a food film lies in the star status accorded to food. Accordingly, the vast array of food-titled films within the corpus of South Asian transnational film might not fit the bill. But the real point of intrigue is not films titled after food, but rather ones in which food orients the narrative toward a critique of race, class, and gender. Unlike the more highly visible films directed by the emergent group of South Asian women directors, such as Mira Nair, Deepa Mehta, and Gurinder Chadha, arguably even Nisha Ganatra, the titles of these films are frequently couched in culinary terms, even as their actual context has little or, in many cases, nothing to do with food per se.[3] Cultural critic Sandip Roy has argued, "the Masalas, the Chai, the Chutneys are not so much the problem because they are there. They are problematic because they are gratuitous and meaningless. There is no chutney in *Chutney Popcorn*. All they do is mark the film as 'exotic other'" (M16). "Chutney," "chai," "masala," and "bhaji" are gratuitous terms, but their continued presence as signifiers of "South Asianness" speaks symptomatically to a larger tendency to frequently use food to signify ethnic otherness.

In contrast to films such as *Mississippi Masala* or his more recent Bollywood hit *Mangal Pandey*, Ketan Mehta's *Mirch Masala* made virtually no mark in the mainstream of Indian films. Despite its lack of mainstream visibility, *Mirch Masala* has provided feminist filmmakers and cultural brokers much critical fodder to negotiate how sites of food production—be they in the restaurant kitchen, or within the walls of factories—are gendered. From its onset, the film announces itself as being fundamentally about land, people, and labor. It opens with a panoramic shot of a bucolic farm scene, gradually focusing in close-up on a single chili plant. In the background, a man's chant ascending in pitch can be heard singing the words quoted in the epigraph. Yet far from being a film about god's volition, the film is about gendered inequities that coalesce around a particular fictionalized event set in 1942, the year of the Quit India campaign.

The film's narrative centers on the resilience displayed by Sonbai (Smita Patil), a peasant woman employed in the local chili factory and locked in a struggle with a tyrannical *subedar* (tax collector) who unrelentingly pursues her. When it becomes clear both to Sonbai and the village folk that the *subedar* (Naseeruddin Shah) will not give up his aggressive pursuit of Sonbai, tensions escalate to the point that the town becomes split in their view of Sonbai. On one hand are the *subedar*'s yes-men, who are willing and able to carry out the *subedar*'s foolhardy wishes; on the other hand are the villagers, who are morally opposed to the *subedar*'s position but who stand to lose their status, property, and livelihoods if they do not capitulate to the *subedar*'s maniacal desire to have firm control over Sonbai. And yet another position emerges among the women of the village, those who have the least strength at their disposal and the most to lose. As the film unfolds, the *subedar*'s powers gradually unravel. As the womenfolk band together in solidarity with Sonbai, they collectively offer the most significant challenge to the *subedar*'s power, eventually halting him in his tracks.

Consider how this narrative plays out during the course of the film.

With considerable arms and support at his disposal, the *subedar* has the upper hand. When Sonbai first resists his sexual advances, he mobilizes his band of soldiers to hunt her down like prey. But she valiantly fights back, eventually taking refuge in the chili factory located in an enclosed fortress atop a hill. In one of the most compelling scenes of the film, Sonbai becomes the hunted prey who tries to evade capture. In a chase scene lasting approximately six minutes, the film captures the mounting tension between Sonbai and her predators. Alternating shots of the *subedar*'s men on horseback encroaching on Sonbai with shots of Sonbai darting between bushes and seeking refuge from the probing eyes of the pursuing soldiers, the sequence depicts the distance between the innocent and the predators. Throughout the sequence, neither Sonbai nor her pursuers appear in the same frame. Instead the film cuts rapidly between alternating shots of Sonbai and the *subedar*'s band. A rapid succession of shot reverse shot repeats as the tension mounts. climaxing at the moment when the men on horseback and Sonbai occupy the same shot. In this final scene of the sequence, the subedar's men occupy the background while Sonbai in the foreground runs toward the safety of the chili factory.

During the chase sequence, long shots of female laborers seated in clusters around the factory courtyard are interspersed with shots of Sonbai masterfully weaving her way toward a safe place by hiding behind large mounds of chilies away from the eyes of the *subedar*'s men intent on capturing her and taking her back to the *subedar*. The parallel shots establish a continuity between Sonbai and the women workers; as the women in the courtyard engage in their work rituals, pouring oil over the chili peppers to aid in the drying process, Sonbai makes her way through and around the formidable mounds of drying chili peppers, hiding behind the stacks. When she finally escapes, she seeks refuge in the chili factory, where Abu Mian, the *chowkidar* (watch man), locks the gates to the factory, promising to protect Sonbai's life.

With this affront to his masculinity and power, the *subedar* steps up his efforts to catch Sonbai. His first action is to enter into a bargain over Sonbai with Jeevan Seth, the chili factory owner. From his words and actions, the *subedar*'s hunger for Sonbai's body is palpable; he likens Sonbai to a spice to satiate his desires. Jeevan Seth, on the other hand, fears that the *subedar* is trying to extract taxes from the earnings of the chili factory:

SUBEDAR: Do you own that spice factory?

JEEVAN SETH: It's not really a factory. They call it that jokingly. It just provides meager work for a few poor women.

SUBEDAR: Well, in that factory of yours there is a certain spice that I like very much. I sent my men for it but your guard locked the gate.

JEEVAN SETH: Locked up the gate, Sir? Tell me what spice, Sir, I'll have whatever you want made up freshly for you.

SUBEDAR: You haven't understood. There's a certain woman inside your factory (*licking his lips*). She's hot as spice. I want her.

Hearing this double entendre, Jeevan Seth quakes with fear, thinking the *subedar* wants a portion of the edible spices in the factory, whereas the *subedar* imagines Sonbai as a spicy commodity to satisfy his libidinal desires. In quick suit, the *subedar* demands that the *mukhi* (village ruler, played by Suresh Oberoi) and the village folk hand Sonbai over to him. While the men of the village passively endorse the more powerful *subedar*'s claim to Sonbai, the aging *chowkidar* Abu Mian refuses to comply with the *subedar*'s wishes. When the *subedar*'s minions demand he hand over Sonbai, he declares, "No, mukhi, I'd rather die than be party to this inhuman act. As long as I'm alive, I won't let this oppression succeed." Abu Mian remains true to his promise, eventually losing his life in a crossfire that transpires when the *subedar* himself penetrates the chili factory in his final effort to capture Sonbai.

Significantly, the only other group to offer resistance to the *subedar*'s wishes comprises the women of the village, led by the *mukhi*'s wife (Deepti Naval). Two features of their attempts to protect Sonbai are particularly telling. When the *mukhi*'s wife learns that Sonbai and the other women are trapped in the chili factory with no food, she takes it upon herself to support their efforts. Disregarding the comments of her detractors, she marches toward the entrance to the chili factory, now a besieged site with no access to the outside world. Upon arrival at the factory's gates, she hands a package of roti to Abu Mian, thus marking her solidarity with the women. But perhaps more significantly, she makes it possible for the women to survive within the walls of their temporary refuge and provides them with a means of sustenance. Upon receiving the package of roti, the women inside the factory appreciatively remark that only a woman would think to bring roti during a crisis. Yet, this gesture of solidarity is not an isolated act. Later in the film, the village women learn that their husbands, fathers, and brothers who have buckled under the *subedar*'s pressure have agreed to storm the chili factory. Once again the *mukhi*'s wife mobilizes the village women, asking them to join her to protest this abuse of patriarchal power. The village women whose labors are primarily confined to the domestic household space transform their everyday objects into tools of protest. Armed with rolling pans, pots, and pans, the women gather together in front of the factory's gates. As they assemble in silent protest, they bang and clang on their pots to mark their opposition to the *subedar*'s abuse of power. Although the tax collector's men forcibly remove the women from their post outside the factory, they stand apart from the men in the village in their willingness to articulate their moral position in opposition to the *mukhi*'s and the village menfolk's passive endorsement of the *subedar*'s practices.

Mehta's imagining of the uses of domestic cooking utensils both touches and expands upon the vision of household domesticity offered in David Dabydeen's culinarily organized novel *The Counting House*. A tale about Rohini and Vidia, an Indian couple who migrate from India to Guyana in the mid-nineteenth century as indentured laborers, *The Counting House* offers glimpses into the culinary logic undergirding cultural practices within and among the diasporized indentured communities of the Indo-Guyanese characters. In a particularly poignant moment laced with undertones of violence, Vidia peruses his home space, allowing his gaze to rest upon various culinary accoutrements: "He looked around the room, noticing for the first time how all the humble implements they used to keep their marriage together—belna, puckni, tawa, cutlass[4]—could so easily become the means of a dozen brutal ways of harming her" (89). Vidia sees himself as an aggressor, brandishing kitchen utensils over his wife, Rohini. As a man who has trouble consolidating any sense of masculine power within his household, it is rather telling that he imagines reasserting himself as the patriarch of the family by transforming his wife's kitchen utensils, ones that aid her in the preparation of household meals, into weapons that he might use not simply to overpower her but to brutalize her. Vidia recognizes the potentially dangerous qualities inherent to these kitchen utensils; the very same items used to keep their marriage together when put to another use can eat away at the edifice of their marriage.

While moments such as those in Dabydeen's *The Counting House* mark cooking utensils as tools capable of further disempowering women, historical narratives about the use of domestic cooking tools offer an alternative narrative. As the environmental feminist Vandana Shiva has argued, symbols of domesticity such as the rolling pin are also "symbol[s] of women's power" (108). The history of this iconic image of

women transforming cooing utensils into objects of protest is also inti-
mately linked with Indian women's movements from the 1970s. In 1973,
the Indian feminist-activist Mrinal Gore, a member of the Socialist Party
of India, joined forces with the women of the Communist Party of India
(CPIM) to establish the Mahagai Virodhi Andolan (United Women's
Anti-Price-Rise Front). Dedicated to countering governmental moves
to increase the escalating price of everyday comestibles and commodities, the protests, as Samita Sen notes, "turned into a mass movement of
women seeking consumer protection" (25). Many activists additionally
credit Gore for her creative protest methods using the *latni morcha* and
handi morcha whereby women would brandish rolling pins and small
water vessels in their agitations against discriminatory gender practices.
Ketan Mehta's film uncovers an important story about female solidarity
coalescing around the means of food production. Resisting a narrative
that might view their tactics as provisional, the link to feminist politics
of the 1970s grounds Mehta's deployment of the iconic image of women
wielding rolling pins and pots.

Despite their best efforts to keep the *subedar* at bay, the women
amassed in front of the factory gates are unable to prevent him from
advancing. He succeeds in penetrating the female enclave, killing Abu
Mian in the process. Certainly this gesture is latently sexualized: large
phallic shaped dowels are used to break down the walls of the factory.
When he finally enters this female space, he approaches Sonbai to claim
her for himself. In contrast to her earlier resilience, Sonbai appears to
have accepted defeat and seems willing to "give herself" over to the subedar. Certainly one cannot overlook the fact that at this point, Sonbai herself does not want to further inconvenience her fellow workers who have
also been under siege without their families or food. Yet in a surprising
turn of events, the factory women who have railed against Sonbai for
having put their lives in danger decide to rally behind her at this critical
juncture. But without muscular strength, guns, knives, or the necessary
technological apparatus, the women are at a disadvantage. In an act of
empowerment, the women turn to the weapons surrounding them: the
baskets full of drying red-hot chilies. As the *subedar* advances toward
Sonbai, the final shot of the film cuts to the women workers as they seize
baskets full of dried chilies, eventually hurling them into the *subedar's*
eyes, causing him to cry in agony at the burning sensation. The final
image of the film centers on the *subedar* screaming in pain, completely
incapacitated by the women's gestures. By targeting his eyes, rather than
any other part of his body, the women of the factory literally burn the

phallic gaze that has looked upon Sonbai as if she were a fiery spice to nourish his sexual appetite.[5]

This moment becomes particularly poignant when contrasted with an earlier event in the film. Following a dance in the village, the *subedar* demands that a woman be brought to him. When she arrives at his home, he plays a record on a gramophone and laughs at her naïveté regarding the new technology. When she naively demands where the voice is coming from, asking him, "Isko kahan chupha raka hai?" (Where have you hidden her?), he patronizingly laughs at the woman, treating her as a simple, unsophisticated peasant girl. By the film's end it becomes apparent that the same simple women who do not have the technological know-how or control over the means of production are not passive victims. Instead, they possess a sense of solidarity and community and have the intellectual acumen necessary to protect one another and to rise up against the abuse of patriarchal power. The chili becomes transformed from an item apparently put on earth to make the world more colorful into a powerful weapon that debilitates the *subedar* more effectively than guns, knives, or brute force.

Mehta's film significantly departs from the conventions of most mainstream films in its refusal to provide a sentimental or moralizing ending. The film ends with a shot of Naseeruddin Shah screaming, in response to having had fine particulates of dried chilies hurled into his eyes. Yet it is not Sonbai who launches this attack on the *subedar*. Rather, the women of the chili factory rally behind her to blind the *subedar*'s penetrating gaze. Sonbai, significantly, does not take up arms at the end of the film. Instead, she is framed in the final shots with a sickle in hand, embodying her position as an agent of revolutionary change. This final image positions Sonbai as another actor in a series of revolutionary acts led by peasant insurgents. While it would be tempting to interpret this as a sign that the women had triumphed over the subedar, the film cannot be so easily contained. The final gesture of the film remains open-ended, not fully interpretable, creating instead a web of potentiality and signification regarding the meaning of the final gesture. As Ranjani Mazumdar also suggests, "Mehta consciously breaks the narrative, to leave it open-ended so that the audience is able to participate and reflect on the issues being raised" (WS 84). Here, we might do well to attend to the complexity of Sonbai's final sphinxlike gesture by recalling the mutable signification of the "circulating chapatti incident." As in that earlier incident, the meanings and effects of which have been buried by the vicissitudes of history, we can entertain a reading that accounts for the open-endedness of the film's closing scene. To recognize this gesture as necessarily un-intelligible is to embrace an alternative narrative: one that recognizes the very undecidability of culinary gestures. The open-ended gesture anticipates and buttresses a narrative of dissent against abuses of power. The complete meaning of this subaltern gesture remains open-ended. Sonbai stands stoically with sickle in hand, and the peasants and disenfranchised subjects are cast as agents of change who are able to use food to counter the hegemonic effects of a patriarchal history.

Ultimately, this film poignantly alludes to how chilies are more than a mere spice, additive, or flavoring. Contrary to the initial musical interlude to the film, chilies figure into this narrative less as objects to make the world "colorful" than as a form of life-affirming fieriness. The commodity which the women labor to produce—dried chilies—is transformed by the film's close into a harbinger of change. The chilies are a source of income and a weapon to resist patriarchal oppression, and the factory is transformed from a mere workplace into a site of struggle. By focusing on the conditions and means of food production, and by elaborating on the societal, political, gendered, and national circumstances surrounding this historical-fictional work, Ketan Mehta's film significantly departs from the conventions of the food film. Certainly the film is far less about food than it is about the conditions of work for those who work with chili peppers to earn a livelihood. Additionally, the film becomes an important point of departure for understanding at least two cultural works produced by South Asian American artists, namely the experimental video *Unbidden Voices* and the poem "The Makers of Chili Paste."

Restaurant Work, Invisible Workers

Released in the mid-1990s, the experimental video *Unbidden Voices* is part of a growing corpus of experimental documentaries produced by feminists of color within the United States. Distributed under the auspices of the Women Make Movies collective, the video was made by two students from the University of Chicago, Deb Ellis and Prajna Parasher. The video focuses on Manjula Joshi, an Indian immigrant woman who labors in the kitchens of an Indian restaurant in Chicago. The film resists easy categorization: it is at once a chronicle of Manjula's life, a critique of gender roles in South Asia and the diaspora, an exploration of how Hindi cinema and television serials produce idealized images of femininity, and a critique of the immigrant wage-structure and working conditions for female restaurant workers in the United States. The thirty-two-minute-long video juxtaposes close-up images of Manjula with subtitles, loose translations of her spoken words. The subtitles alternately scroll along the bottom of the screen or alongside her face with scenes from popular films and television serials, setting in place a radical asymmetry between her utterances and the translations. Throughout the video Manjula extemporizes on the place of women in Indian society, the concomitant changes in familial and gender roles effected by migration to the United States, and her own position as an immigrant worker in the United States. Most urgently communicated in her narrative is the sense of how much she has to labor as a cultural worker. Her life, it becomes apparent, is inextricably bound with the imperative to produce mass quantities of food. There are no scenes of delectable Indian food to propel the video forward, and yet food remains the impetus for the film. But unlike the type of narrative one has to come to associate with mainstream food films, the film's narrative push comes from positioning Manjula's labor as a restaurant worker.

The video begins with a glimpse at food being prepared and is one of the only scenes which enters the space of the restaurant kitchen. The camera then proceeds to hone in on women donning aprons, preparing for the workday ahead, immediately transitioning to a close-up image of Manjula. As she speaks, her words scroll in a looped ticker fashion along the bottom of the screen, translated:

> I come to work at 6 a.m. and 9 or 10 o clock at night . . . How many hours does that make? Think. 6 or 8 o clock depending on the work. And 10, 11 at night. Until 2, 3 we make poories for parties. For a thousand people one has to make at least some 5000 poories, no? One has to make poories? How many hours does it take? Even when 5 or 6 of us make poories, 5, 6, or 7 hours is not sufficient. So much work they make us do and when it comes to money . . . Money they don't give. Indian people have become such crooks.

These subtitles are deliberate and inexact translations of Manjula's words and do not convey how Manjula switches between Gujarati, Hindi, and "Hinglish," an amalgam of Hindi and English. Rather than remaining resolutely faithful to the original, the subtitles approximate Manjula's words. The subtitles rapidly scroll across the bottom of the screen, further underscoring the ephemeral quality of her thoughts: one barely has time to process her thoughts before we are transported to the next scene, thought, or critique. The notion that all experiences are contingently translatable to any idiom reaffirms a patriarchal colonialist view of difference, one that levels all experiences to descriptive assignations. But as feminist translation theorist Tejaswini Niranjana has suggested, translation itself is an act of militancy. Devised as a science to contain the limits of what is knowable about colonized subjects, translation has historically served the interests of those wielding power. Translational practices, in their most productive forms, "inscribe heterogeneity" (186). Through their gestures and movements, translation is most transgressive when it is transformatively reimagined not as a containing force, but as a "disruptive disseminating one" (186). In producing inexact translations, the video signals to the poverty of translation by disallowing the possibility of affirming a voyeuristic glimpse into food preparation. The video operates against a logic of voyeuristic interest in food preparation: scenes of food preparation are always partial, images of food are always blurred or obscured, deliberately blown up, sapped of bright colors—rendered to resist penetrating gazes.

At no juncture does the film allow food to be conceived outside of its labored contexts. In one scene, a *poori* (a deep-fried flatbread) is pressed into shape before being deep-fried in a vat of hot oil. This image is juxtaposed with a deliberately grainy voice-over commenting: "It is women's work that has continuously survived with not only the varieties of capitalism but other historical and geographic modes of production. The economic, political, and legal heterogeneity of the relationship between the definitive mode of production and race—and class—differentiated women's and wives work is abundantly recorded."

In another scene, an image of a simmering pot of dal takes up the screen, as text reading,

kitchens
sustenance
nurture
culture,

interrupts the image of what might have otherwise appeared to be a gratuitous shot of a pot of lentils being prepared for the restaurant's dinnertime meal offerings. Such moments signal to an antipornographic rendering of the image of food. As viewers, we do not consume delectable images of food, nor can we so easily disconnect food from its labored contexts, lodged as it is within a classed matrix contingent on women's labor.

As the film progresses, Manjula continues to speak of inequities in the workplace. She speaks of her untenable work hours, revealing how she is part of a class of laborers alienated from the entrepreneurial class that profits from her labor while causing serious harm to her already exhausted and ravaged body:

> My heart is broken, na? I treated *Annapurna* like my own. That's how I have worked here. Never did I care for my body or anything. For twelve hours I keep on doing my job. Keep on doing my job. I never ever let his work suffer. The last party that he gave, he gave me $85 only. . . .
>
> For these people $15 is nothing . . . to give me an extra $15 dollars in a week is nothing for them. What is there in that? If you don't have, we can understand. We can also understand, no? we are also not the kind of people who don't understand that our boss's condition is like that, that he earns this way. That we also understand and say let's get by this way. It's not like that. You take 5 . . . 500 dollars for a party and sit on it. 5 . . . 5,000 dollars you take for a party. And you give us $85. In $200 you convince all of us.

Manjula's words convey a sense of disappointment that her countless hours of hard labor are not acknowledged by the restaurateurs even as she is lead to believe that she is considered part of Annapurna's family of workers. According to Miabi Chatterjee, this disjuncture between the experiences of the laboring class and the entrepreneurial class is often a strategic attempt to quell dissent among workers. In her rich ethnographic study of Indian restaurant owners and employees in New York City, Chatterjee highlights this narrative rift which allows managers to deploy the metaphor of "family" in reference to their employees even as the workers remain profoundly alienated from their conditions of labor. In analyzing the rhetorical power of this gesture of naming workers as part of the family, Chatterjee suggests, "the family is not just a convenient metaphor, but a managerial ideology, one that attempts to privatize economic relations and screen them from public view and regulation." The language of familiality thus is perniciously used to discourage workers like Manjula from seeking greater workplace equity when that goal runs counter to the profiteering motives of the managerial class. Stories like Manjula's become necessary scripts to understand the kind of invisible labor that women in the restaurant industry perform. As Chatterjee so eloquently states, "when we uncover workplace scripts about race, gender, and ethnicity, we may better understand the difference between conditions of possibility at work or conditions of dread."

As the film draws to a close, Ellis and Parasher insert the closing scene of *Mirch Masala* alongside a final interview segment with Manjula. *Unbidden Voices* fixates on *Mirch Masala's* closing scene, the final act of strength on the part of the women to stand up to the lascivious and toady tax collector as they prepare to face possibility rather than dread. As we repeatedly see his eyes burn because of the chili peppers thrown at him, we also hear Manjula reflecting on the importance of rising up to confront patriarchal abuses of power. Her commentary is about the film but also touches on the exploitation she faces in the workplace preparing *poori* in the restaurant kitchen. I now shift focus for a moment, and consider the mise-en-scène of this sequence of the video:

> [Naseeruddin Shah (*subedar*) is standing in front of the enclave where the women are drying chili peppers. No men, except for the aging Abu Mian (Amrish Puri), the guard, are in this space. This space has been serving as a refuge for Sonbai (Smita Patil), a village woman who resisted the subedar's sexual advances and is taking cover in the factory.
>
> The subedar has just killed Abu Mian, and is on the other side of the factory. He uses a large pole to break down the gate and enters the outdoor courtyard of the factory where the women are drying chilies. He advance to her, walks across Abu Main's dead body, kicks the man and his gun out of the way.]

Cut to Manjula:

> "One thing good is that for our Indian women to protect her honor, she is willing to give up her life? Right?
> "She does not allow her body to be stained, right?
> "That's the thing to be understood in this."
> [As Naseeruddin advances toward Sonbai, the women pick up a large tray of dried chili peppers and run toward the *subedar*. They throw the chili peppers in his eye, and he begins to scream as his hands go to his eyes.]

Cut to Manjula:

> "In order to protect her honor and her character, she fights against him, right?
> "He is after her, no?
> "Naseeruddin, no?

"In order to save herself, she does it—liked this she upholds the woman's pride.

"She says, do it this way.

"If you do something, you'll get something. If you put your head down and go to him, another goes with him. You know?

"Another village girl goes to him and comes."

[The image of the women throwing chilies is repeated twice as we continue to hear the subedar's screams, increasing in pitch and intensity.]

"Yes.

"One goes to him and lets her to go with him.

"She tells him that, no? She doesn't go."

The video returns to an image of the subedar screaming as his eyes burn. It is the same image from before, but we also see him falling to the ground and losing control of his body. In contrast to this is Sonbai, who is standing still without uttering a word.

Unbidden Voices continually translates and interrupts Mehta's film to assert commonalities among cultural workers in locations as geographically distant as India and the United States. The temporal distance between the subjects at hand: Mehta's filmic subjects—women workers in the 1940s and Manjula Joshi, a post-1965 immigrant to the United States—allow for a critical articulation of diaspora as a chronotopic category of analysis: encompassing both space and time. But diaspora emerges as a critical concept, less invested in notions of home and return, and more as a critical strategy to emphasize ongoing labor struggles exacerbated by the vicissitudes of immigration. As the film critic Ella Shohat suggests, *Unbidden Voices* forms part of a corpus of diasporic film/video works that strategically link "issues of postcolonial identity to issues of post–Third-Worldist aesthetics and ideology" (22). Alongside notable experimental feminist films such as Trinh T. Minh-ha's *Surname Viet Given Name Nam*, a film like Ellis and Parasher's "remains anticolonialist while calling attention to a diversity of experiences within and across nations. The films produced in the First World, in particular, raise questions about dislocated identities in a world increasingly marked by the mobility of goods, ideas, and peoples attendant with the 'multinationalization' of the global economy"(22). Manjula Joshi's travails made possible or necessary through the workings of the global economy are rendered homologous, though not identical to struggles of the Indian women peasants represented in Mehta's film who must find other strategies to contain their labor and effort. Against a chronology that might isolate acts of insurgency to specific historical periods, the filmic dance between *Unbidden Voices* and *Mirch Masala* profoundly alters how we might consider diasporic tropes of difference and migration. Rather than separating labor through and across oceans of difference, the cross-fertilization between *Mirch Masala* and *Unbidden Voices* buttresses a metanarrative about South Asian women as cultural workers within a patriarchal order. Struggles for greater gendered equity within the labored contexts of food production become poignantly constructed through and against the strictures of national specificities to establish congruent patterns of exploitation of women workers who populate the world of food production, bringing food to tables.

From Poem to Film: Strategies against Food Pornography

In the previous chapter, I examined how we might revisit Chitra Divakaruni's writing with a view to disarticulate the form of her novelistic writings from the social commentaries entrenched within the inner core of the novel. I want to further extend this point by turning back a page to examine an earlier and typically overlooked work by Divakaruni, "The Makers of Chili Paste," a poem anthologized in her collection *Leaving Yuba City: New and Selected Poems*, a work that refuses to fetishize the immigrant experience in the United States. In its pointed critique of the conditions of labor for women employed in the chili trade, the poem begins the important work of establishing how one might jettison pornographic renderings of food for narratives attuned to the exigencies of class and gender. Unlike the seemingly seamless narratives of migration offered through her fictional works, such as *Mistress of Spices*, or her short-story collection, *Arranged Marriage*, *Leaving Yuba City* is constructed through fissures and omissions. Heterogeneous in its conception, the collection interlocutes with a far-ranging corpus of South Asian literary, expressive, and cinematic traditions ranging from contemporary South Asian film, historical accounts of Punjabi migration to northern California, and Mughal miniature paintings. "Makers of Chili Paste" is part of "Moving Pictures: Poems Inspired by Indian Film," a subsection of the anthology that pays homage to the rich tradition of alternative Indian cinema. Here Divakaruni interweaves an homage to a series of critically acclaimed Indian films including Mira Nair's *Salaam Bombay!*, Satyajit Ray's *Ghare Bhaire* (Home and the World), Adoor Gopalkrishnan *Elippathyam*, Mrinal Sen's *Bhuvan Shome*, and Ketan Mehta's *Mirch Masala*. The words write back to the films and contain critiques of South Asian gendered norms. Divakaruni's choice of films is not insignificant: Beyond these films' formal and stylistic distinctions from Bollywood films, they are linked by their commitment to social justice. Like *Unbidden Voices*, "The Makers of Chili Paste" extracts from *Mirch Masala* a narrative about women as cultural workers, placing emphasis squarely on women's labor and how this particular industry both ravages female bodies and makes them stronger. The naming of the poem "The Makers of Chili Paste" affirms women's position as laborers within a cultural-political economy. The description of the chili peppers emphasizes how physical contact with the peppers takes its toll on the female body. The opening stanza of the poem reads:

> The old fort on the hill
> is now a chili factory
> and in it, we the women
> saris tied over nose and mouth
> to keep out the burning (69)

The third stanza describes how as the wood pestles rise and fall, grinding the chilies into paste, the "Red spurts into air, flecking our arms like grains of dry blood. The color will never leave our skins." Both stanzas emphasize burning sensations and bleeding—vivid images of chili peppers not providing palatal pleasure to bodies but aging them, leaving marks of labor engrained on the skin. The first stanza conveys a picture of burning noses and mouths, addressing a heightening of the senses of smell and taste that eviscerates the body. Their labor leaves indelible marks on their bodies, not so easily forgotten, not so easily erased. As she writes in the second stanza of the poem, " . . . their scarlet / sears our sleep. / We pound them into powder / red-acrid as the mark / on our foreheads" (69). The chili flakes create the appearance of a ravaged bleeding body. The visual power of redness permeates the rest of the poem. The deep scarlet hues of chilies is completely debilitating, searing the women's sleep after they work all day in the chili factory. The redness of their bindis is likened to the acrid redness that burns their hands, noses, mouth as they pound the chilies, turning the long dry chilies into a fine powder. Their work is described as creating red hands which "burn like lanterns." The burn of their touch is positioned, ironically, as something strong enough to keep their husbands away from having forcible sex with them. One of the female worker vows, "we will never lie breathless under the weight of thrusting men, give birth to bloodstained children" (70), conveying her determination to not simply live as one who endures pain.

Such imaginings in the poem closely echo the truth about rural peasant women employed in India's chili trade. A 1988 study of the two thousand women employed in the chili-grinding business in western India highlights the occupational hazards of the chili industry. The study undertaken by the feminist labor organization SEWA (Self Employed Women's Association) gives voice to the lived experiences of the two thousand women employed in the chili-grinding business in Behrampur, Amraiwadi, and Madhupura, three regions adjacent to Ahmedabad, India. Providing demographic details about the women employed in the trade, the study identifies burning bodily sensations as one of the major destructive effects of working so closely with chilies. SEWA's report about the women in this aspect of the spice trade is starkly unromantic. The women work long hours and receive little compensation for their labor. As the article notes, "these women also find sitting near a flame to cook unbearable. If any member of the family—husband or children—comes in close physical contact with the women's bodies, they, too, experience burning sensations. Since the unexposed parts of the body are more sensitive than the exposed parts, they tend to avoid physical intimacy" (34). In introducing this critical vector about women's bodies, the poem turns away from a sentimentalized or romanticized portrayal of food.

The penultimate stanza marks an important change in voice. Here, the poem's speakers insert themselves, stating "we are the makers of chili paste we mix in spices seal it in glowing jars to send throughout the land." This gesture bestows agency upon the laboring women as it refuses to consider food apart from the women who harvest and dry the chilies. As the poem draws to a close, the collective lyric voice emphatically exhorts: "All who taste our chilies must dream of us, women with eyes like rubies, hair like meteor showers. In their sleep forever our breath will blaze like hills of chilies against a falling sun" (70). The strong imperative at the end, all who taste, must dream of "us," has a double resonance. The women are cast within the framework of an easy exoticism and as amazons blazing breath like hills of chilies. The second interpretive horizon challenges us to engage other possibilities. In its iteration of female prowess, the poem calls to mind the scenes in *Mirch Masala* where the basketsful of chilies are hurled into the patriarch's eyes, causing him to descend into a fiery hell. Architecturally the poem mirrors the final stages within Mehta's film in which singular action on Sonbai's part yields to collective organization, where all the women rise up together to fight the *subedar*. The poem's structure allows an alternative interpretation of food through its dialogue with Mehta's film. Unlike *Unbidden Voices,* "The Makers of Chilli Paste" is arguably more cavalier in its "translation" of *Mirch Masala*. The poem uses the language of food pornography to counter a politics of food pornography.

The final stanza of the poem shifts the focus from labor to taste, thus jettisoning a narrative purely determined by the type of food pornography most associated with Divakaruni to a narrative that works through the strictures of food pornography to challenge its very tropes and implications. With their bejeweled eyes and gleaming hair, the women inhabit an all-too-familiar tropic image of South Asian women as fabled exotic beauties. But those who taste chilies and thus dream of exotic women are interpellated within the poem as subjects who must also contend with amazonic women who will haunt their dreams, nightmarishly reminding them of scorching conflagrations of chilies. The strength produced by these final image of warriorlike amazons also recalls Sonbai's final stance in the film, stoically poised, wielding a sickle, the symbol of the disenfranchised peasantry.

Divakaruni's poem moves food outside of a purely consumptive and affirmative cultural economy. Food is reimagined not as a source of unmitigated pleasure but as something produced through the travails of labor. Much like the chilies that physically burn women, in *Unbidden Voices* we also see how endless hours of work take their toll on immigrant women's bodies. If food films are critiqued precisely because they produce palatable versions of alterity, these revisions of Ketan Mehta's film produce antipornographic narratives that are far less palatable. In fashioning a nonlinear narrative about restaurant workers which connects narratives from different discursive spaces, Parasher and Divakaruni reterritorialize the food narrative by laying bare the processes through which Indian food, or ethnic food, is brought to the table. Food itself is not represented in the terms Bower insists consititute the hallmark of food films. Within a film such as *Unbidden Voices*, food is no more representable than the experience of immigration or the conditions of work in restaurant kitchens. In utilizing a nonmimetic approach to chronicling the life and experiences of female workers, wherein we see how working with food transforms the female body, we are left with two narratives that produce strikingly similar narratives if located in different spatial and temporal locations. The palette upon which images are mixed for Parasher and Ellis is not so dissimilar to that which Divakaruni uses for her poetic lines. Neither Divakaruni's poem nor Parasher and Ellis's film mimetically reproduces Mehta's film: what is gleaned through the poem is the process of laboring, this labor's effects on the female body, and, recalling the final lines of "The Makers of Chili Paste":

> All who taste our chilies
> Must dream of us, . . .
> In their sleep forever our breath will blaze
> Like hills of chilies. (70)

That is, the poem insists that consumers must recall the laborers even in a time of slumber. These lines loop back to connect not just with Ketan Mehta's film, but also with Manjula's words in *Unbidden Voices*. During her commentary on *Mirch Masala*, spliced with the image of Naseruddin Shah screaming as chilies are hurled in his face, she states:

> "One thing good is that for our Indian women to protect her honor, she is willing to
> give up her life? Right?
> "She does not allow her body to be stained, right?
> "That's the thing to be understood in this."

The "thing to be understood," as Joshi puts it, is that the women's bodies are not to be stained, whether the damages exacted are psychic or physical. Omitted from the inexact translation is the notion that women's spirits cannot bear staining. For Manjula, being an actor in a film that exposes inequities within the immigrant workplace is a corrective to exploitative work practices. Her voice does not simply break silence. Through her words, she reveals a fundamentally astute perception of the inequities that structure her occupational location. The experiences of the women in *Mirch Masala* mirror and refract her narrative. Similarly, the poetic lines within Divakaruni's ode to *Mirch Masala* also hearken to *Unbidden Voices* in their repeated insistence that women's bodies are colored with redness, blood, labor, sweat, and chilies intermingling to leave behind stained bodies. Divakaruni's poem suggests that these women with stained bodies will blaze nightmarish trails through the sleepscapes of those Orientalists who see chilies and dream of exotically beautiful women.

One resoundingly loud critique of the treatment of food in Asian American literature maintains that it too easily exoticizes Asian American life while rendering palatable the very difficulties and troubles of racialized and classed immigrant lives. In turning to Ketan Mehta's film

to inspire their own tales of food, gender, and labor, Parasher and Ellis and Divakaruni enact transnational cultural translations wherein a
video about collective labor practices in pre-Independence India feeds
into an alternative, and, ultimately, indeterminate rendering of food and
female subjectivity. The chilies do not carry immutable significance unto
themselves: in the vastly different contexts of Parasher and Ellis's video
as well as Divakaruni's poem, the chilies occupy the symbolic and affective space of an object that cleaves a critical space to critique the invisible
structures of food production. Foregrounding women's labor and collective action as organizing thematics linking cultural products from India
as well as the diaspora, *Unbidden Voices* recasts women's relationship to
food to create a consciously antipornographic culinary narrative. Too
often literary analyses of food excise class from their critiques. By using
labor and class as the lens through which to view the place of South Asian
American women, the polylogue between *Mirch Masala*, "The Makers of
Chili Paste," and *Unbidden Voices* prompts a renewed engagement with
how the materiality of food practices can also feed into the literary and
discursive rendering of Asian America, literally exhorting us to see and
taste differently.

Commemorating Labor

Rather than reiterating what each of these cultural artifacts does to
destabilize the genre of the food film, I end this chapter with a brief
analysis of a short experimental film directed by Indian British architect Nilesh Patel. In this way, I hope to signal to the larger continuum
existing between multiple examples of cultural work inspired by those
women who are cultural brokers and whose bodies and lives have been
drawn by their labor within food preparation. Like *Unbidden Voices* and
"The Makers of Chili Paste," *A Love Supreme* belongs to a small corpus
of food-related cultural artifacts sensitive to the exigencies of class, food,
and labor. Patel's short documentary feature *A Love Supreme* stands
apart and distinct from other "how-to" cooking shows, owing in part
to the markedly different production values and audiences associated
with commercial cooking shows such as *Padma's Passport*. Staid commercial cooking shows strategically mine the popularity of Indian food
to strengthen ratings and popularity, unlike independently funded and
filmed works such as *A Love Supreme*, which can offer a counterhege-
monic narrative sensitive to the exigencies of class, labor, and food production. These differences aside, it is difficult not to read *A Love Supreme*

against these commercial cooking shows, if only because both Patel's film and programs like *Padma's Passport* and *Oliver's Twist* are imbricated within cultural systems that promote the late-1990s fascination with all things Indian. Consider, for example, the penultimate show of the first season of *Oliver's Twist*. Aired in 2002, the episode titled simply "Bollywood" is a paean to Indian food and music. Oliver's culinary quest to present Indianness begins with a trip to an Indian restaurant, where he picks up freshly made chutneys and pickles; he then returns home to set the context for his Bollywood Indian feast. This episode showcases select Indian dishes: what Oliver names "Bombay Potatoes," a South Indian red curry and his own homemade paneer. Midway through the episode Oliver announces the arrival of friend, Honey Kalaria, a London-based choreographer who has also spearheaded bhangra aerobic workout videos in the United Kingdom As Kalaria gushes over Oliver's food, the two converse easily about Hindi film and Indian food. Most episodes of *Oliver's Twist* end with the presentation of food; the assembled social group gather around the food, before the end credits roll. This episode, however, ends with Kalaria taking center stage, leading Oliver's guest in a Bollywood-bhangra style dance. Ashley et al. suggest that Jamie Oliver's cooking shows "encourage the viewers to think of cooking and eating as part of a wider lifestyle" (184), while Rachel Moseley notes that Oliver's cookings shows sell a "lifestyle through a discourse of accessibility and achievability" (qtd. in Ashley et al. 184). With Oliver's acceptance of Honey Kalaria into his circle of friends, Bollywood is rendered chic, even emulatable. *Oliver's Twist* thus recruits consumers into its fold by creating a dance of sorts between food and Bollywood, showcasing the seamless integration of an achievable Indianness and Bollywood culture in Jamie Oliver's espoused lifestyle. Where *Padma's Passport* and *Oliver's Twist* might be noted for fetishizing a culinary chicness for things Indian, *A Love Supreme* offers a far more complex narrative. In the space of nine minutes, the film documents how one woman's life's work becomes engrained on her body while calling attention to what is at stake in producing cooking shows.

Shot entirely in black-and-white, the nine-minute, eleven-second-long film is as much about Nilesh Patel as it is about the subjects of the film, samosas and his mother, Indumati Patel. The film focuses entirely on Indumati's hands as she deftly prepares samosas, deep-fried Indian pastries filled with spiced vegetables. Organized into ten sections, almost mimicking the deliberate stages one encounters in cooking shows, the film captures the complex simplicity of Indumati Patel's craft. Unlike the commonplace television cooking shows that are the mainstay of the Food Network, *A Love Supreme* resists the penetrating gaze of consumers who look to firmly apprehend Indianness through a visually rich register, complete with delectable Indian bodies. Entirely absent from the short film are faces: all that is depicted on-screen are an Indian woman's hands slicing chilies, rolling dough, sautéing vegetables. The image in no uncertain terms refuses to allow food preparation to be divorced from the craft of labor. Promotional literature about the film also explains how and why Patel was intent on making a film about the labor of samosa making. About his mother, a woman who spent most of her adult life working as a lock-stitch machinist in knitwear factories, Patel notes, "my mother suffers from Rheumatoid Arthritis, in her knees and shoulders, and my film was made in case her affliction spread to her hands. I did not want to simply record my mother's hands, but make a film which recreated the sense of extraordinary speed and strength I had observed as a child, and the grace, precision appreciated when older" (Patel 2005). But *A Love Supreme* is not about simply representing the act of samosa making. As the camera closes in on shot after shot of dough being rolled and potatoes frying, the film quietly weaves a compelling narrative about the toll Indumati's labor has taken on her body. Beginning with distance shots, one sees a "ballet of the hands" as Indumati's hennaed hands deftly roll pastry and slice vegetables. Subsequent close-up shots reveal hands that have been weathered by years of work, both within the home and in the world of garment factories. These images disturb the now-commonplace and commodified image of henna as Indian cool. The hennaed hands do not suggest that Indumati is indulging in cultural nostalgia. Rather, the close-up shots of her hands convey how she transcends "race, gender, generation and a disability" to lovingly prepare samosas (Patel 2006).

Visually the film's name harkens to John Coltrane's musical oeuvre. Coltrane's influence on the film can be detected through the film's composition, which moves through the stages of the samosa-making process. Coltrane's famous musical suite, which in its original form includes elements of chant, raga, and modal jazz blended into the four compositions of *A Love Supreme*—"Acknowledgment," "Resolution," "Pursuance," and "Psalm"—inspires the composition of Patel's film, even if its music is wholly absent from the film. The tribute to Coltrane underscores a history of polycultural admixtures, one in which Black American jazz musicians, most notably Duke Ellington and John Coltrane, turned to the "East," notably India, to draw inspiration. Speaking to his musical collaborations with renowned sitarist Ravi Shankar, Coltrane notes:

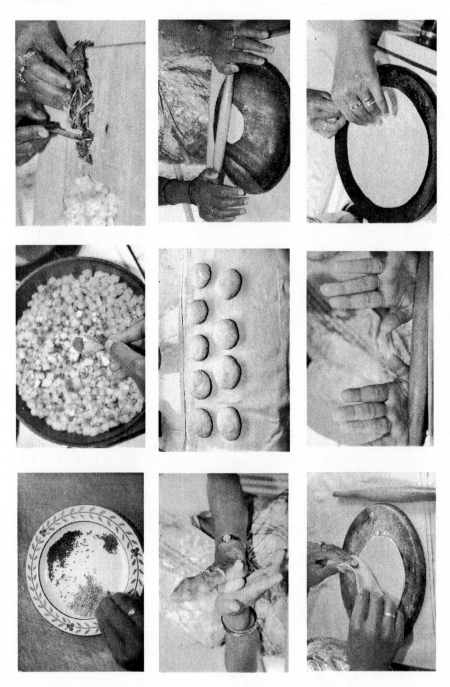

FIGURE 1 Storyboard images from *A Love Supreme*. © 2001, Nilesh Patel.

When I hear [Shankar's] music, I want to copy it, not note for note of course, but in his spirit. What brings me closest to Ravi is the modal aspect of his art. Currently, at the particular stage I find myself in, I seem to be going through a modal phase . . . There's a lot of modal music that is played every day throughout the world. It's particularly evident in Africa, but if you look at Spain or Scotland, India or China, you'll discover this again in each case. If you want to look beyond differences in style, you will confirm that there is a common base. That's very important. Certainly, the popular music of England is not that of South America, but take away their purely ethnic characteristics—that is their folkloric aspect—and you'll discover the presence of the same pentatonic sonority, of comparable modal structures. It's this universal aspect of music that interests me; that's what I am aiming for. (Porter 211)

Coltrane's music, which evokes the spirit of Ravi Shankar, forges a diasporic connection between Black America and a progressive Indian culture of the 1960s and 1970s, albeit one that also rehearses an Orientalist fascination with the "East," or what Bill Mullen has termed "Afro-Orientalism." As Madhav Chari puts it: "even though Coltrane did not use specific devices of Indian music, his own work was influenced by the 'spirit,' 'energy,' or 'essence' of Indian music. He was aware of the different tonal possibilities of Indian scales, and his awareness of the manner in which Indian classical musicians developed melodic ideas informed his own conception, especially in the development of his own improvisations, by extending and elaborating melodic motifs" (268).

Patel enters the diasporic dance between Coltrane and Shankar by forging his own diasporic connection to Coltrane's album. Coltrane's music is not infused into the film but into the composition of the film. As Patel notes, "the concept and representation of memory was central to its development, and would be explored through five sets of relations, memory and subject, filmmaker, viewer, community, and cinema." These five relations through which Patel's film moves connect to the four stages of Coltrane's *Love Supreme*.

Interestingly, there are no voice-overs in the film that might lead consumers to think of it as a "how-to" exercise in the craft of samosa making. The recipe is not one that can be easily duplicated: viewers can perhaps only watch in sheer astonishment how deftly the hands prepare samosas. Added to that is the fact that the film inhabits a space that is neither the domestic kitchen nor the professional restaurant kitchen. Rather, it is a provisional in-between space, a makeshift kitchen in Nilesh Patel's bedroom created explicitly for the purpose of recording Indumati Patel's craft. As such, she is positioned neither as a cultural worker producing meals in the home nor a cultural worker producing meals for public consumption. Rather, she occupies the space of someone for whom cooking can occupy the status of craft. At the same time, her on-screen presence cannot be confused with that of cooking show hosts, who painstakingly take viewers through the stages of food preparation. Quite simply, her face is never revealed on-screen for reasons that become legible less through visual registers than through the film's audioscapes. It is not a coincidence that the musical number opening and closing the film, "Bhor Bhaye Panghat Pe," is taken from the Bollywood film hit of the early 1980s, *Satyam Shivam Sundaram,* in which 1980s screen icon and siren Zeenat Aman plays a disfigured village woman who captivates all those around her with her facility as a singer. Her face can never be revealed: the transformative potential of her music and art must come from a refusal to disclose her visage to her suitor who seeks to aggressively penetrate her space and privacy by being able to see her face. The music Shashi Kapoor's character hears seduces him into falling in love with her, but upon fulfilling his desire to see her, Aman's suitor turns away from the voice (and body) that has brought him sensory pleasures that exceed the visual horror her face produces. Shashi Kapoor's demise in this film comes from his refusal to disengage from his desire to see her face: it is the pornographic gesture Zeenat Aman strives to keep at bay which gestures toward a connection with *A Love Supreme*. Patel's film deliberately and strategically refuses to disclose his mother's face. The ballet of her hands, analogous to the melodic rapturousness of Zeenat Aman lip-synching Lata Mangeshkar's voice, captures a poignant critique of privileging the ocular to contain perceptions of abject figurations of difference.[6] We never see her face, only the hands that work so diligently and loving to prepare samosas.

In ending this chapter with this brief exploration of *A Love Supreme*, I mean to gesture toward ways in which the film concerned with the production of food can buttress a critique of race, class, and labor. At heart, any understanding of Patel's film must provide a critical analysis malleable and yet supple enough to see how *A Love Supreme* inhabits the space of the cooking show genre while deterritorialzing it to capture the role of women's labor in producing delectable commodities. While Patel's mother does not prepare samosas for commercial distribution, her products bear the culinary imprimatur of an exotic cool. Yet where cooking shows like *Oliver's Twist* present Indianness as a commodifiable essence that has made its way seamlessly into a British metropolitan culture which revels in its consumption of difference, one cannot view Patel's film without reflecting on labor and love. The film closes with a dedication, "Dedicated to my Mother, her Mother and your Mother," poignantly creating a community of women bound less by a simple gynocentric logic than by a logic of labor. As Patel notes, "the formal presentation enables viewers to project an image on their own mother, grandmother, daughter, wife, sister, or aunt onto the isolated images of hands at work. This enables them to recall memories of similar labour-intensive dishes, observed and consumed, whether they be dim-sum, artisan pasta, or the perfect apple pie" (*"A Love Supreme* and Memory" 2). Communicating the spirit of labor-intensive cuisines becomes the rallying cry of the film. Through its unwavering gaze on Indumati Patel's deftness and dexterity in preparing samosas, Patel offers a stunning film exposing what goes into the process of making food: a vehement articulation, in the final analysis, of a love supreme.

PART THREE

THEORIZING FUSION IN AMERICA

5 / Eating America: Culture, Race, and Food in the Social Imaginary of the Second Generation

In this food-obsessed world, Anthony Bourdain has carved out a distinct place as a gastronomic Indiana Jones.

—DISCOVERY.COM [1]

Thanks to the Immigration Act of 1965, Roosevelt Avenue is the sort of place where someone who has just downed some Filipino barbecue may emerge from the restaurant, and in the next block or two, be tempted to follow that up with an Afghan shish kebab, a Mexican torta, an Indian dosa, and a Tibetan momo before making the decision about whether to go with Korean or Uruguayan baked goods. For devout chowhounds, the route of the No. 7 is El Camino de Santiago.

—CALVIN TRILLIN, "NEW GRUB STREETS"

For the last three years, I have taught Nilesh Patel's *A Love Supreme* to my students in a seminar titled "Food and Culture." As they watch this film, brought to them from across the shores of the Atlantic Ocean, many students respond with delight to see samosas prepared with love and care on-screen. If Patel's loving homage to his mother's samosas speaks to members of the second generation, it is in part due to the fact that Patel's film recasts Indian food as something to be viewed with desire, love, and care.

Such a rendering of food prepared with love has clear echoes in Jhumpa Lahiri's much-acclaimed debut novel, *The Namesake*. As Ashima Ganguli, the mother of second-generation protagonist Gogol Ganguli, prepares to leave her home in suburban Massachusetts to take up residence in India, thus enacting a form of return migration, she holds a dinner party at her home to bid farewell to her community of Indian friends and to the house she has inhabited for thirty years. Her final act of communion with the desi community is one that, unsurprisingly, centers on sharing food. Lahiri painstakingly takes us through Ashima Ganguli's careful culinary preparation for the evening's celebration:

> Ashima Ganguli sits at her kitchen table, making mincemeat croquettes for a party she is throwing that evening . . . Alone, she man-

ages an assembly line of preparation. First she forces warm boiled potatoes through a ricer. Carefully she shapes a bit of the pota-to around a spoonful of cooked ground lamb, as uniformly as the white of a hard-boiled egg encases its yolk. She dips each of the croquettes, about the size and shape of a billiard ball, into a bowl of beaten eggs, then coats them on a plate of bread crumbs . . . Fi-nally she stacks the croquettes on a large circular tray, a sheet of wax paper between each layer . . . She remembers making the first batches in her kitchen in Cambridge . . . her husband at the stove in white drawstring pajamas and a T-shirt frying the croquettes two at a time in a small blackened saucepan. She remembers Gogol and Sonia helping her when they were small, Gogol's hand wrapped around the can of crumbs, Sonia always wanting to eat the cro-quettes before they'd been breaded and fried. (274–75)

With loving attention to the process of cooking and the labor involved in producing these seemingly commonplace Indian snacks, Jhumpa La-hiri's and Nilesh Patel's portrayals of culinary practices stand in stark contrast to the more staid but commonplace images produced by Holly-wood films such as *Indiana Jones and the Temple of Doom* (hereafter *The Temple of Doom*) in which Indian food might be presented as distaste-fully spicy or simply inedible. For second-generation Indian Americans raised on a diet of Hollywood film in the 1980s, *The Temple of Doom* occupies a curious and painful position within our cultural psyches. The second installation of the Indiana Jones Trilogy was, after all, re-leased in 1985, when the post-1965 generation was in early adolescence. One of the most infamous scenes in the film is the banquet scene set in the sumptuous dining hall of the Maharajah of Pankot. While Indiana Jones is engrossed in a conversation with Chattar Lal, an Indian mem-ber of the court intent on keeping the Thugee cult a secret, Jones's two sidekicks, Short Round and Willie Scott, are fixated on the food before them. A succession of stomach-turning delicacies are presented before the American guests. The main course, "snake surprise," a large python stuffed with live snakes that crawl out of its belly, is followed by a plate of dead beetles. While the Indians at the table greet the dishes with oohs and aahs, Willie politely declines the offerings, declaring, "I had bugs for lunch." When she makes a request for "anything simple . . . like soup," the server returns with soup. Again, she is unable to stomach the soup as she sees eyeballs float to the surface of the samovar. The scene culminates with the presentation of dessert—individual monkey heads stuffed with chilled monkey brains are served to each person seated at the table. At the thought of consuming such unpalatable fare, Willie faints.

Though set in a mythologized colonial India, the film resonates with North American viewing publics. While Americans may be more likely to consider Indians as vegetarians rather than voracious consumers of live animals, this scene produces a form of disgust that positions the Americans as the normative subjects while casting the Indians as the aberrant heathens. Blond-haired, blue-eyed Kate Capshaw, the normative subject par excellence, becomes the focal point of this scene. As the greedy Indians devour snake and monkey brains, Capshaw looks horrified at her hosts, who, though seemingly "civilized," betray their barbaric nature by relishing such inedible fare. The successful demonizaton of the persons of Pankot is rendered legible through a visually marked culinary idiom; Indians eat food that leads to them being viewed with suspicion whereas Americans consume "normal" food. In the scene, Short Round, played by Jonathan Ke Quan, an Asian American actor, provides some relief to squeamish Asian Americans. Though cast as Chinese, Quan is Vietnamese American and part of the second generation of Asian Americans. His disgust in the scene renders visible an Asian American repudiation of consuming inedible fare.

In this scene, a culinary idiom buttresses racial and ethnic rhetoric. However, repeated viewing of this film makes it clear that the actual foodways of Asian subjects do not help us to better understand why popular understandings of racial and ethnic subjectivity are so frequently rooted in the language of eating and consumption. Where Asian America is concerned, Asian American food can be both a source of disgust and embarrassment (think dog eating) at the same time that Asian American cuisine can engender ethnic pride. On college campuses across the United States, the most common feature of any cultural show organized by Asian American student groups (besides the fashion show) is the consumption and display of ethnic food. Annual summertime food festivals held in North American cities and small towns are often the closet analogue to the college ethnic food heritage celebrations. Critics, however, do not converge in their readings of these public displays of Asianness. Cultural critic Sneja Gunew contends that "one of the few unthreatening ways to speak of multi-culturalism is in relation to food . . . the usual way in which this diversity is acceptably celebrated is through a multi-cultural food festival" (16); but for Uma Narayan, North American food festivals are "one of the rare public events where one is visually, viscerally, and positively conscious of the range of diverse ethnicities and identities that in fact constitute us as a community" (185).

Despite my own varied misgivings, *The Temple of Doom* is an undeniable part of the cultural legacy of the second generation of South Asian Americans. Although Americans may no longer consider South Asians to be indiscriminate consumers of offal and other culinary unmentionables, there is an element of truth to the notion that South Asian American youth might defensively retort back to challenge these bowdlerized myths of South Asian American foodways. The sense of racial abjection produced through and against the viewing of films like *The Temple of Doom* almost always produces narratives of repudiation and disavowal. Motivated by a desire to correct the mainstream misperception of South Asian foodways, cultural responses viscerally and politically aim to position South Asian Americans as normative subjects who consume regular "American" fare. Part of this quest to establish normalcy might well be prompted by the desire to show how well one has assimilated to the norms of a larger mainstream American culture and to counter narratives of culinary excess. But in equal measure the sense of discomfort that emerges about such apparently racist narratives like those in *The Temple of Doom* serves as a visceral reminder of the kind of otherness that leaps from the screen to become grafted onto the bodies of young Indian Americans.

In recent years, some of the most compelling studies of South Asian American life are those chronicling the vast array of subcultural practices of the second generation (Maira 2002; Joshi 2006; and Shankar 2008). But where rave clubs and popular culture allow an older age group of second-generation individuals to adopt and resist cultural identity so as to reflect a more politicized and disruptive praxis of cultural identification, food marks the racialized body in more traumatizing ways. When the subjects are school-aged, with less cultural and political arsenal to shape their cultural terrain, opting to eat certain foods that carry the stigma and smell of otherness viscerally marks the body in disastrous ways. Negotiating the exigencies of racism for these younger bodies may take a markedly different form and shape than it might for older youth, who are better able to render culture malleable to the specificities of their encounters with racism. But ethnic food rears its ugly head more than subcultural practices precisely because its effects are visceral and often manifest at an early age. Anthropologist Sunil Bhatia, one of a handful of cultural theorists who has completed ethnographic work with children from kindergarten through high school (as well as their parents) notes that the second-generation Indian American child's lunch box is often a site of "disruptive otherness." One of Bhatia's informants, a parent who included chutney sandwiches in his daughter's lunch box, notes that:

> he changed his daughter's lunch menu after she reported that one of her school friends said her chutney sandwich smelled bad . . . Rohan said that this was one of the most significant moments in understanding how his children differed . . . From that moment on, [Rohan and his wife, Asha] made sure that their children's lunches were vegetarian and he decided that one way to shield them was to give them lunches that made them feel part of a group rather than excluded . . . For Rohan the move from the exotic to everyday involved repackaging Indian food in a way that fit in with the lunch practices of his children's white schoolmates. (141)

A variation of this can be found in the *New York Times* review of Jhumpa Lahiri's short-story collection *Unaccustomed Earth*. Michiko Kakautani zeroes in on the collection's thematization of second-generation Indians in a review titled "Wonder Bread and Curry: Mingling Cultures, Conflicted Hearts." This title seems out of place given that the collection has little to say about food. Indeed, the review's title stem from a lone moment in the story "Only Goodness" when the narrator, Sudha, laments how her mother's foreignness finds its way into her lunch box: "Her parents had always been blind to the things that plagued their children: being teased at school for the color of their skin or the funny things their mother occasionally put into their lunch boxes: potato curry sandwiches that tinted the wonder bread green" (143). To consider the chutney sandwich a sign of "disruptive otherness" is to invest heavily in the ability of food to produce and contain difference. For Bhatia's informants as well as some of the characters who will be the focus of this chapter, Indian food is wholly unredeemable within the framework of mainstream America; the smell and color of Indian food marks a kind of visceral difference analogous to the indelible traces race leaves on the immigrant body. Otherness feels more disruptive for younger Indian Americans less able to exert agency in shaping cultural practice to reflect a dynamism to their racialized otherness.

Consider the short story "School Lunch" by Indian American author Pooja Makhijani. The editor of the collection *Under Her Skin: How Girls Experience Race in America,* Makhijani is one of the select few among the throngs of South Asian writers concerned with producing viable writing for and about adolescents and young persons of color. "School Lunch" appears within the pages of *Women Who Eat,* a collection of food writing by North American women of all ages and races. Makhijani's narrative tells a story about a young Indian American girl who is unable, perhaps unwilling, to consume the Indian foods her mother prepares for her to take to school. "I don't want her lunches," the narrator notes: "I want to touch a cold, red Coca-Cola can . . . I want to pull out a yellow Lunchables box so I can assemble bite-sized-sandwiches with Ritz crackers and smoked turkey. I want to smell tuna salad with mayonnaise. I want bologna on white bread, Capri Sun Fruit Punch and Cool Ranch Doritos in a brown paper bag . . . But I am too scared to ask her. I know she will say 'no'" (41–42). The narrator's culinary dilemma is complicated by the fact that the foods she covets are overtly coded as American. She believes Doritos, tuna salad, and bologna are the types of culinary accompaniments that will facilitate her assimilation into the mainstream whiteness of her surroundings. However, when she befriends Aisha, a newly arrived immigrant from Pakistan nostalgic for the tastes of home, her culinary dilemma appears to be at the brink of resolution. For Aisha, a girl who finds herself having to purchase "chicken nuggets, a spoonful of corn, sticky peach halves floating in sugar syrup and a tough dinner roll" (46) at the cafeteria, trading meals with the narrator proves to be more than ideal. As the days progress, the narrator swaps her mother's homemade *aloo tikkis* for Aisha's American cafeteria fare.

At play in Makhijani's story is the notion that the feelings of racial abjection produced by the narrator's shame for her mother's food can be eliminated through a simple bartering of food; she jettisons her mother's *aloo tikkis* for what she truly covets—"American" fare. In this daily culinary exchange between the girls, ethnicity becomes represented as an easily transacted commodity. What is undesirable can be traded in for something else to create an apparently even terrain of difference. Her arrangement, a clever solution to everyday discomfort with race, is a temporary palliative that reinforces a binarism between Indian and American. To properly become American, the narrator of Makhijani's story must learn to engage in a form of deception which seems to delight, rather than vex, reviewers. Not surprisingly, the mainstream press seizes upon the binary nature of the struggle the character faces as indicative of the conundrum in which young desis find themselves. A review in *USA Today* notes, "delightful authors include . . . Pooja Makhijani, who longs to swap her fresh raisin bread and warm tamarind-infused lentil soup for chicken nuggets, pizza bagels or Hostess cupcakes."

But Makhijani's story all too easily weaves a seamless narrative, complete with a recipe for the much-loathed *aloo tikkis*. This is a curious move, given that the potato dumplings are the invisible protagonist of this story, the abject food item that confounds the narrator's sense of herself as an American. In the process of creating a narrative where bartering resolves the narrator's dis-ease with Indianness, made manifest through her repudiation of *aloo tikkis*, Makhijani produces a narrative that writes back to a film like *The Temple of Doom* insofar that it yearns to show how the second-generation Indian American subject is resolutely normal. The Indian American subject in Makhijani's pages longs for nothing more than to belong to the cultural terrain of the United States and to rid her body of the stigma associated with otherness.

The creative dilemma Makhijani's story enacts closely echoes the culinary vexations that plague the narrator of Geeta Kothari's critically lauded essay "If You Are What You Eat, Then What Am I?" In this short meditative piece on food, family, and Indian-Americanness, Kothari productively mines those moments of culinary discomfort to weave a narrative rife with moments of discord and unhappiness that can only be understood by casting a wider net around the larger set of culinary conundrums which so frequently become vital moments in making teenagers confront their sense of self. Kothari maneuvers away from an easy binarism pitting tamarind soup against chicken nuggets, chapatti against chips, or dal-roti against tuna fish sandwiches. Kothari's essay first appeared in the pages of the *Kenyon Review* and was later included in *Best American Essays of 2000*. Despite the fact that the volume has been an annual staple for over two decades, Kothari's essay remains one of the few works in the series to be written by an Asian American. While it is positioned as one that can speak emblematically to the experience of race in the United States, the essay's deep ambivalence about any form of culinary isomorphism between taste and national-ethnic identity undercuts the notion of speaking for one's community. Addressing the deep divisions that mark Indian Americans as "other" within the North American racial landscape, Kothari's essay offers a poignant glimpse into what it means to try to become "American" by consuming foods that are overtly coded as "American." Through a series of interlocking vignettes, Kothari stages the movements of her life through a culinary register. Beginning with a moment in the kitchen of her childhood home, she navigates through the intimate space of the kitchen, and the (at times, foreboding and cold) space of the school lunchroom to chronicle her own angst-ridden process of trying to apprehend how her sense of ethno-national identification has recourse to her complex culinary history. Fundamentally, the essay asks, can one articulate one's culinary proclivities with national-ethnic identity?

At first glance, Kothari essay's title seems formulaically to echo the tired cliché that has inspired so many scholarly works on food and consumption. Yet in its syntactic maneuvering, the cliché "you are what you eat" is reformulated as a question rather than as a smug statement of fact, unearthing a deeper ambivalence about food, race, and ontology. Her title interjects doubt, complicating a neat alignment between eating particular foods and claiming an identity rooted in, and routed through, race and ethnicity. Implicitly, this interrogative title challenges the logic of linking food with ethnicity so commonplace in many works of fiction by second-generation South Asians who write about identitarian issues using food as the signifier of ethnicity.

Take, for example, the work of second-generation Indian British author Nisha Minhas. Her novels, which might be most appropriately described as racialized chick lit, casts identity within a culinary frame. Most saliently expressed in *Chappati or Chips?* and *Passion and Poppadums,* Minhas's novels stage the second-generation quest for finding oneself as a facile brokering between East and West. In almost all of her novels, second-generation women in their twenties are depicted as individuals freighted by the burdens of an unrelentingly patriarchal vision of South Asianness. For the feisty second-generation desi, rescue comes in the form of a white young man. Within Minhas's novels, food takes on a metonymic function, banally representing East and West. There is little room to question how and why chapattis and poppadums represent South Asianness or why they are placed in diametric opposition to chips or something as amorphous as passion. In Minhas's novels, food becomes the easiest and most profitable way to represent ethnicity within the popular genre of chick lit. [2]

Against such easy renderings of difference, Kothari's essay opens with an epigraph from Michael Ignatieff's *Blood and Belonging* (1995)—"to belong is to understand the tacit codes of the people you live with"— drawing attention to how immigrants must work to unravel the unwritten codes and rules of U.S. society. Kothari's coming-of-age story is structured as a series of vignettes in which she continually turns to food to find ways of being included and, by implication, appearing less foreign to her American friends. In a discussion over tuna fish sandwiches, Kothari reveals:

> I want to eat what the kids at school eat: bologna, hot dogs, sala-mi—foods my parents find repugnant because they contain pork and meat by-products, crushed bone and hair glued together by chemicals and fat. Although my mother has never been able to tol-erate the smell of fish, my mother buys the tuna, hoping to satisfy my longing for American food. Indians, of course, do not eat such things.
>
> The tuna smells fishy which surprises me because I can't remem-ber anyone's tuna sandwich actually smelling like fish. And the tuna in those sandwiches doesn't look like this, pink and shiny, like an internal organ. In fact, this looks similar to the bad foods my mother doesn't want me to eat. She is silent, holding her face away from the can while peering into it like a half-blind bird . . .
>
> "What's wrong with it?" I ask.
>
> She has no idea. My mother does not know that the tuna every-one else's mothers made for them was tuna *salad* . . .
>
> There is so much my parents don't know. They are not like other parents, and they disappoint me and my sister. They are supposed to help us negotiate the world outside, teach us the clues to proper behavior: what to eat, and how to eat it . . .
>
> We throw the tuna away. This time my mother is disappointed. I go to school with tuna eaters. I see their sandwiches yet cannot explain the discrepancy between them and the stinking oily fish in my mother's hand. We do not understand so many things, my mother and I. (5–6)

Tracing the contours of Kothari's troubling encounters with tuna fish, it is the whiteness of the tuna fish sandwich, a fitting signifier of middle-class whiteness, that confounds both Geeta and her mother. The tale of making tuna salad out of oily canned tuna fish is one of failed assimila-tion. Geeta, the child, wishes to eat tuna fish sandwiches because she thinks it will allow her to fuse seamlessly with her friends and move beyond her racial identity, an external mark of her difference. If she eats like them, then she becomes more like them. Her attempts to assimilate are predicated on internalizing a hegemonic view of middle America's notion about the form of a tuna salad sandwich. But ironically, her failure to follow the implicit recipe further accentuates her difference instead of facilitating her inclusion into the world of the second grade within the lunchroom cafeteria. Unmistakable in its symbolism, the whiteness of the mayonnaise corresponds to the whiteness of mainstream America Geeta covets. In her tale of a botched recipe to produce whiteness, neither she nor her mother understands that a pink oily fish must be mixed with mayonnaise before it acquires the creamy white texture characteristic of the tuna fish sandwiches that her white friends routinely consume for lunch. Kothari's anxiety about tuna fish sandwiches poignantly captures the tensions that arise from eating foods that might be deemed unusual. Kothari's essay focuses on the everyday as the site that racializes Indian Americans. It is not in some elaborate eating ritual that Kothari comes to understand her difference; it is through the mundane act of making a tuna salad sandwich, that most white of foods, in her mother's kitchen that she confronts the implicit culinary hegemony of white middle-class America, and how consumption alone cannot dismantle her racialized experiences of feeling Indian.

The stark beauty of Kothari's narrative resides in her refusal to provide a definitive space of culinary comfort. While Geeta is confounded by tuna salad (and, by extension, other American foods), she remains equally vexed about Indian culinary matters. For both Kothari and Makhijani, adolescence and school lunches in particular pose particular challenges in understanding the complex negotiations between "Indianness" and "Americanness"; within Makhijani's story, that narrative trajectory adheres to a binarism, while Kothari's story resolutely unsettles that binarism in refusing to provide a space of absolute culinary comfort for the narrator. Rather than providing an unmitigated definition of Indian Americanness predicated upon an embracing of particular foods and a disavowal of foods deemed too ethnic, Kothari's essay thoughtfully inquires into the vexing nature of culinary desires. In essence, a simple desire to consume, a bartering of "Indian" for "American," is rendered suspect such that culinary desires do not flatten out to facilitate one's easy access or move into a narrow definition of Americanness. In the nuance of Kothari's story is a rendering of Indianness within the United States that takes stock of heterogeneous taste regimens that do not blindly adhere to a simple disavowal of what Indian Americans eat or do not eat. Kothari's story mines deep to understand what prompts a desire to consume those foods which come to occupy the hegemonic status of Indianness so as to mark the culinary transaction between India and America as more complex than a simple repudiation of the perceived excesses of Indian food. Latent in the expressions of culinary preferences in these narratives is an unabated desire to be able to identify with normative expressions of citizenship.

Culinary Maladies: Food in *Interpreter of Maladies*

I like cooking and eating all different kinds of food . . . And I come from a very food-oriented family. Like most children of immigrants, I'm aware of how important food becomes for foreigners who are trying to deal with life in a new world. Food is a very deep part of people's lives and it has incredible meaning beyond the obvious nutritional aspects. My parents have given up so many basic things coming here from the life they once knew—family, love, connections—and food is one thing that they've really held onto.—JHUMPA LAHIRI, "FAMILY VALUES"

Even this most preliminary exploration of second-generation angst about culinary practices reveals the absolute centrality of food to the imagination of everyday life. Such imaginings about how food shapes the narrative vision of second-generation authors, however, cannot be restricted to narratives where the protagonists are of the second generation. Rather, an exploration of second-generation culinary narrative must also consider the larger cultural field of writing in which second-generation South Asian Americans are active participants.

No second-generation Indian American—or, for that matter, South Asian American writer—in the early years of the twenty-first century has been cast as the representative voice of a populace as much as Jhumpa Lahiri. With the publication of her first collection of short stories, *Interpreter of Maladies*, she shot from complete obscurity to occupy a prominent place within the national and international spotlight. In part, *Interpreter of Maladies* has appealed to a large segment of mainstream reading publics and won literary accolades because it skillfully evokes the ordinariness of the immigrant existence. But the poignant, at times heart-wrenching tales of alienation that provide subtly pointed critiques about the racialized underpinnings of Indian American immigrant experiences are also easy to lose within the pages of a collection that has been lauded for being so universalist. And yet, one might ask, what can be found within the pages of a collection authored by Asian America's most celebrated second-generation voice that illuminates the intersections of food, race, and abjection? As Lahiri reveals in an interview, food lends meaning to the lives of immigrants uprooted from familiar cultural contexts. Unlike the stories discussed thus far in this chapter, Lahiri's short fiction, at first glance, steers away from presenting food as much beyond the apparent backdrop to immigrant life. The opening story of the collection, "A Temporary Matter," tells the story of Shukumar and Shobha, a young South Asian couple on the brink of divorce. A freak loss of electricity in the neighborhood over the period of a week causes the estranged couple to share more time together during the nights, leading to their eventual separation. As the week wears on, the couple—one a second-generation Indian American, the other a graduate student from India—find their way back to each other to share a meal at night. Each meal is prepared with love and care, each meal rendered more complex than the previous one. But when the lights come back on, the couple sever ties. Marred by the tinge of failed love and a sense of betrayal, food is only able to create a sense of community between husband and wife when all else around them has fallen apart. Once life returns to normalcy, food loses its ability to keep the couple together.

If "A Temporary Matter" is a tale of failed beginnings, the closing story of the collection, "The Third and Final Continent," is a story about the redemptive power of immigration. The unnamed narrator of the collection's closing story is the prototypical immigrant who comes to America in search of the American Dream. As he waxes about how far he has come from his modest beginnings as a young librarian to live a life beyond his imagination, the narrator of "The Third and Final Continent" is able to imagine "arrival" in specifically gendered terms. It is the narrator, not his wife, who imagines "arrival." Unlike this final story, "Mrs. Sen's"—a story that sits unobtrusively in the middle of the collection—does not easily settle questions about arrival, inclusion, or exclusion. Literary critics have largely overlooked the story precisely because it seems to present a mundane problem that does not "travel" easily. And yet this piece strikes a chord when it comes to chronicling how the second generation works through food to understand race and belonging, less because of the story's actual content than because of what the story means to Lahiri. In an interview with Vibuthi Patel of *Newsweek International*, Lahiri remarks that "Mrs. Sen's" was her attempt to imagine what life might have been like for someone like her mother, a young South Asian immigrant cast into the silent vastness of a largely white America of the 1960s: "one character is based on my mother who babysat in our home. I saw her one way but imagined that an American child may see her differently, reacting with curiosity, fascination, or fear to the things I took for granted" (60). "Mrs. Sen's" thematizes an alternative narrative of migration for the immigrant woman who works within the home and must implicitly uphold the burden of maintaining traditions from the "homeland."

Set during the era immediately following the relaxation of stringent anti-Asian immigration policies that had been in place since the 1920s, when the Supreme Court had ruled that South Asians were to be excluded from naturalization, "Mrs. Sen's" evocatively narrates an encounter between a prepubescent boy, Eliot, and Mrs. Sen, the young immigrant wife of an Indian professor at a small liberal arts college in New England. Over a series of afternoons, Eliot passes time with Mrs. Sen, his babysitter in the latter's home. Routed through Eliot's perception, the story reveals how the two characters develop a subtle yet powerfully affective bond that crosses lines of age, race, gender, and class. Initially, Eliot passes his time within the confines of the Sen apartment, which overflows with the sights and smells of Mrs. Sen's home in Calcutta, and Mrs. Sen is slow to allow him complete access to that world. She is a lonely immigrant who yearns for a connection with her home and family; she spends her days imagining what she might best prepare for the evening meal, typically comprised of Bengali cuisine. At the same time, she recognizes that her makeshift universe of the Indian kitchen can be safely observed by Eliot, a child, but that it must be carefully hidden from the sight of his mother. Eliot marvels at Mrs. Sen's culinary prowess, but before Eliot's mother comes to fetch him, all signs of Mrs. Sen's otherness, notably the smell of difference and foreignness, are carefully covered up. Floors are scrubbed, vegetable peels are removed, and the odor of food is masked. She does her utmost to lessen the appearance of strangeness by systematically removing anything that might reinforce her status as an other.

When Mrs. Sen ventures to the outside world, it is primarily to purchase food for the week's meals. On one occasion when she succumbs to the pressures of cultural nostalgia, she takes Eliot with her to buy fish, a staple of her culinary repertoire. As she puts it, "in Calcutta people ate fish first thing in the morning, last thing before bed, as a snack after school if they were lucky. They ate the tail, the eggs, even the head" (124). Because she cannot drive, she and Eliot take the bus. As they travel on the bus, Mrs. Sen is gently reproached for carrying fish, with its pungent odor:

The driver turned his head and glanced back at Mrs. Sen. "What's in the bag?"

Mrs. Sen looked up, startled.

"Speak English?" The bus began to move again, causing the driver to look at Mrs. Sen and Eliot in his enormous rearview mirror.

"Yes I can speak."

"Then what's in the bag?"

"A fish," Mrs. Sen replied.
"The smell seems to be bothering the other passengers. Kid, maybe you should open her window or something." (132–33)

When the bus driver startles Mrs. Sen with his offhanded question, he assumes that her quizzical look means that she cannot speak English. Instead of addressing Mrs. Sen, he speaks to Eliot, at once erasing Mrs. Sen's presence and reminding her of her status as a racialized outsider. Even though she understands the bus driver's words, she does not comprehend that she is expected to suppress the fishy odor of otherness, so latently offensive to the other passengers on the bus. The next time Mrs. Sen decides to obtain fish, she opts not to take the bus—presumably out of a desire not to be cast as the racialized outsider who does not understand the tacit rules of society; instead, she braves her fear of driving, and ventures to the store with Eliot in tow. The outcome, though not grave, brings a screeching halt to her affiliation with Eliot. Mrs. Sen loses control of the car, hitting a telephone pole. The tentative meeting of these different worlds is instantly demolished; Eliot is taken out of Mrs. Sen's care, and she returns to a world where she negotiates the pangs of loneliness and alienation that she feels as a woman with no real community located far away from her family.

Like Kothari, Lahiri evocatively stages the everyday as a scene of dramatic racial encounters. The mundane acts of preparing the evening meal and purchasing fish cause Mrs. Sen to reflect on her position as a racialized immigrant. Little in this story can be easily digested without thinking about racialized bodies out of place in monochromatic American suburbia. In Lahiri's culinary suburbanscape, Mrs. Sen's Bengali foodways are not rendered exotic and colorful; indeed, Mrs. Sen must take pains to hide all visible signs of difference lest she is deemed an unfit caregiver. Culinary nostalgia becomes a conduit to convey to the experiences of one who has seemingly banal, everyday concerns. There is nothing exotic in this tale about a woman who feed her nostalgia for India by purchasing malodorous fish. Further, "Mrs. Sen's" does not "travel" easily; it gives shape to Mrs. Sen's particular experiences as an Indian immigrant woman, but even more to her position as a Bengali American. As sociologist Krishnendu Ray notes, "dinner is often one of the few spheres left in an American world where a Bengali can reproduce her Bengalihood actually and materially" ("Meals" 118). Ray argues that the drive toward commodification and the demands of Bengali patriarchy code meals as either "American" or "Bengali," "traditional" dinners or "American" breakfast. Mrs. Sen's almost obsessive need to prepare a fully Bengali dinner must be read in light of her position as an immigrant woman wedded into a system of Bengali heterosexual patriarchy. Eliot, for instance, takes note of the care with which she prepares each meal, "eventually a collection of broths simmered over periwinkle flames on the stove. It was never a special occasion, nor was she ever expecting company. It was merely dinner for herself and Mr. Sen" (117).

"Mrs. Sen's" is not a universalist feel-good story that emphasizes the underlying humanity of the character. Instead, it subtly calls attention to how Mrs. Sen's dislocation is further complicated by the implicit pressure to assimilate. Mrs. Sen, a new immigrant, is unable to find a place for herself in her new home and goes to pains to observe the tacit codes of mainstream society but fails because she calls attention to herself and all of the ways in which she and her foodways do not belong in this new America. Thus, while legislation may have opened its doors to new immigrants after 1965, the culinary prejudices against those immigrants who are now "welcomed" into America remain in place. For an immigrant character like Mrs. Sen, a simulacrum for many South Asian immigrant women of the 1960s, a failure to observe the tacit rules of life in America can have grave consequences. By the close of the narrative, the tentative community established between two unlikely allies comes to a grinding halt as the two embark on separate, but parallel lives, with no hopes that their paths might ever intersect again. Mrs. Sen's singular attempt to brave life on the outside has devastating effects, and she is once again relegated to make do with life within the confines of her small apartment. Her simple desire to reproduce a little piece of her Bengali identity in the sleepy New England town is indefinitely suspended such that her own "arrival" in the United States is far less momentous, far less triumphant, and largely unremarkable.

"Mrs. Sen's" remarkableness might be best understood through its understatedness. Food in this particular immigrant narrative does not represent a struggle between "East" and "West" in the terms familiar to the youth literature genre. In its deft maneuvering through Mrs. Sen's culinary world, the narrative does not produce a "foodie" narrative complete with recipes to lessen the impact of otherness. Rather, food is the backdrop, but a vital one, to address the very processes of abjection immigrants experience while attempting to cleave a cultural space within Americanness. Lahiri's spectacular achievement in a story like "Mrs. Sen's" is in refusing to adhere to food pornography. Neither food pornographer nor culinary guide, Lahiri depicts food to anchor the vexing nature of Mrs. Sen's life as a newly arrived immigrant in a largely homogeneous United States of the 1960s.

But following her meteoric rise to fame after securing the Pulitzer Prize, Lahiri's writing has lessened the racially affective impact of stories like "Mrs. Sen's." Why, one might ask? Her writing has become commodified perhaps because it presents a palatable version of multiculturalism, one that reaffirms the view that Indian Americans enter the wider terrain of American culture easily, even though stories like "Mrs. Sen's" suggest the opposite. Lahiri's immediate post-Pulitzer writing venture was a short piece in 2000 titled "Indian Cookout" that appeared within the pages of *Food and Wine*, a leading magazine in the food and beverage industry. In this short piece, Lahiri chronicles her family's relationship to food, paying close attention to how the changing nature of immigration patterns has altered her family's culinary practices. The essay begins with a thick description of how the Lahiri family negotiated the absence of Indian foodstuffs within the marketplace of 1970s America. Lahiri describes her parents as "pirates" running the equivalent of an ancient spice trade, transporting spices from India back to her home in Rhode Island in a vintage portmanteau dubbed the "Food Suitcase." Reminiscent of the *Mistress of Spices*, the foods alluded to in "Indian Takeout" are exotic spices and unusually colored powders. Excised from this narrative are the smelly fish of her earlier parable about immigrants and food. The immigrant experience in "Indian Takeout" commemorates nostalgic encounters with their foodways. The story thus engenders a form of ersatz nostalgia, enabling readers without particular lived experiences or connection to particular collective historical memories to feel a sense of loss for the ways of life that have been forgotten as Indians become more at home on alien soil.

Where the stories in *Interpreter of Maladies* unearth the racializing tendencies of food, the failure of consumption, and the ways in which immigrants like Mrs. Sen fall outside of our imaginations, "Indian Takeout" creates a more palatable narrative of multicultural inclusion. In this new multicultural America, Indian American immigrants travel easily, and affirm nostalgia for their homelands through their consumptive practices. Lahiri dishes up a narrative for a public that is hungry for visions of culinary alterity that can be considered tasty, colorful, and "exotic." Moreover, Indian Americans can be seen as the consummate minorities at ease and at home in the United States who have efficaciously carved a niche for themselves; all that they seek to consume is comfortably within reach in suburbia. The hallmark of arrival is chronicled by the placement of the last vestige of olfactory otherness; the food suitcase, Lahiri notes, "sits in our basement, neglected, smelling of cumin" ("Indian Takeout" 304). The lingering smell of cumin coats this story with an enticing veneer, and all that is smelly, distasteful, foreign, violent, or abnormal is carefully kept out of the story to produce a version of Indian American modernity modulated by a palatable multiculturalism that avoids intimating that Indian Americans are also racialized by the foods that they choose to consume.

With "Indian Takeout," Lahiri forays into the genre of culinary tourism, assuming the posture of culinary tour guide. Now that she has secured a base of fans and readers, curiosity abounds about her own life. What better way to introduce her Indianness to her hordes of readers than to speak of culinary traditions within her family? The juxtaposition of these two styles of writing—the short story about immigrant life for South Asian Americans and the short culinary memoir—hint at a radical instability within the ways Indian immigrant life is rendered legible to the mainstream. More than with any other genre, as Frank Chin was quick to note, Asian Americans are frequently heard and read when their writings focus on the culinary. Yet in castigating or looking askance at the genre of culinary tourism, one radically diminishes the possibilities for considering public, and often gendered, negotiations with diasporic citizenship. Culinary tourism, after all, is a cultural form that has become tooled in vastly different ways, thus producing seemingly dissonant narratives about the ethno-racial identity about the erstwhile foodie. In the final section of this chapter, I juxtapose two radically different works that might be loosely defined as works of culinary tourism. Crafted with Indian Americans at the forefront, these narratives deliberately and strategically produce a kind of obsession with food mediated by the experience of race and racialized difference, therein carving a niche for Indian Americans within the space of culinary tourism.

Being American, Feeling Indian

Overt connections between the second generation of ethnicized Americans and food can be found on the now defunct show on the Food Network titled *My Country, My Kitchen*. The half-hour show takes a culinary tour of the world in each episode. Typically, the hosts own restaurants or have authored cookbooks, and the show also functions to earn publicity for their culinary ventures. On each show, the hosts—usually first- or second-generation ethnic Americans—journey on camera to their immigrant homeland to sample the diversity of that cuisine. During the show's first season, episodes devoted to the cuisines of China, Japan, India, Vietnam, Morocco, France, Italy, and Greece were hosted by a person deemed to have insider/native informant status. Subsequent shows focused on subregions within the United States such as Hawaii, the American South, and New York. Such attention to regionalism is not restricted to the episodes on the United States; the episode on India hosted by Maya Kaimal, a South Asian American cookbook author, focuses on the regional cuisine of the southern Indian state of Kerala. The show is billed as the representative episode on "India," whereas the various U.S.-centered shows actively acknowledge that the cuisine of the United States is not monolithic but subject to regional variation. Such attention to regional variety at the domestic level is at odds with the vision of other countries as homogeneous culinary zones. The "here," the United States, is a pluralistic melting pot; the "there," the immigrant homeland, is a homogeneous monolith. In the case of India, a nation-state that contends with the hegemony of the Hindi language, *My Country*'s gesture of locating the cooking show in Kerala, an unyieldingly non-Hindi space, punctures the narrative of a seamless India for the American audience.

As a biracial Asian American subject suspended between Asian and white, or native and non-native, the host of the episode on India, Maya Kaimal, apparently embodies the melting pot ideal of ethnicity and the fusion or agglomeration of difference. Despite being racially "fused," her cuisine is unequivocally "Indian," and all traces of her New England whiteness are strategically submerged. Kaimal may be Indian American, but her cuisine originates from Kerala. As a second-generation Indian American, she appears to be well-positioned to introduce Indian cuisine. As the episode begins, Kaimal explains: "I'm taking you up the spice coast of India. This is what Columbus was looking for when he stumbled upon the New World. It's where my father was raised and where I've been visiting since I was a child. This is *my* Kerala" (emphasis added). The first leg of her journey, titled "My Story," begins with a shot of Kaimal in the distance, walking against the direction of pedestrian traffic along a busy street in Kerala. As she approaches the camera, she explains, "I grew up in Boston, Massachusetts, and Boulder, Colorado." Her words "my father is from South India and my mother is actually from New England" can be heard in the background while black-and-white photographs of her parents are superimposed on the left portion of the screen. As Kaimal walks toward the camera, she comes into clearer focus. She ends, "I grew

up feeling very much American, but I had a really strong connection
to my Indian side." After this early reference, Kaimal's mother drops
out of the narrative. Instead, Kaimal's affective journey to her "homeland" reaches back to her father's past; as she delves into that past, the
browning of Maya Kaimal goes into full effect. Despite being the Indian
American daughter of an Indian immigrant and a New Englander, her
father's racial identity is routed through his national identity—he is irreducibly "Indian," and her white Indian mother is apparently nonethnic,
a "native" New Englander, white, and therefore American. While her
mother's whiteness grants Kaimal the legitimacy to claim Americanness, her connection to her father grants her greater authenticity as an
Indian subject. Discussing the imbalance that affects biracial children,
sociologist Yen Le Espiritu explains that often, "multiracial Asians are
deemed more 'Asian' when their father, rather than mother is Asian"
(29). In its efforts to cast Kaimal as a subject who properly meets popular
requirements for being Indian, the episode mines this racial asymmetry
that grants greater authenticity to children with Asian fathers.

The half-hour show hosted by Maya Kaimal is presented as an emotionally charged journey back to the homeland. The show begins with
Kaimal wearing a *salwar-kameez*, traditional Indian clothing; she is exu-
berant and upbeat, and promises to give viewers a tour of "my Kerala,"
adding, "I am addicted to this place." Infused with a vibrant air of intoxi-
cation, Kerala consolidates Kaimal's identity as an Indian. Within the
space of a half hour, Kaimal takes viewers through the myriad culinary
scapes of Kerala. She eats dosas (sourdough crepes) on the street, samples
food on the houseboats of Kerala, "cruising through the canals of Kerala
like my ancestors did," and finally travels to her aunt Kamala Nair's
kitchen to prepare food for Onam, a Hindu harvest festival. As Kaimal
travels through the Kerala countryside to her aunt's house, the voice-
over announces, "over the rivers and through the palm trees, to aunty's
house I went." A rewriting of the poetic ode to Thanksgiving penned by
the abolitionist and women's rights activist Lydia Maria Childs, Kaimal's
words bear the affective quality of a child well versed in the lore of American schoolchildren but adept enough to transform her knowledge to suit
her movement across the Kerala landscape. The harvest festival Onam
stands in for Thanksgiving, a form of cultural translation that subtly fo-
ments links between Kaimal's India and America. Adhering to a logic of
multiculturalist egalitarianism, this gesture of replacing Thanksgiving
with Onam simultaneously erases the violence of Thanksgiving and the
historical differences between the two in order to render Onam legible

within a U.S. domestic frame while also producing a logic of sameness that would construct the South Asian American subject as being safely different.

Thanksgiving is a particularly appropriate site from which to imagine a form of safe multiculturalism. One only need consider Gurinder Chadha's paean to Thanksgiving, *What's Cooking?* to detect how the symbolism of Thanksgiving can accommodate ethnic difference without necessarily transforming the racial logic of alterity. Set in a middle-class Los Angeles neighborhood, *What's Cooking?* follows the lives of four families of different ethnic backgrounds as they prepare to celebrate Thanksgiving. Mindful of Thanksgiving's whiteness, the film begins with a shot of an advertisement that appears on the sides of a Los Angeles bus. The advertisement depicting a white middle-class family carving turkey offers stark contrast to the passengers riding the bus—low-income people of color. Cutting from this scene where Thanksgiving is portrayed as incongruous with multiracial Los Angeles, the film transports us into the worlds of the four families that are the focus of this film, the Nguyens, Avilas, Williamses, and Seeligs. From here the film remains determined to show how Thanksgiving can become a symbol of ethnic inclusion for the Vietnamese, Latino, Black, and Jewish American families. As Chadha tellingly notes: "I wanted to make a film that could celebrate the diversity of Americans today. The American films I'd seen that actually dealt with race were almost always about problems and conflicts. We wanted to move away from that and show how the differences between cultures can actually underscore similarities" (qtd. in Rich). Just as Thanksgiving becomes a signifier of a positive and inclusive multiculturalism in Chadha's film, Onam becomes associated with Thanksgiving, representing a positive multiculturalism between Indian Americans and Indians.[3]

The final and longest segment of the episode of *My Country, My Kitchen* on India is devoted to establishing the filial bonds that tie Kaimal to her Indian aunt. When she arrives, Kaimal disembarks her auto rickshaw and is welcomed by three women. The camera zooms in on Kaimal and her aunt Kamala as the two women embrace. The remainder of the show is spent in Aunty Kamala's kitchen. In the kitchen, Kaimal suggests the two women who speak different languages are able to bridge the distance between India and Indian America, and can "understand each other perfectly." It is not insignificant that Kaimal's connection to India is routed through the figure of "Aunty Kamala." The matriarchal figure here stands in for her own mother while also simulating the figure of Mother India. Aunty Kamala passes on culinary wisdom and wit to Maya in the mythologized tradition of mothers and daughters—an all-too-familiar trope within Asian American literature. Marianne Hirsch suggests that an examination of the mother-daughter relationship plunges one into "a network of complexities, to attempt to untangle the strands of a double self" (73). For Maya to emerge as an authentic and recognizable Asian American subject, her narrative is strategically reframed to position her within the mother-daughter trope so prevalent in Asian American literature. And yet for this affective maternal connection between aunt and niece to emerge, Maya's biological mother must carefully be excised from this picture of monochromatic, indeed, monoracial harmony. Actual affective ties between mother and daughter notwithstanding, the narrative demands that Maya's mother be removed from this familial narrative to pave the way for Maya to connect to her homeland—both her "authentic" fatherland and her chosen motherland—by interweaving the strands of her history with those of Aunty Kamala.

Unlike *Padma's Passport*, a cooking show that foregrounds the host's ability to travel internationally, *My Country, My Kitchen* places emphasis on feeling allegiance to a singular national space. And for Kaimal, an Indian American whose identity refuses a kind of singularity, that space cannot be India. Like the show, Kaimal's cookbook foregrounds her Indianness, downplaying her status as a biracial Asian American woman. Following the conventions of cookbook authors like Madhur Jaffrey, *Savoring the Spice Coast* intersperses recipes with personal narrative. The cookbook begins with a fragmented narrative about Kaimal's family that delves into only her father's history. In the opening pages of the book, where one might expect a childhood picture of Maya Kaimal, is a family photograph depicting two children and two adults posed around a formal couch. The mother, wearing a sari, is seated on the couch holding a baby in her lap, and her husband is perched on the edge of the couch, with a boy toddler sitting in front of him. But the sepia-toned photograph, circa 1933, is not of Maya Kaimal's immediate family but of her father's family. The baby is his sister Kamala, and the adults are his parents, Maya's Indian grandparents. Here the family stands in for the nation—a distinct, coherent unit that is unmistakably "Indian"—monoracial, unified, and heterosexual. Kaimal's father's family also stands in for her own family. With its biracial, heterogeneous character, a photograph of Kaimal's immediate family would be incommensurable with an image of an essentialized, and pure (unfused) India that is monoracial. In order to produce a palpable narrative about South Asianness as an enduring and timeless essence, Kaimal's whiteness is strategically de-emphasized in favor of establishing Maya as a properly brown subject. The photograph is used to document authentic cultural and racial lives and to legitimize the present through the manipulation of an apparently monolithic narrative. Readers will perhaps accept the veracity of the sepia-toned photograph. It is a snippet of history, taken from the leaves of a private, faded family album that, when brought into public purview, authenticates Kaimal's Indianness. But in an age of digital reproduction, the photograph is no longer a certificate of presence. Unlike the purported veracity of earlier photographic styles including the sepia-toned family portrait or the daguerreotype, photographic scenes of contemporary life require an additional dimension to render them authentic. Although highly stylized photographs typical of contemporary cookbooks predominate, one full-page illustration approximately halfway through the book is constructed as a montage of photographs that lends authenticity to Maya Kaimal's culinary ventures. Proofs with the number indexes still in place are haphazardly arranged. A crudely drawn line separates the page into two sections. Handwritten captions, "Beet Thoren" "Fish Curry," "Pullao w/ onions," "Dosa," "Adda prep," "Roll #32," accompany certain images, affirming the presence of a human actor behind these photographs. Kaimal's narrative, as it emerges in the cookbook and the television show, leaves little space to imagine a more complex personal history, one that braids together the multiple and contradictory strands of her existence. Cuisine emerges in bifurcated terms—it is either Indian or American. And it becomes impossible to imagine where these worlds might meet. As the episode of *My Country, My Kitchen* ends, Kaimal says:

> uncovering recipes from the markets, the locals, and my aunty is like a history lesson of my culture and my family. I grew up loving food, but it's the trips to India that influenced me to become a food writer. When I return to New York, my suitcase is filled with recipes and stories for new chapters. I feel as though I have passports to two vastly different cultures and I'm very lucky. But, sadly, each trip is bittersweet because at some point I have to say good-bye (*voice begins to break*). My aunty always says she counts the days until I come, and then when I come, she counts the days until I go. But I always come back . . . yeah . . . I always come back . . .

A rapid succession of images from the half-hour show—scenes of a street vendor preparing dosas, the cook on the houseboat preparing shellfish, women milling in a crowd, Kaimal eating roasted peanuts at a market,

Kaimal reclining in her houseboat, Aunty Kamala walking with Maya, picturesque sunsets—cut to a picture of a teary-eyed Kaimal, visibly saddened at having to leave her Indian home. As she reaches the end of her narrative, her voice begins to falter. The scene segues into a shot of niece and aunt walking hand in hand away from the camera before the final shot cuts to a picturesque sunset as the end credits begin to roll on the screen. Feeling beyond the nation in Kaimal's case only extends to feeling a connection with one part of her heritage. New York is her "here," and Kerala is her "there." The only thing connecting Kerala and New York is Maya Kaimal. She is both positioned as, and embraces her role as a broker of Indianness. She may literally and racially embody fusion, but that narrative is carefully submerged, both in her cookbook and on the television show, in order to grant Maya Kaimal the legitimacy to speak authoritatively about Indian cuisine and to claim a "home" in India. Such formulations—*because Maya Kaimal is biracial, her Indianness must be amplified*—cast national identity into parochial terms. As such, it rehearses the notion that Indian Americanness is derivative, inauthentic, and diluted if it is subject to other forms of fusions.

My Country, My Kitchen is myopically focused on the articulation of one cuisine for one nation. The show emphasizes the singular; plural cultural or culinary contacts are implicitly disallowed. As Maya Kaimal establishes herself as an American who feels connected to India via its food, the show's narrative stages her movement as one in which the borders of the nation do not collapse into one another. If feeling Indian requires a communion with its food, that communion also takes place on Indian soil. Moreover, that connection to India can only be renewed in India; nowhere does she intimate that the tastes of India will be brought into the United States save in the pages of recipe books and stories.

Here then, the second-generation subject's quest for a place to belong is couched in no uncertain terms as being about food and culinary matters. In order to become a legitimate American subject, Kaimal must first reveal her comfort with being considered a racialized subject and only then find home in Indian food. There is little in Kaimal's quest for food that is tainted by the issues that vex Kothari's narrator. Her clear articulation of "feeling American" but being connected to her Indian side renders a connection to India palatable, unremarkable, and ordinary. Thanksgiving and Onam can be seamlessly interchanged with a modification of a few lines of Lydia Marie Child's poem and a few Keralan dishes to replace the American meal. Lest the effects of a diasporic affiliation seep in to muddy the whiteness of America producing a kind of excess of Indianness, difference in this show is carefully managed to show that alterity exists safely elsewhere. For Kaimal, a racialized and ethnicized subject, that affirmation of self takes place through an easy communion with "Indian" food. Such a rendering of ethnicity becomes an iterative gesture to affirm how and why the Indian American subject becomes a cultural broker who allows Americanness to be protected from the influences of diasporic effect and connections to an "elsewhere." At the very least, the terms under which diasporic ties to an elsewhere—in Kaimal's case, India—need to be very carefully policed. Kaimal can claim Americanness, but she is not cooking American food or confusing the culinary borders between India and America. In a stunning application of the importance of affect, Maya Kaimal can use the language of emotion and affiliation to express her Americanness. Her expression of feeling and affiliation to Americannness is what makes her tie to a diasporic identity manageable and less dangerous. In this way, she is not an unruly second-generation subject who confuses the lines of diasporic influence; rather, she protects Americannness from the brown diaspora. Diaspora, in the context of Kaimal's narrative, is central because when amorphously imagined and diffuse in structure, it messes and confuses racial, national, and cultural borders. To protect the nation from its own otherness, there must always be a way to affirm American exceptionalism while recognizing the presence of mixed and racialized bodies. To this end, many second-generation texts seem to pledge culinary allegiance to the United States because that gesture of avowal implicitly repudiates a connection with an elsewhere. And yet, paradoxically, the only safe way to articulate otherness might be through a culinary register, but only if eating otherwise happens over there, and not here. In the same breath, Kaimal intimates that second-generation subjects belong in America, while acknowledging that America is different from its diasporic populations. Diasporic affect here becomes a way to manage ties to other spaces, both spatially and temporally.

In the context of a history where U.S. courts legislated to keep a certain type of subject off American soil, and in a climate where the Asian laborer must be kept out of America to protect the nation from the purportedly untoward gestures of the Asiatic race, Kaimal's own narrative about being American enacts a kind of exclusion through omission. To her white viewers, she is not American but Indian. To her Indian American viewers, she is the type of American one might aspire to become: comfortable in Indian spaces, connected to India, but also affectively very much American. Indeed, in this shift from thinking about citizenship as state-legitimated to conceiving of it as culturally legitimated, Kaimal can continue to be American only as and when she announces the cleaving, "I feel American but I'm connected to India." The episode thus works against the effects of racial complexities and miscegenation that might produce subjects who confuse and muddy the borders of the national body and the national palate. Where her body might confuse the borders of the U.S. nation-state, her claims on cuisine remain culturally recognizable as Indian. Through the particular tooling of the genre of culinary tourism, Kaimal is able to affect a kind of inclusion as an American citizen without having to disavow Indian tastes or claim American food in any way.

Moving forward, it becomes vital to consider whether the opposite holds true—that is, what might a narrative about second-generation Indian Americanness look like when the claim to Americanness is made via the pursuit of an all-American culinary icon? How indeed might Indian American cultural citizenship allow for the claiming of Americanness that does not necessarily other the palate of America within the borders of the nation-state? To examine this, I consider how the film *Harold and Kumar Go to White Castle* puts the genre of culinary tourism into crisis through the claim its Asian American protagonists make on that most American of culinary icons, the hamburger.

Feeding an Asian American Yen

Hamburgers are never defined as exotic in the United States.—LISA HELDKE, "EXOTIC APPETITES"

In the world of food writing, culinary tourism—the act of writing about one's deliberate and engaged efforts to travel to other places to document the culinary particularities of non-normative subjects—has earned a particular cachet. But even more popular than brown bodies returning to present the culinary traditions of their homelands are shows in which white bodies travel to the far-flung reaches of the world to present their take on culinary exotica. While shows like *My Country, My Kitchen* endured for one or two seasons, shows about culinary adventuring enjoy far greater staying power on the Food Network. And why not, some might argue? After all, Anthony Bourdain's culinary adventures frequently take him to remote spaces in the barely civilized world where he must traverse difficult terrain to find the ultimate culinary treasure, "braving" particular and peculiar culinary delicacies that are, more often than not, the mainstay of people of color, both in the United States and abroad. In *A Cook's Tour*, Bourdain tellingly notes: "I wanted adventures, I wanted to go up the Nung River to the heart of darkness in Cambodia. I wanted to ride out into a desert on camelback . . . I wanted kicks—the kind of melodramatic thrills and chills I'd yearned for since childhood, the kind of adventure I'd found as a little boy in the pages of my *Tintin* comic books. I wanted to see the world—and I wanted the world to be just like the movies. Unreasonable? Over-romantic? Uninformed? Foolhardy? Yes! But I didn't care" (5). Inserting himself into the plot of an adventure novel, Bourdain flagrantly displays how he wants the non-Western world to function as the backdrop to his adventuring. On the televised counterpart to his memoirs, Bourdain can be seen savoring all manner of culinary fare as he travels to his culinary heart of darkness, traversing the deserts of Rajasthan, the crowded metropolises of Kolkata and Mumbai in search of hidden Indian treasures. Rarely is Bourdain or his audience disappointed. Whether he is treated to a meal cooked for him by a maharaja or an exquisite martini prepared at the bar of a lake palace converted to a hotel, or simply sampling culinary oddities like sheep's brain or gorging on all manner of street food, his food choices are always about the superlative—the most pristine, the most extreme, the most outrageous. Rarely is his food adventuring about the everyday. More pervasive instead is the sense that either his person or his GI tract is routinely put in danger through his travels and travails across "brown" and "black" spaces of the non-Western world. Against this type of food adventuring, one rarely, if ever, encounters the other type of travel: the person of color traversing North America to eat what Vietnamese American author Bich Nguyen refers to in *Stealing Buddha's Dinner*, her culinary memoirs of growing up in Grand Rapids, Michigan, as "White American Food" (53).

So what does it mean that one of the most intriguing films to present a South Asian American character engages food in a manner that does not stage the encounter with food to be one that is deeply vexing, connected to issues about one's identity as a racialized subject in America? Reading culinary tourism against itself, I want to focus the remainder of this chapter on an unlikely subject: the film *Harold and Kumar Go to White Castle* (hereafter *Harold and Kumar*). Why? I am interested in exploring how to use this definition of culinary tourism to understand how the film pushes forward a critique of extreme cuisine and gastronomic otherness brought to life in the writings of Calvin Trillin and Anthony

Bourdain. Recognizing the very different contexts in which culinarily touristic writings and films arise, my analysis unpacks the driving force of this film—the quest to find the elusive White Castle burger. *Harold and Kumar* is a film guided by the racialized subject's impulse to "eat back." The deliberate recasting and reframing of which foods are deemed "exotic," un-American, and desirable can be read as a strategic attempt to understand and undermine the continuing link between Asian Americans and their foodways.

So what, one might ask, does a stoner film have to do with food? Beyond the rich interpretive possibilities of analyzing the scatological humor in *Harold and Kumar*, the surprise hit offers a rare opportunity to think about the place of food in films about Asian Americans even as the film is directed by a non–Asian American like Danny Leiner. My interest in this film stems mostly from a scene close to the end. I do not offer an exhaustive reading of the film per se, but instead use this one scene to push forward a critique of the genre of adventurous eating and to consider how it masterfully allows racialized subjects to lay claim to an icon of American fare without rendering it "other."

The central drama of the film begins in the pair's living room with the two watching television. After what has been a trying day for the somewhat uptight Korean American character, Harold (John Cho), and his roommate, the more free-spirited South Asian American, Kumar (Kal Penn), the two twenty-somethings are sprawled on a couch with little to do on a Friday evening. Upon seeing a commercial for White Castle, they are reminded of their fondness for the establishment and its signature sliders and impulsively decide to drive to New Brunswick, New Jersey, where they believe there is a White Castle restaurant. Once in New Brunswick, they learn that it has been converted to a Burger Shack. As they pull into the drive-through, the Burger Shack employee tells them that the burgers there just "don't cut it" compared to those from White Castle. With the Burger Shack employee's help, Harold and Kumar learn that the nearest White Castle is located in Cherry Hill, a forty-five-minute drive away. The trip takes far longer than forty-five minutes, and along the way the pair make numerous unanticipated stops, several of which involve run-ins with local authorities and encounters with the local New Jersey "white trash."[4] As Harold and Kumar approach their destination, they encounter a final obstacle. They can see the establishment in the distance located at the foot of the hill below them. In hot pursuit of them is a police officer. With White Castle in plain sight, their only option for evading capture is to take hold of a hang glider and descend the hill. At the moment when the decision is about to be made, Kumar finds himself having to quash Harold's doubts. Addressing Harold's trepidation, Kumar waxes:

> So you think this is just about the burgers, huh? Let me tell you, it's about far more than that. Our parents came to this country, escaping persecution, poverty, and hunger. Hunger, Harold. They were very, very hungry. They wanted to live in a land that treated them as equals, a land filled with hamburger stands. And not just one type of hamburger, okay? Hundreds of types with different sizes, toppings, and condiments. That land was America. America, Harold! America! Now, this is about achieving what our parents set out for. This is about the pursuit of happiness. This night . . . is about the American dream.

The humor in this sequence resonates because Kumar's words parody the notion that America is the land of plenty: he takes a familiar adage about immigration and couples it to an idea of American consumerist excess, one in which happiness becomes yoked to having one's choice of burgers and condiments. The scene familiarly stages the narrative that exhorts the second generation to do right by the first generation and to take advantages of the opportunity that generation afforded them. Through this parodic reiteration of these cliché values that characterize Asian American families, the scene's humor acquires legibility. Kumar's proposition seems absurd precisely because he frames the need to complete their journey to White Castle through a hyperbolic narrative of filial and national responsibility. Identifying them as sons of immigrants, Kumar implores Harold to respect their parents and to pursue the American Dream embodied here in the image of a White Castle slider. A crucial element marking this particular quest to down a series of White Castle's signature sliders as humorous is that the restaurant acquires the status of an out-of-the-way hidden treasure rather than a ubiquitous fast food chain. With the two protagonists engaged in this quest to feed a rather idiosyncratic "yen," to paraphrase the title of Calvin Trillin's best-selling narrative about food adventuring, the humor of the film derives from the fact that White Castle hamburgers are not considered worthy of this kind of avid pursuit.

Harold and Kumar's unrelenting pursuit of the all-American hamburger thus mimics the type of culinary adventuring one encounters in masculinized culinary travel writings (and their televisual offshoots) such as those of Anthony Bourdain and Calvin Trillin. Much of Trillin's best-selling *Feeding a Yen* illustrates how its author will feed his need for gastronomic delights and "blaze trails combing gleefully through neighborhoods for hidden culinary treasures." In the short essay "New Grub Streets," Trillin praises the rich culinary treasures located within the varied ethnic enclaves of New York City. In the essay, Trillin waxes poetic about a sandwich made of leafy greens that can only be purchased at a tiny establishment in New York's Chinatown at the corner of East Broadway and Forsyth before he launches into an explanation about the importance of the Immigrant Act of 1965. For Trillin, the 1965 act is remarkable because it opened American shores to more immigration: "prior to the Immigration Act of 1965 . . . this country's immigration [was] based on a system of national quotas reflect[ing] not simply bigotry but the sort of bigotry that seemed to equate desirable stock with bland- ness in cooking . . . serious eaters [like myself] think of the Immigration Act of 1965 as their very own Emancipation Proclamation" (71). Trillin's assertion that the removal of racist laws of exclusion allow adventur- ous eaters like Trillin to become "emancipated" from bland food thus suggests that an inclusive multiculturalism is best when it makes white America happy.

But why does Leiner's film hone in on the White Castle burger in par- ticular? Why is the McDonald's burger—a more ubiquitous symbol of American corporate success in the wake of globalization—not the object of desire? The answer lies in the history of White Castle in the 1920s. Da- vid Gerard Hogan explains that before the establishment of White Cas- tle, hamburgers were not connected to American identity. During the 1920s, when White Castle rose to prominence as the first fast-food chain (well ahead of McDonald's, which only opened in the 1950s), hamburgers were introduced as a standardizable fast-food item because of the ways in which immigrant entrepreneurs had altered the nature of the restau- rant industry. In the 1920s, concerns about the safety of eating ground meat of an edible grade, as well as the popular understanding of burg- ers as food for the poor, made hamburgers an unpopular choice among mainstream middle-class American eaters. So who were the consumers and producers of what we now think of as the quintessential American food? Hogan explains that immigrant vendors would sell "quick foods" to workers in industrial cities. This mobile form of food entrepreneur- ship paved the way for investors to think about creating larger, but less mobile businesses that would still dish out quick foods to a larger Ameri- can public. Hogan concludes that it was within this environment, where fast foods were becoming more and more of an option (thanks in large part to the pioneering efforts of immigrants), that establishments such as White Castle were able to thrive and market themselves as quintessentially American. When White Castle opened its doors for business in March 1921, under the official name "The White Castle System of Eating Houses," it did so through the collaborative efforts of the Wichita, Kansas–based businessman Billy Ingram and Walt Anderson, a second-generation Swedish American grill cook based in Wichita. As Hogan's study provocatively suggests, White Castle had strong ties to American ethnic immigrant practices. This synoptic history gestures to the ways in which the White Castle burger is intertwined with a history of immigrant entrepreneurialism to underline what Hogan suggests: that it was immigrant labor that eventually (though not causally) paved the way for Walt Anderson, also the son of immigrants and White Castle's founder, to imagine and eventually profit from selling fast foods to the American public.

With this cognitive mapping of White Castle as a business entwined with a history of immigration, it is difficult to separate the fast-food establishment's roots within American ethnic history from the implicit ethnicity anchoring *Harold and Kumar*. In some ways, the film might rehearse a simple multiculturalism: the notion that these two guys are just like "us" because they like to get stoned and eat hamburgers. But through its focus on the hamburger. the film strategically critiques the type of writing that casts its penetrating gaze upon Asian American foodways and, by extension, Asian Americans. Quite unlike narratives like the ones Jhumpa Lahiri or Maya Kaimal produce, *Harold and Kumar* takes pleasure in showing the hamburger as the food most capable of feeding nostalgia for second-generation Indian Americans. At the same time, we cannot consider the film's framing of hamburgers without also considering how works like Trillin's *Feeding a Yen* almost unquestioningly position Asian Americans as cultural workers who dish up alternatively strange and delectable commodities for the white consumer.

Harold and Kumar thus unsettles a relationship which positions Asians as culinary tour guides who will render their foods legible to the mainstream gaze. The Immigration Act of 1965 that Trillin elegizes in "New Grub Streets" has resonance for characters such as Harold and Kumar precisely because they are part of that second generation of Asian Americans whose parents emigrated from India and Korea owing to the loopholes made possible by the 1965 legislative act. Reading the scene from *Harold and Kumar* against Trillin's words, one cannot help but notice the startling asymmetry between their respective positions. For Tril-

lin, the 1965 generation is to be celebrated for paving the way for America
to diversify its palate. Through the labor and efforts of the 1965 generation, a new era of restaurants opened up their doors, allowing Americans
to benefit from the new immigration from Asia. And yet Harold and
Kumar's quest for the elusively ubiquitous burger disrupts that narrative
in compelling ways. Kumar's parodic words insist that he and his family
are not cultural workers who will make Indianness or ethnicity available
for consumption. Instead, his quest is about unabashedly satiating his
desire to consume. Kumar evokes his family's history (a story in which
he emphasizes how his family came to the United States in order to consume) to appeal to Harold's sense of adventure and to view the quest for
White Castle burgers as a means of achieving the American Dream.

Harold and Kumar Go to White Castle thus opens up a space from
which to critique the mechanisms by which we interpret the food-ad-
venturing genre. For Trillin, hopping on the number 7 train to Roosevelt
Avenue to be served "authentic" Asian foods by "real" Asians is something to celebrate. Immigration is good because it brings Trillin palatal
pleasure and happiness. In this light, Kumar's desire to be served mass-
produced American food in Cherry Hill, New Jersey, ruptures narratives
like Trillin's, which position Asian Americans as objects dishing up foreignness for white Americans to consume. In casting Asians as consumers and producers of American taste mechanisms, the film provides a
counternarrative to the notion of Indian Americans as authentic brokers
of Indian food at the same time that it exhorts us to reexamine the easy
homologies one might construct between food and ethnic identity.

Eating and the "Children of 1965"

Food, typically configured as that which augurs and cements a feeling
of belonging, presents an array of startling complexities when cast into
the context of narratives which present food not as a source of identification and comfort, but as something that occasionally yields to a more
varied set of feelings, including those of abjection and alienation. In her
careful analyses of the affective life of citizenship and belonging, Ann
Cvetkovich astutely describes "structures of affect," naming those processes and structures through which affective life is incorporated into
notions of citizenship, outside of the institutional practices we custom-
arily associate with citizenry. Engaging Cvetkovich's point, this chapter
works to unravel the threads that together weave a tapestry of Indian
Americanness while also calibrating the underacknowledged role of the

affective life of food within the Indian American bildungsroman and narratives produced by second-generation Indian Americans. A reading sensitive to the vagaries of racialized life for children and young adults in the United States might well reorient our thinking about ritual performances of culinary citizenship such that we become more attuned to the links between race, food, generation, and citizenship. My interest in thinking through the public and affective life of food comes from a growing awareness of how the culinary functions as an important cultural site from which to articulate comfort (or discomfort) for what Min Hyoung Song has aptly dubbed the "children of 1965." In a provocative reading of Jhumpa Lahiri's *Namesake*, Song reframes the legacy of 1965 to theorize how this group of second-generation Asian Americans positions itself vis-à-vis Americanness. Song coins the term "children of 1965" to name the demographic group of immigrant professionals whose parents migrated to the United States after the passage of the 1965 Immigration and Nationality Act. In an era during which multiple groups clamor to be considered "aggrieved minorities," Song suggests the children of 1965 are "remarkable exactly because they fit so neatly—perhaps too neatly—into the ideal of mainstream American life" (354). They are remarkable because of their strong impulse to provide a counternarrative to the experience of a racially based form of aggrievement. Harold and Kumar might want to eat hamburgers as much as Lahiri's characters want to disavow Wonder bread and curry. Geeta Kothari's unnamed narrator may feel confused about her desire for tuna fish sandwiches as much as Pooja Makhijani's narrator jettisons *aloo tikkis* in favor of American fare. Without simply recycling the trope of "you are what you eat," these narratives set in motion a complex array of questions that seek to puncture the notion that fitting into the ideal of American life necessarily manifests as a full-blown acceptance of what mainstream America stands for.

When read collectively, these texts thematize the burdens of feeling torn between a hegemonic polarity that demands that allegiance must always be rendered to a singularly defined identity. To consider a slightly different example, Wenying Xu's analysis of John Okada's *No-No Boy* hints that the Japanese American author is unable to resolve his protagonist Ichiro's identity crisis because of "the absence in the 1950s of an alternative discourse to American assimilation or Japanese nationalism" (*Eating* 24). The no-no boys are disciplined by a particularly unfair form of racism set in motion by the internment camps, where the only choices open to young Japanese Americans of the 1940s and 1950s were to affirm their loyalty to America or repudiate Japaneseness. The no-no boys are caught in a no-man's land, making the body of the Japanese American a metaphoric battlefield and site of racialization. Choice becomes a not-choice dovetailing with that "most detrimental form of racism—self loathing" (*Eating* 26). As Xu points out, the scarring effects of this kind of racism manifests in the culinary preferences of the characters. In a racial climate where one's Japaneseness becomes reason enough for violent social and political censure, it is no surprise that eating American food such as lemon meringue pie, roasted chicken, and salad brings more happiness to the second generation than the consumption of Japanese fare such as tea, rice, and eggs fried with soy sauce. Enjoyment, Xu suggests, is vitally linked to the purported Americanness of the food on the table (*Eating* 26–27). Without enjoyment, the risks of claiming ethnic identity become that much more troubled.

Certainly Harold and Kumar lay claim to the most mainstream of American icons, the hamburger, but not before defamiliarizing it and positioning it as the ur-text for all immigrant palates. Enjoyment of hamburgers for Kumar is doubled through the gesture of claiming it, parodically, as the very food for which his parents left India. Kaimal may claim kinship with Indian food, but not before positioning herself as an American subject who affectively bonds with India through Indian food. Equally remarkable about this subgenre of Indian American culinary writing is that it refuses to succumb to the dynamics of a simple reversal and repudiation. The effectiveness of this group of writings by the children of 1965 comes from the kind of narrative thickness that results from clustering these texts together. Producing a kind of multiplicity in lieu of simple assimilationist dynamics in order to foment one's connection to America is but one way in which this subset of Asian American literature turns to the culinary to produce narratives that understand food to be about more than comfort or discomfort. To read each narrative as one that teleologically orients itself toward a politics and poetics of assimilatory inclusion is to ignore the asymmetry of the narratives and the contradictions within each set of culinary narratives. Despite the apparent desire to espouse American foods, each of these narratives contains a highly vexed meditation on what it means to be a child of 1965, pledging allegiance to the United States through one's choice of eatables.

The unevenness of the narratives I have examined in this chapter serves as a reminder of the dangers inherent in simply flattening out difference. The term "children of 1965" must not become reduced to a simple moniker that levels out the differences among the larger demographic cluster.

The value in Song's conceptual framework is that it insists on a praxis of unevenness; the term must be expansive enough to accommodate the multiplicity of narratives produced about the children of 1965 while retaining a core political sensibility about the ideological, literary, and political necessity of such a category of identification. The differing attitudes delineated in each narrative is suggestive of a far richer and more heterogeneous narrative tradition than heretofore conceived. As much as some of the children of 1965 stake a claim on distinctively American fare in order to claim a place at the table, there are narratives which do not aim to resolve the contradictions that are part of this corpus of writing. Food becomes part of the conversation about the literary legacy of the children of 1965. But without resorting to an easy duality or hybridization of identity, these texts collectively yield much interpretive ground to consider that inclusion alone is insufficient. The contradictions inherent within the notion of Indian American should not be resolved through a politics of eating that only valorizes hybrid duality; nor should hybridity be elevated as the exemplary corrective to racist narratives about Asian foodways. These narratives unsettle the notion that hybridity is the necessary modus operandi for the second generation. In carving a space to theorize the meanings of Indian American and the "children of 1965," we need to not simply consider where and how hybrid identities resolve themselves and come home to roost; we also need to follow the murky terrain and trails of where and how culinary icons of Americanness travel to produce narratives of multiplicity where Indian American taste mechanisms are concerned.

6 / Easy Exoticism: Culinary Performances of Indianness

If *Harold and Kumar Go to White Castle* was so successful because it parodied an overtly "white" genre, the culinary-adventuring travelogue, it bodes well for parody's ability as a literary-political mode to cleave a space to critique how interest in Indian American foodways is installed as a positive outcome of the purported mutualism engendered by multicultural liberalism. An overt parody of the runaway success TV show *Queer Eye for the Straight Guy*, the *Badmash* comic reproduced here targets the fashionability of Indian cuisine by focusing on how Ravi, an Indian immigrant, is made over by the Fab Five. After the clothing expert modeled on Carson Kressley drapes Ravi in an "India-inspired" outfit from Versace, the gourmand modeled on Ted Allen (the culinary aficionado on *Queer Eye*) informs the "straight guy" of the inadequacy of his mode of consuming tea. Ravi, the food expert suggests, is consuming a product that might be authentic, but is not trendy enough for his tastes. Allen updates Ravi's tastes by elevating his mundane tea into something more contemporary, a chai tea tai chi latte, explaining: "I am the culinary expert on this show—your tea tastes great but the presentation is WAY off, and the price is TOO low. Here is some vanilla chai tea tai chi latte in a champagne flute," signaling to the poverty of Ravi's understanding of Indianness, at the same time that it impresses how India is "in."

Like *Harold and Kumar Go to White Castle*, *Badmash*'s parody of *Queer Eye* reinserts South Asian Americans as participants within American cultural exchanges wrenching the power of the gaze cast upon

FIGURE 2   *Queer Eye for the FOB Guy.* Badmash Comics © 2004,
badmash.tv.

"exotic" Indian bodies onto whiteness itself. Whereas *Harold and Kumar* refocuses the notion of culinary gaze to render White Castle burgers as exotic fare, *Badmash* calls into question the culinary-cultural authority conferred upon "white" experts. The irony in this comic strip resides in the purported knowledge of the wardrobe and culinary experts and their strategy of professing to "know" India better than the Indians. Here, the Indian chai Ravi consumes is seen as hopelessly unhip and in need of the white gaze to elevate its status to "ethnic cool." And yet the parodic undertones of the comic strip mark an opposition to the point of view of the lifestyle experts who presume that these signs of Indianness need to be mediated by the consumerist capitalist complex in order to be rendered legible for Western tastes. In exposing the conditions of its repackaging, the comic strip recognizes the currency of Indo-Chic while also critiquing its racist and racialized structures. Television shows like *Queer Eye* which have participated in promoting how Indianness can be mediated by Western eyes for Western tastes disarticulate Indian signs and tastes from Indian bodies. In alluding to this history, *Badmash* reinserts the voices of those from whom culture is being appropriated less to suggest that the only response is to dismantle those efforts to appropriate signs of Indianness than to create a critical space from which to engage those histories that have so easily led to the appropriation and commodification of Indian signs for mainstream consumption.

Formed in 2003 by a group of second-generation Indian Americans, the weekly Web zines and the comic strip *Badmash* have emerged as an important venue to offer political and social critiques about issues affecting South Asian Americans. The comics cover an impressive range of topics from the commodification of Indianness to the racial profiling of South Asian Americans. As Nimesh Patel, one of the founders, notes: "*Badmash* works because it speaks to second-generation desis, and goes beyond the 'who am I?' identity struggles recycled every week in your typical Indian-American newspaper youth section. It will affectionately jeer at things we grew up with and were embarrassed by, but are now somehow cool, like the typical Indian family party" (qtd. in Shah). It is this desire to "affectionately jeer" that sets *Badmash* apart from other cultural responses to the commodification of Asianness.

"Queer Eye for the FOB Guy" bears witness to another history: that of transnational mobility and the movement of labor and capital between the United States and South Asia. Ravi is presented as a new immigrant who finds himself having the cultural artifices of his identity reinterpreted and packaged upon traversing the physical borders of the nation-state. Even though food has been traveling and traversing the world for years, the fetishizing of the present has led to an upsurge in considering fusion and its concomitant admixtures as a hallmark of a new cosmopolitanism. Fusion cuisine produces an affective language to think and feel beyond the nation. The proliferation of fusion cooking styles on cooking shows as well as in writings about South Asian American culinary citizenship at the turn of the twenty-first century remaps and reterritorializes the easily constructed homologies between nation and cuisine, often imagining an end to the viability of the "nation" as a culinary discursive possibility (Fairchild 3). Such logic would posit that national cuisines are no longer rigidly in place; where one would expect to find the clear demarcation between "Indian," "French," "Cambodian," and "Thai" cuisines, one finds hybridized cuisines that fuse one or more different culinary styles. In a period of rapid and rampant globalization and as corporate America finds it more efficient to outsource both capital and labor, the contours of geopolitical nations have been remapped and reconfigured. McDonaldization and Coca-Colonization have altered aspects of the domestic food and beverage market in South Asia; similarly, though not necessarily in equivalent ways, migrant labor from South Asia has altered the nature of culinary practices and cultures in North America. Emerging as part of larger immigrant urban working-class structures in North America, South Asian immigrant labor often participates directly—albeit invisibly—in the changing face of America's culinary market through the work of laborers in kitchens of restaurants and cafeterias. Thus, in an era when migration and movement between the United States and South Asia have altered the racial and ethnic composition of homogeneously conceived national spaces, it becomes increasingly suspect to unflinchingly adhere to narrowly defined visions of national cuisines. In problematizing the category of the "national" within the culinary realm, we might ask what happens to theorizations of national cuisines in a "postnational" world. I ended the previous chapter with a consideration of how Cvetkovich's notion of "structures of affect" might orient the ways in which the cultural legacy of the children of 1965 seems inescapably bound with culinary matters. Beyond a polarity of aggrievement or affirmation, claiming particular foods becomes tied up with the act of establishing one's Americanness. My thinking about the public and affective life of food grows out of an awareness of how cookbooks have become important cultural sites from which to articulate (dis)comfort concomitant with being a racialized minority during a political moment when South Asian brown bodies most associated in the

United States with particular ethnicized cuisines have been subject to scrutiny through more pervasive and invasive forms of surveillance.

For many other immigrant communities, food becomes a tool to articulate tensions that emerge through the chaffing of identity vectors of "home" and "diaspora." Such exoticizing narratives about food which render race palatable paradoxically emerge alongside narratives about South Asian Americans as undiscerning consumers of unpalatably fiery fare. As Floyd Cardoz, executive chef at Tabla, puts it, Indian food in the United States is understood through its extremities, "too oily, too hot and full of mushy mysterious ingredients" (xv). These perceived excesses also extend to the senses beyond taste; in matters of smell, Indian food is routinely derided for being malodorous. In the episode of the hit television series *Sex and the City* briefly discussed in the introduction, the character Carrie Bradshaw, played by Sarah Jessica Parker, turns her nose up at an apartment located above an Indian restaurant. Smells of masala and "curry" waft into the overpriced apartment, leading Carrie to question how she can justify paying so much money for an apartment she dubs a "shit hole." Bradshaw's aversion to the smell of Indian food suggests intolerance for smells that do not know their place: in Bradshaw's mindset, strong pungent odors do not belong in the same space as her Mahnolo Blahniks and Jimmy Choos. Ethnicity becomes spatialized through a sensory framework and is maligned for entering the private space of the white upper-middle-class home. Indian food thus becomes defined through its excess (Indian food is too spicy; Indian food smells too much like "curry") and needs to be disciplined to fit within North American tastes and expectations.

Echoing this scene is a moment from Lauren Weisberger's *The Devil Wears Prada*. As the protagonist, Andrea Sachs, prepares to move out of the apartment she shares with two Indian Americans, she notes, "I loved Indian food, but I did not love the way the curry smell had seeped onto everything I owned" (157). Like Bradshaw, Sachs can tolerate Indian bodies but not the smells their food produces. So egregious is the mingling of smells with her personal effects that she opts to move out of the apartment. Martin Manalansan's rich ethnography of smells in the immigrant home provides insight into the racialization of space enacted in this scene in *Sex and the City*. Through interviews with realtors in Queens, a borough of New York home to several immigrant communities, Manalansan comments on how potential homeowners react violently to "the heavy aroma of food linger[ing] in the hallways" ("Immigrant Lives" 47). A telling interview with one realtor reveals the strategies for managing this olfactory excess: "A Korean American realtor, Mr. Kim advised the homeowner to cook something American such as pot roast or, even better, apple pie . . . He argued that while many of the homebuyers are Asian themselves, they were upset when confronted with what they believed to be permanent olfactory "damage" (47).

For Asian Americans, the space of the home becomes associated with the excess associated with Asian American tastes. The threat of excess, though seemingly benign in the framework of an episode of *Sex and the City*, becomes violently exclusionary when we consider dimensions of racially and ethnically embodied excess that go beyond the culinary. In a post–9/11 United States, brown bodies are paradigmatic instances of excess: after all, the archetypical figure of the "terrorist" is nothing if not an excessive aberration against all that is palatably American. Thus, while food is often the most palatable index of alterity, the signs of excess that lend an ethnic flavor to culinary traditions—spiciness, pungent odors, sourness—need to be strategically managed in order for Indian food to be rendered palatable. In negotiating the epistemological and political meanings of palatability, it becomes vital to consider the psychic and material costs and benefits for racial and ethnic communities to create the conditions for palatability to emerge. A turn to palatability within a culinary frame, however, must not be equated with a tolerance for the brown bodies associated with those foods.

Fusion cuisine, an innovative approach to cooking, is arguably all about celebrating the ways in which foods intermingle to carve a space for new tastes and flavors; as such, it offers intriguing possibilities for thinking through the politics of palatability in a racial-ethnic-culinary frame. Cookbooks are particularly fertile sites for cultural inquiry for the ways in which they manage to broach issues of belonging without overtly calling attention to the anxieties of this process. Cookbooks specializing in fusion cuisine put Indian gastronomy on the map of American eaters by refocusing commonplace narratives about fiery Indian cuisines. But in positing Indian cuisine as nuanced, thoughtful, and complex, these cookbooks and their innovative approach to cuisine produce a culinary logic that implicitly espouses a politics of assimilation in which foreign excess must be translated into easily digestible and overtly domesticated signs of difference for it to be palatable to sensitive palates. When we consider that, historically, South Asians have been excluded from psychic, juridical, and social definitions of citizenship because they are seen to be too "alien," or "foreign" or "inassimilable," how can we interpret the vogue in fusion cuisine that celebrates the coming together of so called

"Asianness" and "Westernness"? Within the context of U.S. multicultural and racial discourses about Asian Americans as model minorities who are to be emulated because they have so readily assimilated, what does it mean to celebrate fusion cuisine while the U.S. state apparatuses and governing bodies such as the Bureau of Citizenship and Immigration Services (BCIS) actively foment a culture of suspicion that renders the brown bodies producing the food so suspect? My object of study here is a novel by the Denmark-based Indian author Amulya Malladi titled *Serving Crazy with Curry*. Malladi's novel, set in Southern California, examines how a version of fusion cuisine takes on a therapeutic function for a suicidal Indian American. Far from viewing fusion as a palliative for cultural schizophrenia, Malladi's novel stages the difficulties involved in ascribing an ameliorative psychic capability to cooking. I read narratives about fusion cuisine against this novel as a way to suggest that the trope of fusion expands the vision of the second generation to accommodate narratives that speak to moments of racial abjection, produced against the experience of negotiating the muddy and often complex terrain of feeling like a failed version of an Asian American subject.

The cookbooks I focus on in this chapter—Raji Jallepalli and Judith Choate's *Raji Cuisine: Indian Flavors, French Passion,* Floyd Cardoz's *One Spice, Two Spice: American Food, Indian Flavors,* coauthored with Jane Daniels Lear, and Padma Lakshmi's *Easy Exotic: A Model's Low-Fat Recipes from around the World* and *Tangy, Tart, Hot and Sweet: A World of Recipes for Every Day*—widely differ in their approach to cuisine; the common threads woven through each cookbook are the extensive narratives about how to adapt Indianness to American palates and tastes that preface the larger collection of recipes. But a quick journey through this culinary landscape will reveal that radically different political meanings of cultural identity emerge from these cookbooks. Negotiating what it means to adapt one's tastes to Americanness and how such a narrative might be buttressed by a rhetoric of assimilation is the first step one might take in order to arrive at a more careful understanding of the place of the culinary within the immigrant psyche.

The term "fusion" is muddied and muddled, open to multiple and often contradictory definitions. Once considered the new vogue in cuisine, fusion cuisine is no longer an emergent phenomenon and has garnered a posse of vocal critics who frequently decry fusion cuisine as faddish and "inauthentic." A wave that swept through California and the West Coast in the 1980s in the form of Japanese-French or Chinese-Italian-French restaurants, fusion cuisine made its mark on East Coast culinary culture in the 1990s (Lovegren 420). Beginning in the late 1990s, fusion cuisine restaurants have been proliferating in cities, and are now also becoming a presence in smaller towns and cities in the United States. Thanks to fusion cooking shows on the Food Network during the 1990s and the first years of the twenty-first century, such as *East Meets West, Padma's Passport,* and *Nuevo Latino,* fusion cuisine became more of a household name. But what is fusion? Norman Van Aken, who claims credit for having invented the term "fusion cuisine," defines it as "a harmonious combination of foods of various origins" (Dornenburg and Page 22). Offering the more precise definition that circulates in the restaurant industry, Andrew Dornenburg and Karen Page describe fusion as "a melding together of the cuisines of more than one country" in a single dish (302). Food writer Sylvia Lovegren argues that the popularity of fusion cuisine is a symptom of improving ethnic relations in the United States. "American cooks," she conjectures, "feel increasingly comfortable combining ingredients and techniques from around the world, without worrying about 'authenticity' anymore" (420). Lovegren's gesture toward inclusiveness is undercut by a narrow definition of Americanness. Implicitly subsumed under the rhetoric of whiteness, Americans are defined as white middle-class subjects who are experimenting in the kitchen. Whether or not the taste of "difference" coming from Asia is negatively or positively valorized, food is irreducibly foreign and not American unless it is mixed or combined with recognizably "American" ingredients by persons who can unproblematically claim a legitimate stake to the United States. Insisting that Americans have always been fusion cooks (chili con carne, jambalaya, spaghetti and meatballs are cited as examples), she concludes, "contemporary American cooking, however, differs in one important respect; we are now consciously melding cuisines rather than simply adapting foreign foods to American tastes and ingredients" (420). Her optimistic vision of a harmonious American society leaves little room to imagine how Asian Americans or other immigrant or ethnic American groups might cook. "We" references mainstream white America, othering Asians and Asian Americans foodways.

Fusion cuisine, the coming together of different culinary practices, can also be understood in the terms used in the *Oxford English Dictionary.* The *OED* defines fusion as "the union or blending together of different things (whether material or immaterial) as if by melting, so as to form one whole; the result or state of being so blended." An alternative definition rooted in the psychological usage of the terms describes fusion as "a blending together of separate simultaneous sensations into a new complex experience or qualitative perception; the process whereby a succession of similar stimuli produces a continuous response or the sensation of a continuous stimulus." Fusion cuisine, however, is not merely about combining different types of foods. Blending together, forming a whole, creating a complex or qualitative experience: various acts of fusion are intended to produce palatable effects, allowing persons to experience what happens when disparate elements come together in new and unusual ways.

Ming Tsai, host of the Food Network shows *East Meets West* and *Ming's Quest*, offers a slightly different take on fusion cuisine. According to Tsai, "so-called fusion cooking [con-*fusion* cooking some of us call it] produces chaos on the plate and in the mouth. This results from not respecting a culture's ingredients and the traditional techniques that turn them into wonderful eating. Successful East-West cooking . . . finds just the right, harmonious way to combine distinct culinary approaches . . . When a dish is not just new—but better—when I can find a superior way to celebrate oxtail's earthiness, say, or the deep sour tang of preserved lemons, and then join the two—that's real East-West cuisine" (1). Tsai's commentary is still coated in terms of the promise of inclusion. Fusing different cooking styles eventually makes for a better final product. In almost all of the recipes included in his book, Tsai muses on how ingredients from the "East" can improve "Western" cuisine, hinting at the uneven flows between "East" and "West."

Race, Assimilation, and Multicultural Foods

While fusion cuisine has a history different from that of race in the United States, the rhetorical strategies used to describe fusion cuisine can be better understood by placing it in the context of the racial and ethnic debates about diversity, difference, and assimilation in the United States. In juxtaposing the rhetoric of fusion cuisine with the rhetoric of popular and legal discourse around race and ethnicity, I seek to debunk the myth that discourse about fusion cuisine can be separated from the related political issues. In an article that appeared in the July 14, 2000, edition of the *Chronicle of Higher Education* titled, "Why I'm Sick of the Praise for Diversity on Campus," Roger Clegg, general counsel for an anti–affirmative action group, the Center for Equal Opportunity, argues against racial and ethnic diversity on college campus. Including food in his diatribe against race-based affirmative action policies, he notes: "It's fine to eat different kinds of food and to have pride in óne's ancestors. But in matters of language and our civic culture—as well as, more broadly, our manners and morality—assimilation should be the goal. An America that is multiracial and multiethnic, yes. Multicultural, no. E pluribus unum: *Out of many, one.*" Although this is a small part of a larger argument about multiculturalism and U.S. national character on the right, Clegg makes it clear that people of color and immigrants are welcome in America provided they assimilate to the norms and expectations of white English-speaking United States. Here Clegg presents an all-too-familiar argument about racial and ethnic difference, presupposing that the only useful contribution of people of color is in the culinary world.

Commenting on this phenomenon, culinary historian Donna Gabaccia argues: "multiculturalism has its outspoken critics, especially among those who fear the abandonment of a unified national culture and the concomitant 'disuniting' of a great nation, to use Arthur Schlesinger's phrase. So too does multi-ethnic American eating have its critics" (224). But Clegg's contention differs in one important respect. Culinary multiculturalism is acceptable to Clegg only if it does not morph into a politics of nonassimilationist racial inclusion. Gabaccia, on the other hand, is not so quick to dismiss the potential for thinking of culinary multiculturalism as politically enabling. Clegg's evocation of food in a discussion about racial diversity is hardly surprising given the frequency with which people of color and "ethnic" communities are reduced to their foods. In the popular press, for instance, it is often argued that racial interaction and tolerance are improving because the larger public is more comfortable eating "foreign" or "ethnic" food. A 2001 issue of *Bon Appétit* titled "America Goes Global" has editor-in-chief Barbara Fairchild proclaiming: "We're eating off the same plate and enjoying ourselves immensely. It has been said that the problems of the world might be solved more easily by talking around a dinner table than a conference table. We agree" (42). In reality, "we" are not eating off the same plate. Immigrants who prepare food in restaurant kitchens do not eat off the same plate—figurative or literal—as the editors of *Bon Appétit* or celebrity chefs who own fusion restaurants or host fusion cooking shows. It is seductive to think that racial inequities and national differences can be overcome by sitting down and sharing a meal, but food alone cannot effect a politics of inclusion, particularly if assimilation is the primary motivating force.

In her landmark *Immigrant Acts: On Asian American Cultural Politics* (1996), Lisa Lowe offers a useful critique of multiculturalist liberalism and promises of inclusion for previously marginalized groups. For Lowe, multiculturalism establishes itself as an "assert[ion] that American culture is a democratic terrain to which every constituency has equal access and in which all are represented, while simultaneously masking the existence of exclusion by recuperating dissent, conflict, and otherness through the promise of inclusion" (86). Lowe incisively comments on the inherent dangers of presenting inclusion—cultural, legal, and economic—as the force that will necessarily enable better access to the benefits of American citizenship. The rhetorical construction of fusion cuisine as that which brings things together engenders an oversimplified framework for thinking about the racial positioning of South Asian immigrants in the United States. Different people come together as one, leaving behind all traces of foreignness and difference. That which cannot be assimilated must be left behind.

For South Asian immigrants and South Asian Americans, the logic of "assimilate or be left behind" has also informed their ability to be seen as "American" within the legal setting. While legal history and culinary history are not coeval, the terms of inclusion and exclusion that have been debated in Asian American legal and historical studies offer a useful perspective from which to think about how inclusion and exclusion are at work in the fusion culinary world. The oscillation between "white" and "nonwhite" in the legal history of the racialization of South Asian America has been framed around questions of inclusion and exclusion. At a session of the Forty-seventh Congress in 1882, it was determined that Chinese would be denied entry into the United States on the grounds that they were inassimilable; in 1917, the "Asiatic Barred Zone," running from west of the 110th meridian and east of the 50th meridian, was demarcated as a way to curb emigration from Asia and the Middle East, and in 1924, the exclusion of Asians culminated in the passing of the Immigration Act of 1924. The enactment of this legislation was anticipated by two landmark Supreme Court cases that dealt specifically with the question of assimilation and eligibility for citizenship—the 1922 case *Ozawa v. United States* and the 1923 case *United States v. Bhagat Singh Thind*.

Ozawa v. United States, deeming that Japanese immigrant Takao Ozawa was ineligible for citizenship on the grounds that he was not white, laid the groundwork for excluding persons of Japanese origin from acquiring citizenship in the United States because they were seen as inassimilable. On the heels of this case, the 1923 Supreme Court case *United States v. Bhagat Singh Thind* determined that Asian Indians were ineligible for citizenship because they, too, were culturally and racially inassimilable; Bhagat Singh Thind filed a petition to be allowed to naturalize as a citizen on the grounds that as descendants of Aryans, Asian Indians could be racially classified as Caucasian, but his request was denied on the grounds that a common understanding of race precluded Asian Indians from being considered in the same category as white Caucasians of European descent.[1] These two cases are key not only because they detail how the notion of assimilability is linked to constructions of American citizenship but also because they historically anticipate the 1924 Immigration Act, which curbed immigration from Asia altogether.

Following *United States v. Bhagat Singh Thind*, South Asians (then identified as Asian Indians) were defined as nonwhite. In 1970, South Asians were reclassified as "white." But in the wake of affirmative action legislation and post-1965 immigration, Indian Americans sought to be classified as nonwhite. Strategies of inclusion and exclusion have thus functioned as an important thread in the flexible racial positioning of South Asians in America. As Kamala Visweswaran writes, flexible citizenship "can be seen as both strategy and outcome of South Asian class positioning on the one hand, and active negotiation of pre- and post–civil rights designations on the other" (21–22). South Asian Americans who fit into the "model minority" stereotype of being upwardly mobile and with middle- to upper-class income are seen to be more "flexible," while working and immigrant classes—less proficient in English and less upwardly mobile—are not as "flexible."

In the United States, narratives of racial passing have often been embedded within discourses of "black" and "white" with scant attention paid to how nonwhite subjects, notably Asian Americans, inhabit positions along these "color lines." In the judicial arena, South Asian Americans in particular have oscillated across color lines. The history of race for South Asian Americans often has its symbolic ethnogenesis with the 1923 Supreme Court case *United States v. Bhagat Singh Thind*. Thind, an immigrant from Punjab, India, filed a petition to naturalize as a citizen of the United States owing to his status as a "Caucasian." Under existing law, "Hindus," the generic appellation for immigrants from the Indian subcontinent, were considered Caucasian. But federal regulations dating from the 1790 Naturalization Act dictated that naturalization be limited to those who could be considered "free white persons." Whereas earlier prerequisite racial cases had failed to conclusively determine whether Asian Indians as Caucasians were "white" or "nonwhite," *United States v. Bhagat Singh Thind* was the first legal case to decouple the link between Caucasianness and whiteness, setting a legal precedent for deeming Asian Indians to be nonwhites, and therefore ineligible for naturalization. Although *Ozawa v. United States*, which had been decided a year earlier, set a precedent for this case, the actual meaning of "Caucasian" was not debated at length prior to *Thind*. According to the legal scholar Ian F. Haney Lopez, two approaches predominated prior to *Thind* in the discourse within the courts pertaining to immigrant petitions to file for naturalization. An understanding of race based on "common" understanding or "scientific understanding" was the primary mode through which the judicial arena adjudicated whether Asian Indians as Caucuasians were "white," and therefore eligible to naturalize, or "nonwhite," and thus barred from seeking the privileges of U.S. citizenship. *United States v. Thind* marked an important historical moment in the racialization of South Asian persons in the United States because it challenged the ambiguity inherent in the racial prerequisite cases, many of which had determined that Asian Indians were alternatively white (*United States v. Dolla, United States v. Balsara, In re Mohan Singh, In re Thind*) or not white (*In re Akhay Kumar Mozumdar, In re Sadar Bhagwab Singh, United States v. Akhay Kumar Mozumdar*), and demarcated the color line, placing Asian Indians squarely within the nonwhite category. If in the 1920s the court was the site that determined one's Americanness, in the era of late millennial culture, the kitchen and the culinary become new sites of racialization.

A recent issue of *Bon Appétit* showcases successful restaurateurs Neela Paniz, owner of Bombay Café in Los Angeles, and Floyd Cardoz, co-owner of Tabla in New York, as denizens of the new culinary culture. Cuisine is no longer about "good food" alone, it is also about traveling, crossing old boundaries, and forging new alliances in the kitchen. If fusion cuisine is heralded as the democratic melding of cuisines, it is largely because it is a type of culinary culture that seems to challenge the sanctity of national boundaries and fixity. Fusion cuisine is a less potent threat because it is enacted in the cultural realm, where mixing is always only ephemeral and not capable of transforming the structural nature of race in the United States. Differences are rendered palatable, easily consumed and digested. Fusion cooking is an arena in which hybridity, cultural interaction, and assimilation are omnipresent, precisely because it celebrates the coming together of different cultures and cuisines. It is seen as the apparent tribute to successful multiculturalism in the United States—different ingredients come together to create something new. More often than not, it is also described as a fusion of different national styles, combining one national cuisine with another.

Within the American culinary landscape, Asian fusion cuisine has typically combined East Asian cuisines with French cuisine. Fusion chefs Ken Hom and Ming Tsai, in particular, have been credited with making visible strides in the world of fusion cuisine. Until recently, South Asians have been relatively absent from the fusion-cooking arena. With the proliferation of restaurants, South Asian fusion cuisines have been gathering more national attention and are celebrated as the cuisine of choice for cosmopolitan urban dwellers. In part, the rise of fusion cuisine in the North American urban metropolis can be understood as part of the trend toward high-income gentrification within certain sectors of the urban landscape in cities such as New York, London, and Tokyo. In *The Global City: New York, London, Tokyo* (2001), Saskia Sassen usefully explores the types of class differentials that sustain the demand for "cuisine" rather than "food" (341) in such global cities. Sassen describes this emergent class of "spenders"—high-income workers with a propensity to spend rather than save or invest their disposable income—as important players in the market for high-priced goods and services. She connects their consumption patterns and demands with the presence of an immigrant working class, often from Asia and the Caribbean, hypothesizing that "economic inequality in major cities has assumed distinct forms in the consumption structure, which in turn has a feedback effect on the organization of work and the types of jobs being created. There is an indirect creation of low-wage jobs induced by the presence of a highly dynamic sector with a polarized income distribution. It takes place in the sphere of consumption (or social reproduction)" (285). Sassen describes this version of "high-income gentrification" as labor intensive. "Behind the gourmet stores and specialty boutiques," she argues, "lies an organization of the work process that differs from that of the self-service supermarket and department store" (285). Gentrified classes in these cities that demand varied cuisines in restaurants exert a new type of pressure on the service sector that makes it necessary for immigrants to satisfy the demands of high-income gentrified workers located amid the "new cosmopolitan work culture" (341).

But is it possible to fashion a language to theorize fusion cooking in terms of race and assimilation without the celebratory rhetoric so predominant in reviews of, and discussions about, fusion cuisine? Heeding Lisa Lowe's cautionary remarks about the dangers of falling prey to the seductive appeals of a malleable, and all-too-easy multiculturalism, this chapter offers concluding remarks about food and South Asian Americanness, arguing that it is important to understand the sociopolitical conditions that render fusion a distinct possibility—not just theoretically, but materially and discursively.

Madhur Jaffrey: Introducing India

Before fusion cuisine captured the fancy of restaurant goers, Madhur Jaffrey, long considered the grande dame of Indian cuisine, was introducing Americans to the tastes of Indianness. The prolific cookbook author who came to the United States from India in the 1960s via England has published over a dozen cookbooks focused on Indian cuisine and is credited with introducing "authentic" Indian home cooking to American culture, writ large. Her earliest cookbook, *An Invitation to Indian Cooking* (1973), sets about to create authentically Indian food while aiming to defamiliarize Indian food by rendering it legible to American cooks. Adorning the cover of the cookbook is an image of a young Madhur Jaffrey clad in a formal silk sari, hair swept back in an elegant chignon. She is seated at a kitchen table slicing vegetables and invitingly smiles at her reader. The book cover states, "Classic Indian dishes . . . carefully worked out for American cooks in American kitchens," suggesting its author will render Indian food less foreign to American cooks and palates. Within the first few pages of the book, Jaffrey launches into an explanation of why Americans need help understanding Indian food. Indian food, in Jaffrey's estimation, is vastly misunderstood by Americans thanks to the lack of diversity showcased within the handful of Indian restaurants in the United States of the late 1960s and early 1970s. Jaffrey notes, "there is no place in New York, or anywhere in America where top-quality Indian food can be found—except, of course, in private Indian homes" (3). Published within a decade of the Immigration and Nationality Act of 1965, the cookbook implicitly anchors its understanding of Indian food within the context of legislation that paved the way for Indians to immigrate to the United States. Positioning herself as one of the few patriotic Indians within a newly Asianized New York to care about the authentic taste of Indian food, Jaffrey uses her cookbook to demystify Indian food, moving it out of a narrow formulation of culinary choices—"mild, medium, hot" (3)—into a space that allows for palatal nuance. As a diasporic subject who has adapted her cuisine for American kitchens, she enables cooks in American kitchens to take pleasure in the complexity of Indian flavors that might be easily created with American spices and ingredients. In her vast culinary enterprise which has followed in the thirty intervening years, Jaffrey has come to occupy the space of Indian culinary expert—someone who understands how to bring the nuance of Indian cuisine to the American palate without compromising the essential qualities of Indian flavor. Thus, through her concerted guidance and efforts, she helps make Indian food palatable: Through her recipes and gentle suggestions, Indian flavors are able to move away from their extremities to occupy the realm of nuanced palatability.

Raji Jallepalli: Indian Flavors

Such a focus on palatal nuance and Indian flavor dominates the landscape of fusion cuisine. Consider that two of the preeminent chefs specializing in fusion cuisine accent "Indian flavors" in the titles of their cookbooks. For Raji Jallepalli, French passion is fused with "Indian flavors," and for Floyd Cardoz, American food is fused with "Indian flavors." For the late Jallepalli, executive chef and owner of the Memphis-based Raji, fusion is not "foie gras and curry" but a "rather quiet melding of vastly different cultures, philosophies and cooking techniques" (3). Heralded as one of the pioneers in South Asian fusion cuisine, chef, restaurateur, and author Raji Jallepalli was not as visibly recognizable in circuits of U.S. public culture as Padma Lakshmi, one-time host of the Food Network's *Padma's Passport* and current host of Bravo TV's *Top Chef.* Before her death in February 2002, Jallepalli made a strong mark in U.S. culinary culture, receiving favorable reviews in industry periodicals for her innovative approach to cooking. Although she did not host her own TV show, she had been featured on the Discovery Channel series *Great Chefs of the World,* and she was included in the canon of great chefs along with a handful of other women.[2] Jallepalli received accolades for her culinary innovations in mainstream publications ranging from the *New York Times* and *Wall Street Journal* to *Food and Wine* and *Food Arts*; and she was also nominated for the prestigious James Beard Award in 1996 and 1997. She opened her first restaurant, Restaurant Raji, in 1989 (then named the East Indian Trading Company), a French-Indian fusion cuisine restaurant in Memphis, Tennessee, and in 2001 opened Tamarind, a restaurant serving traditional Indian food in New York City. Despite her formidable success in the world of culinary culture, Jallepalli did not make her presence felt in the same ways as other multicultural hosts such as Ming Tsai or Padma Lakshmi.

Jallepalli's cookbook, *Raji Cuisine: Indian Flavors, French Passion* (2000), collects recipes from her award-winning Restaurant Raji. A narrative of culinary mixings and tales of "Indian flavors fused with French passion," the cookbook situates itself at the crossroads of two international culinary cultures. The cover image of vegetarian spring rolls and mezclun green salad defies easy national classification: it is not discernibly "Indian" or "French." The front matter of the text, including the foreword by Chicago restaurateur Charlie Trotter and Jallepalli's extensive introduction, carefully establishes Jallepalli's connections with the "Eastern" world of India and the "Western" world of France. For Jallepalli, working with food has more to do with what she learned after becoming diasporic than with the lessons learned in the kitchen of her land of ancestry. While her approach to cuisine narrativizes a nonessentialist approach to Indianness, it is one that emphasizes the immigrant's ability to forge a new identity in the diaspora. In the context of the South Asian diaspora in the United States, Jallepalli's contributions to the world of fusion are marked by how she changes French cuisine and not how French cuisine changes Indian cuisine, suggesting that fusion, as it is defined here, is a unidirectional process. Fusion cuisine is more about how Jallepalli's culinary practices can enhance the flavor of the West with the piquancy of the East. Linda Burum, a Los Angeles–based food writer and author of *The Guide to Ethnic Food in Los Angeles,* describes *Raji Cuisine* as one of "the best examples of intelligent mixed cultural cooking today." Offering an explanation about Jallepalli's early influences, she continues, "as the daughter of a diplomat who exposed his children to the cultures of the world, Jallepalli inherited, as she puts it, 'the freedom to venture into areas trained chefs would be reluctant to follow.'"[3] As a diplomat's child, Jallepalli self-admittedly comes from a background where it is unnecessary, or at least optional, to deal with the exigencies of citizenship and crossing borders—complicated matters for those without diplomatic immunity and the privileges that affords. Choosing to emphasize her diplomatic background earns her a secure place in upper-class categories, placing her in a prime location to be able to embrace fusion and to be more dismissive of confining "authentic" and "traditional" notions of home.

But markers of Indianness emerge in subtle but important ways in Jallepalli's cookbook. Jallepalli mentions her frequent trips to France to indulge her love of classic French cooking and wine as a way to establish her connection with Europe. But more problematic is the way the book's dust jacket copy mentions that before becoming a restaurateur, she "immersed herself in a career in microbiology." Her own explanation as to why she became a cook—"perhaps the only answer is kismet; even as I was standing in the laboratory, incubating tissue, fate had framed my future and it was not under my control at all" (1)—is coated in self-Orientalizing terms eliding issues of class privilege. Jallepalli's flexibility is thus deeply rooted in her class positioning. She can fuse, meld, and adapt cuisines, and change careers partly because she has the resources to be able to do so, not because cosmic forces in the universe allow her to do so.

A quick glance through her cookbook begins to gastronomically map how this melding takes places. Among the hors d'oeuvres one finds Sevruga caviar and dal blinis, crab crustillant with raspberry sauce, and foie gras with French lentils. Salads include carpaccio of cured beef with baby greens and mung bean polenta or corn compote in a pappadum bowl. For an entrée, one might sample cassoulet of veal with tempered lentils and Provençal herbs or halibut with lime-leek beurre blanc and cauliflower bouquets. And for dessert one might relish the sweetness of cardamom crème brûlée or lemongrass sorbet with sweet spice madeleines. The culinary offerings here remap French cuisine by adding accents of Indian flavors and tastes; in Jallepalli's definition of fusion, one does not find ways for French flavor to accent Indian home cooking. In the process of fusing flavors, Jallepalli suggests that the "assertive flavors of [her] homeland" are lightened up to yield "menus that are bursting with flavor yet delicate, healthful yet complex and naturally low in fat but exceptionally satisfying" (2). Here, then, the perceived excess of Indianness is eliminated. The "quiet melding" explains how Indian flavors enter French gastronomy. French dishes confer status on Indian food through this particular marriage of flavors. Such rhetorical strategies are eerie echoes of model minority discourse. Asian Americans, notably Indian Americans, receive high praise for quietly assimilating into the American landscape. The analogous movement for Indian flavors is stunning. Through fusion, assertive Indian flavors are lightened and rendered delicate; the flavors, in other words, eliminate the signs and smells of immigrant excess. Thus, where Jaffrey focuses more on offering alternatives to "excess," Jallepalli's version of fusion aims to remove the stigma of "heaty excess" from Indian flavors by allowing its taste to assimilate into classic French cuisine.

Floyd Cardoz: Indianness Incorporated

While Memphis may have been an early witness to the renaissance of Indian cooking, it was in 1998, more than thirty years after the publication of *An Invitation to Indian Cooking*, that New York City saw the emergence of a new ambassador for Indian cuisine, and a new generation of Indian restaurants as the fusion-style restaurant Tabla opened its doors for business. Tabla is part of the group of restaurants owned by Danny Meyer, and its executive chef is the Goan-born Floyd Cardoz, who trained at Lespanisse in New York City. Adjacent to 11 Madison, Tabla became one of the first upscale restaurants in the United States to serve Indian food and is also celebrated as one of the first to delink Indian food from the schemata Jaffrey abhors—"mild, medium, hot" (3). Tabla has quickly risen to prominence as one of the most visible restaurants specializing in fusion cuisine, where Indian tastes fuse with American flavors. Floyd Cardoz has quickly earned the stamp of approval of many in the restaurant-reviewing business. When the cooking show host Rachael Ray takes in the tastes of New York City during a segment of her television show $40 a Day, she lunches at Tabla, granting the restaurant a particular visibility within the national landscape. Ruth Reichl, former restaurant critic of the New York Times, gave Tabla "3 Stars," describing it as a dining experience that amounted to "love at first bite." Both Ray and Reichl are impressed with how Tabla is not just fusion but a particular instance of how American food is infused with the flavors of India. Reichl notes, "This is American food, viewed through a kaleidoscope of Indian spices"; similarly, Ray notes, "Chef Floyd Cardoz's menu is a perfect example of what is so great about New York dining—its ethnicity, its diversity." For both, Cardoz's fusion is truly "American" because it combines the tastes Indian immigrants and Indian Americans hold dear with the best of American nouvelle cuisine.[4]

But what makes Tabla's conversation about fusion morph into a conversation about class? The architecture of the restaurant provides the best answer to this question, for in Tabla's unique design, which segments one large space into two restaurants under one roof, class becomes spatialized. Tabla's Web site announces, "guests may choose from two different dining experiences: the balcony-level Dining Room, offering refined New American cooking infused with Indian spices or the bustling street level Bread Bar, which serves home-style Indian cuisine." While the two "dining experiences" cater to different budgets, the Main Dining Room, specializing in New American cooking in which Indianness fuses into Western taste, commands higher prices and carries the moniker "refined," whereas the "Bread Bar," which offers home-style Indian food, is cast as a "bustling" space, rhetorically calling to mind Third World excess produced through the culture of bazaars and markets. A glance through the menu reveals a curious alignment of class with race. Where the Bread Bar offers familiar Indian dishes like makai ki roti, shahi basmati pilaf, an assortment of raitas and chutneys, chicken tikka, and mango lassi with prices ranging from four dollars to twenty-one dollars, the Dining Room offers a markedly different experience. Among the appetizers are dishes named Hudson Valley duck samosa served with shaved fennel, blood orange, and holy basil; seared foie gras with quince "cheese," cashews, candied ginger, and bacon. The main course offerings include rawa-crisped skate with rock shrimp, sunchokes, savoy cabbage, bacon, and kokum brown butter jus and spice-crusted flank steak with local Swiss chard, scallion-potato rösti, smoked bacon, and horseradish raita. In the Dining Room, no dish is priced below nine dollars, and entrees cost an average of twenty-one dollars. The food showcases how Indian flavors might subtly enhance the flavor of Western cuisine; indeed, it seems as if the marriage of Indian flavors with Western cuisine is what elevates Indian food from the type of mere bazaar food served on the lower level of the Bread Bar to the type of nouvelle cuisine that earns high praise from Reichl. While both spaces offer tasting menus, it is only in the Bread Bar that tasting menus are served family style, as if to mimic the free flow and simplicity of the bazaar the Bread Bar emulates.

Within less than a decade, the chef and co-owner of Tabla, Floyd Cardoz, entered the culinary writing marketplace with the publication of his cookbook *One Spice, Two Spice: American Food, Indian Flavors.* His cookbook, a paean to the Main Dining Room, includes recipes for many of the dishes on the menu served in the Main Dining Room—Goan crab cake, black-peppered day boat cod, rawa-crisped skate, tapioca-crusted shrimp and scallops, black spiced roasted chicken, and fricassee of wild mushroom. The Bread Bar thus becomes illegible within the cookbook. While there may be space for the excess associated with Indian food within the space of the restaurant at 11 Madison Avenue, the Bread Bar is not the public face associated with Tabla's carefully managed tastes. As Ruth Reichl notes: "At the [Bread] bar downstairs, people lean into conversations as they watch cooks grilling roti and naan in crazy flavors . . . when they are ready for dinner they climb a wide staircase made of padauk, a gorgeous red wood . . . Graceful servers stroll the room." Even in Reichl's glowing review of Tabla, it is clear that the Bread Bar is a space of carnivalesque excess: to find graceful order where one's Jimmy Choos can coexist with appropriately expressed flavors and tastes, one must turn upward, literally, to the Main Dining Room, the space that uses American food to elevate Indian flavors from its colorful but slightly déclassé, bazaarlike excess.

Flexibly Exotic: Padma Lakshmi and
New Cosmopolitanisms

Although Padma Lakshmi, better known as host of Bravo's *Top Chef*, does not own her own restaurant, she is arguably more of a media presence in public circuits of culture than South Asian restaurateurs including Jaffrey, Cardoz, and Jallepalli. Her face has graced the covers of international fashion magazines from *Marie Claire India* (October 2007) *to Newsweek* (March 6, 2006). *Newsweek*, in fact, presents Lakshmi on the cover of its special issue on the "New" India. In the face of globalization and a rapidly changing India, *Newsweek*, and to a lesser extent *Marie Claire India*, hone in on Lakshmi as the face of the new India—young, mobile, attractive. Before her career as host of the hit cooking reality show, Lakshmi hosted a short-lived television show, *Padma's Passport*. Generally organized around a specific topic, either showcasing types of food to be consumed and prepared for special occasions and outings such as picnic lunches and aphrodisiacal food, each episode creates culinary fusion by juxtaposing dishes from disparate national culinary cultures. Her two cookbooks, *Easy Exotic: A Model's Low-Fat Recipes from Around the World* (2000) and *Tangy, Tart, Hot and Sweet* (2007), instruct cooks how to bring cosmopolitanism to one's everyday palate. Part of the success of the cookbooks rests with the way in which Padma Lakshmi is positioned as an ideal ambassador for a benign (and unthreatening) culinary cosmopolitanism. Lakshmi is presented as a South Asian American subject for whom race matters are less relevant because she brings her worldliness to bear on her approach to cuisine without corrupting the domestic sanctity of American cuisine with unpalatable fiery foreignness. Unlike the chefs whom she engages on *Top Chef*, Padma Lakshmi deals more with everyday foods, easily re-created in the home kitchen in less than thirty minutes. Her first cookbook, *Easy Exotic: A Model's Low-Fat Recipes from Around the World*, takes a global approach to cuisine in its framing of Lakshmi as a transnational citizen. Part cookbook, part memoir, the work opens with Lakshmi's nostalgic memories of growing up and learning to cook in the company of female relatives in South India, thus rooting her identity in Indianness. As the book progresses, it follows the routes Lakshmi has taken in traveling; this movement is mirrored in the cookbook's organization into separate chapters on the cuisines of Spain, France, Italy, India, Asia, and Morocco. Intriguingly, the cookbook positions Lakshmi not as an "immigrant" with all of its classed implications but as a savvy world traveler. Her background in modeling, her ability to speak five languages, and her racially ambiguous appearance position her as a formidable ambassador for (Indian) fusion culinary culture. With such an overt connection to the world, the cooking show upon which *Easy Exotic* is based carefully constructs Lakshmi as a legitimately American subject. Like *Easy Exotic*, *Padma's Passport* does not produce the same kind of fusion as Cardoz or Jallepalli; rather, it produces "fusion" through juxtaposition. The titles of various episodes—"My Mother's Cooking," "Late Night Suppers," or "Aphrodisiac Foods"—represent the thematic focus. The recipes for dishes prepared are included in *Easy Exotic*, and culinary fusion is created through a juxtaposition of national styles. A single episode, for instance, will include an Italian, Moroccan, and Indian dish. The episode "Light Luncheon" instructs viewers how to prepare carpaccio di pesce, Parisian chicken salad, spaghetti di Capri, and mango parfait, whereas the episode "Casual Buffet" delves into the intricacies of Spanish stuffed bell peppers, honeyed chicken legs, pesce spada, and Chambord berries in cream. Episodes with raunchier titles such as "Aphrodisiacal Foods" showcase recipes like oysters with an Asian mignonette, saffron and preserved lemon-scented shrimp pilaf, and pan-seared cinnamon bananas over vanilla ice cream, while "Hot n' Spicy" goes into the specifics of preparing nimbu rice, spicy Szechuan stir-fry, and Thai soup. Only on the episodes "My Mother's Kitchen" (coconut chicken, *kheema* [Indian spiced ground veal and beef with peas], *rajma* [vegetarian chili]) and "Indian Feast," (Rani's rice pilaf, Turan's tuna curry, and tandoori chicken salad) do we see apparently unfused Indian food. In the former, dishes are subtitled with an American twist as if to foreground that while many of the foods before us may be Indian in origin, they are not irreducibly foreign. *Kheema* and *rajma*, respectively, are described as "an Indian version of the American sloppy joe and a hearty vegetarian chili." As she moves through the episode, she comments on just how American-like these dishes are:

> When I would come home from school (it's funny now that all these dishes are meat dishes because my mom's actually a vegetarian). But when I was going to school in this country, elementary school or, you know, junior high, I would eat all these things in the cafeteria like sloppy joes, and I would come home and my mother—my poor mother—would have to reproduce them for me. And I would say, "Well, that's not what all the other kids eat. You know.

That looks like what the other kids eat." So this is her version. She would basically throw this *kheema* between two slices of bread and say, "Here. Here's your sloppy joe." And, in fact, it is very similar.

In the cookbook, however, she introduces the *kheema* recipe with a different narrative, one that positions the dish of ground meat and peas as comfort food that is unmistakably Indian: "When my mother and I first moved to California, we lived near an Indian couple, Nirmal and Pratima. As my mother worked late in the evening, I often dropped by their house for dinner . . . when I first started eating meat, it was Pratima's kheema that I liked best. I suppose the ground beef didn't look like meat to me and the taste was exquisite. Even as a girl, I had an appetite for fiery fare and Pratima was happy to oblige by slicing chilies up for me to mix into my kheema" (74). In the cookbook, Lakshmi's Indian neighbors in California introduce *kheema* into her culinary repertoire. She describes it as "fiery fare," whereas on *Padma's Passport*, *kheema* becomes domesticated and is presented as Lakshmi's mother's answer to American cafeteria lunchroom food. The cleaving between the two narratives for this particular recipe is telling: the show carves a niche in the American palate for Indian food by presenting Indian cuisine as a form of accented American cuisine rather than as a transaction between diasporics. Toward the end of the show, Lakshmi explains just how American these dishes can be: "When I was growing up in America, my mother made a great effort to incorporate a lot of the flavors that I was getting at school and at other people's houses into our cooking so that I would feel more in tune with what my friends were eating at home, and it made me feel more international. And she was good at going to all these restaurants and picking up a Thai thing here, a Mexican thing there, and joining that into our cuisine."

These moments present Lakshmi as a subject who has become disciplined by the mechanisms of U.S. cultural citizenship; absent, however, is a sense of negotiated loss that so often characterizes the immigrant's entry into the racial and ethnic order of the United States. Her chili and sloppy joe seem like clever twists on old American favorites, but the narrative is crafted so as to depict Lakshmi as a good model minority for the ways in which she and her mother attempt to assimilate their tastes into Americanness without compromising American national or culinary character. She may have a culinary passport to travel, but she always comes home to America and its food.

Sylvia Lovegren dubs the 1990s the "fusion" decade, but from her description of how fusion cooking has changed the nature of American culinary culture it is apparent that fusion is not exclusively about bringing different types of cuisines together. She concludes: "in America, we have the bounty and the culinary heritage to cook and eat virtually anything we wish. Whether we choose to nourish ourselves with a meal of frozen fish sticks and fat-free brownies, or with food—whether simple or sophisticated—that is chosen and prepared with love and respect, is up to us" (421). The language of entitlement pervasive here, the notion that "we" as Americans pick and choose want "we" want to eat, fits into the rhetorical construction of America as the land of plenty and blurs distinctions between fusion, assimilation, and appropriation. Padma Lakshmi's take on this type of choice is free of the notion of entitlement but skillfully manages to insert its author as part of an everyday cosmopolitanism. In her second cookbook, *Tangy, Tart, Hot and Sweet*, a much longer and more elaborate cookbook than *Easy Exotic*, Lakshmi delves into her culinary philosophy in more detail. Organized into courses rather than national cuisines, the cookbook enacts Lakshmi's culinary philosophy, "a little of this and a little of that" (xix). Lakshmi's view of America espouses an easy culinary cosmopolitanism. She notes:

> we are all a little bit Chinese, a little bit Mexican, a little bit Italian and French . . . most of us do not eat a single cuisine all the time . . . one day sushi, another Thai, a third Italian, and the fourth day . . . maybe Mexican, or how about Moroccan? . . . I want to eat a rice dish that transports me to the paddies of Indonesia, a couscous dish to remind me of mysterious Marrakech, and a fiery curried broth to evoke my lost childhood in the deep lushness of the South Indian rainforest. Like most of us, I have been influenced by the people around me. A Peruvian babysitter, a Korean college roommate, an Italian lover and a Swiss aunt have all affected my cooking and I am grateful to them for making my life in the kitchen more robust and complicated. (xviii–xix)

Within the pages of the cookbook's poultry section are recipes for dishes from Mexico, Morocco, China, India, Jamaica, and the U.S. South. Similarly, the salad section includes offerings from Alpujarra, Spain, and Pondicherry, India, as well as a recipe adapted from an Iranian American's repertoire. This easy multiculturalism where one can slide in and out of varied ethno-national contexts with a simple pinch of cumin or sprinkle of zaatar, while certainly seductive, flattens out the unevenness of multiculturalism in America. All cuisines are positioned as equally accessible. Eating widely is equated with embracing a visceral diversity among the company one keeps, and, most importantly this communion with culinary diversity is celebrated as quintessentially American. As she phrases it: "I believe the American palate is the most open and inviting audience for the world's flavors. The best thing about an immigrant culture is the choice and variety of tastes and ingredients it offers" (xvii–xviii). Recalling Calvin Trillin's words discussed in the previous chapter, Lakshmi's words celebrate immigrants for the culinary, reinforcing Barbara Fairchild's belief that the world would be a better place if we could simply share one another's food. Moreover, this narrative of transnational mobility also privileges a particular class experience.

Lakshmi's ability to travel in and out of the worlds of international cuisine, built on her class privilege as an upwardly mobile subject, contrasts with the realities of many Bangladeshi workers in Indian restaurants in New York. Many of the working-class Bangladeshis who work in "Indian" restaurants have to embrace a more transnational identity, subordinating their Bangladeshi identity to an Indian one, not because they are transnationally mobile, but because "Indian cuisine" carries more cultural capital than "Bangladeshi cuisine" (Bhattacharjee et al. 14). As Munir, a Bangladeshi employee at a restaurant in Queens, New York, reveals, "we have to work in restaurants because we do not find other jobs" (qtd. in Bhattacharjee et al. 14). Working in the food business is anything but glamorous for immigrants like Munir, who have to strategically reposition their ethnic and national identity in order to make a living. But instead of reading the subordination of Bangladeshi to Indian as completely disempowering, we would do well to look for spaces where Bangladeshi restaurant owners disrupt seamless narratives of Indianness. As Naheed Islam notes, "Older Bangladeshi restaurants bear names such as Tandoori Nights, or Gate of India, for they reach out to a clientele who can not, or does not, distinguish between peoples of different South Asian nations and commonly misidentifies then as Indian. Bangladeshis play on such mistaken identities, but at the same time—as in the case of the restaurant Gate of India, where a Bangladeshi artist has painted a mural of a 'typical' scene in Bangladesh—they find ways to assert their own construction of identity" (qtd. in Kumar 83).

The need to reinvent and reframe ethnic identity stands in direct contrast to Lakshmi's ability to posit Americans as having the world's most open palate. The rhetoric in Lakshmi's cookbooks presents Asian cooking styles as ones that might be easily appropriated by those looking to add some diversity to their palates. Let me be clear that I also read the culinary rhetoric in these varied cookbooks as a way to collectively insist that Asianness need not be understood as an inassimilable presence within the United States but as something that can assimilate quietly and subtly into the U.S. culinary landscape. The *OED* defines assimilation as "the action of making or becoming like, the state of being like; similarity, resemblance, likeness" as well as "the process of becoming conformed to," and "conversion into a similar substance; especially the process whereby an animal or plant converts extraneous material into fluids and tissues identical with its own." This literal definition of "assimilation" invites the question, how does fusion cuisine blur the boundaries between fusion, an ostensibly democratic coming together of cuisines, and appropriation, which involves actively taking from the ethnic heritages of people of color, including Asian Americans, and divesting cultural production of any racialized implications?

As one way of answering this question, I would reemphasize that assimilation, and particularly the notion of assimilating quietly, cannot be divorced from the study of race and ethnicity in Asian America. The culinary maps onto the racial because the two discursive modalities are mutually constitutive. Racial language in the United States has always evoked culinary tropes, and as is clear in the examples from the cookbooks by Cardoz, Jallepalli, and Lakshmi, the culinary is a palimpsest on which the language of race leaves its traces. As I suggested earlier in this chapter, the term "assimilation" is historically significant in terms of legislation and the juridical mechanisms regulating the racialization of Asian Americans. In the early years of the twentieth century, numerous Asian groups were excluded from American citizenship because they were deemed "inassimilable." In the context of a legal historical understanding of Asians as inassimilable because they are racially different, when cuisine is described in laudatory terms precisely because it is so readily assimilable, it starts to mirror the rhetoric of racial discourse. Focusing on how the taste of Asia can assimilate into America is one way to elide larger issues that might suggest that working-class Asian Americans do not always enjoy the rights and privileges afforded to the younger, high-income gentrified subjects that they serve—albeit invisibly. Further, the continued post–9/11 profiling of Arabs and Arab Americans, Muslim Americans, and South Asians and South Asian Americans suggests that a fear of the "other" can be strategically mobilized to position Asians as the perpetual outsider in America who can pose a threat to the sanctity and safety of the American citizenry. The unruly immigrant, the terrorist, the smelly immigrant, the undocumented restaurant worker—these are all paradigmatic examples of undisciplined excess. Much as Indian food is understood through its extremities, the prototypical immigrant is a figure whose difference must be lessened or eliminated in order to render him or her palatable to mainstream America.

Fusions and Leftovers

We went to lunch at a place that wasn't Indian but had things like elderberry chutney and mango coulis (which the waitress pronounced "coolie" to my mother's perturbation) and charge a lot for a salad with leaves called endives that were so bitter I nearly spit my first and last bite out. We left vastly unsatisfied and bought chestnuts from the Indian guy on the corner.—TANUJA DESAI HIDIER, BORN CONFUSED

The novelty of cardamom crème brûlée, elderberry chutney, tamarind consommé, and pineapple-lemongrass martinis has not failed to capture the fancy of restaurant and cookbook critics; on occasion these new mixings give rise to raised eyebrows among skeptics of unholy culinary alliances. As Hidier suggest, not everyone is enamored of fusion cuisine. "Consumption" as Pierre Bourdieu notes, is "a stage in a process of communication that is an act of deciphering, decoding, which presupposes practical or explicit mastery of a cipher or code" (2). Consuming fusion cuisine, then, can only have meaning for those who have the cultural know-how. If we think of fusion cuisine as a form of artistry, it "has meaning and interest only for someone who possesses the cultural competence, that is, the code into which it is encoded . . . A beholder who lacks the specific code feels lost in a chaos of sounds and rhythms, colours and line, without rhyme or reason" (2). In many of the more popular fusion cookbooks, there are unwritten rules about what ingredients can be fused and what the end product must look like. Fusion cuisine has its signature dishes: crème brûlées, ragoûts, cassoulets accented with a palatably foreign or exotic touch. Is this "authentic" fusion cuisine or merely an attempt to showcase the facility with which Asianness can be incorporated into haute cuisine? Ultimately, hybrid cuisines do not trouble me; rather the discursive terms by which we navigate hybridizitization figure as problematic. Smoking poussin on sandalwood chips and serving it with Israeli couscous à la Raji Jallepalli may indeed be considered an example of French passion fused with Indian flavors because it sits comfortably within the American culinary landscape, but, following Bourdieu, knowing how to consume and enjoy fusion cuisine necessitates a familiarity with its codes and conventions.

The "arrival" of Raji Jallepalli's restaurant in New York after making an initial debut in Memphis, Tennessee, and the arrival of Tabla in New

York have been read as signs that South Asian Americans have "made" it.[5] These stories attest to the success of Asians in America. But to read the popularity of South Asian cuisine, fused or "pure," as a mark of arrival is troubling because this type of fusion cuisine is described by Jallepalli as a "rather quiet combining of vastly different cultures" and thus aligns with the laudatory rhetoric that praises Asians for assimilating quietly into American culture. Quietly combining suggests that the mixing of Asianness and "Americanness" is best when it is subtle, silent, and unobtrusive. Roger Clegg's essay "Why I'm Sick of the Praise for Diversity on Campus" implicitly suggests how people of color should "enter" the American racial landscape: like good "model minorities," South Asian Americans should "enter" quietly and unobtrusively, adhering to that old ideal *E pluribus unum*: out of many, one. While Jallepalli and Lakshmi do not necessarily create one out of many, their respective approaches to cuisine make it possible for an assimilatory version of fusion to emerge. In so doing, the perceived excesses of South Asianness are kept at bay and the United States retains its place as the central clearinghouse for managing diversity.

Managing Excess: Black and White and Brown

I had also slipped back into conceiving of the United States as Culinary Central—as the place through which any foreign cuisine would have to pass ... How could Thai food have made it to Kenya without any (apparent) help from Us? How could two cultures interact with each other without the United States being somehow involved?—LISA HELDKE, *EXOTIC APPETITES*

Reading the rhetoric and culinary logic of Jallepalli's and Cardoz's approach to fusion cuisine, it becomes clear that excess is managed to produce palatability. Like Jallepalli's, Cardoz's version of fusion aims to temper the "assertiveness" of Indian flavors. "When melded together" with traditional Western food, Cardoz explains, Indian flavors become "subtle and sophisticated" (xv). During his apprenticeship with Gray Kunz at Lespinasse, he learned that Indian flavors didn't "taste right in its new setting" of Lespinasse; "the black cardamom was too strong ... the chilies were too extreme" (xv). Kunz, he explains, "encouraged [him] to tone down the chilies and the rest of the ingredients" (xv) in order to bring balance to the plate. In no uncertain terms, Cardoz suggests that Indian flavors and spices acquire upward mobility, even the title of sophistication, within the classed world of restaurant dining and gourmet cooking when combined with American and French cuisine.

Some of New York's more recent restaurants, most notably Bombay Talkie, a fascinating homage to Indian cinema, have been praised for creating menus that allow unpalatable fieriness to be modulated for the more subtle (read sophisticated) palate. The *New York Magazine* profile for Bombay Talkie describes the restaurant's food as "straightforward Indian (as opposed to wacky Indian fusion)." The culinary offerings, it is suggested, "evoke the vibrant universe of Indian street food. There is a 'street bites' section on the menu, a 'curbside' section, and one called 'by the roadside.' You can take the edge off these moderately fiery dishes with several temperate desserts, like carrot halwa, and an excellent selection of ice creams and gelati." It thus remains that even in this restaurant which refrains from producing "wacky Indian fusion," the reviewers seek to find tastes to modulate a sense of overwrought spiciness endemic to street food and all of its excesses.

But it is also clear that American or French cuisine is tinged by its whiteness. While Jallepalli's and Cardoz's fusions might create a transaction between the tastes of "India" and "white" America, other combinations with "Black" cuisine are not intuitively understood to be part of the culinary dance into which Indian flavors enter. For Jallepalli, Black America enters her culinary repertoire in a rather curious manner. She introduces her recipe for South Indian barbecue with collard greens and black-eyed peas with the following narrative: "This recipe began as a joke. One evening a regular customer called to see if we had any tables open for dinner. After I assured him of his favorite spot, he went on to say that he was having a difficult time deciding whether to eat at Raji's or hunt up some great barbecue. Since he opted for Raji's I created this especially for him so he could have the best of both worlds" (xv).

South Indian barbecue might well represent "the best of the both worlds"; the optimist in me—inspired by Bill Mullen's path-breaking analysis of Afro-Asian connections in *Afro-Orientalism*—wants to read this recipe as an acknowledgment of the possibilities in fusing Indian food with Black culture, but the realist in me thinks this might be a nod to Restaurant Raji's location in the South; after all, what is more quintessentially "southern" than barbecue? Moreover, the caveat—this recipe began as a joke—suggests that this recipe's eccentric location requires explanation. Unless it is qualified as a joke, a recipe for an Indianized version of barbecue served with quintessentially Black food—collard greens and black-eyed peas—would be viewed as excessive and eccentric within the purview of delicate and sensual fusion cuisine.

Such nods to Blackness, however, are wholly absent on Tabla's menus.

This omission of Black tastes within Cardoz's repertoire is particularly startling in light of the fact that *One Spice, Two Spice* notably begins, "I was named after Floyd Patterson, the late great African-American boxer," hinting that Cardoz's vision of fusion accommodates a more radical history of cultural admixture between Black America and India. The restaurant's name, Tabla, as Danny Meyer notes, is not the French way of saying "table" but is named for the Indian drums that enact a "fascinating synchronicity of the Western and Indian music forms" (xii). Descriptively, Cardoz's vision of fusion bears the imprimatur of American music traditions; most notably in jazz. With its history of blending Indian musical elements into its compositions, jazz represents a unique blending of cultural tradition between Black America and India. As but one example, the African American jazz saxophonist John Coltrane represents a particularly expansive notion of fusion, one that fuses Indianness with the rich traditions of African American jazz. As the Kolkata-born jazz pianist Madhav Chari notes, "even though Coltrane did not use specific devices of Indian music, his own work was influenced by the 'spirit,' 'energy,' or 'essence' of Indian music. He was aware of the different tonal possibilities of Indian scales, and his awareness of the manner in which Indian classical musicians developed melodic ideas informed his own conception, especially in the development of his own improvisations, by extending and elaborating melodic motifs" (268). With its nominative nod to African American jazz and the legacy of Floyd Patterson, Cardoz's culinary offerings fall short of the mark of a truly integrative approach to fusion; at the end of the meal it remains that the only fusion that "counts" to enhance the palate is that which combines Indianness with whiteness. Blackness enters this culinary dance to characterize fusion, but not to transform its underlying logic.

While culinary rhetoric is by no means an index of changing racial norms, its nuances and articulations are suggestive of ways in which to conceive of difference. By juxtaposing culinary rhetoric with discourses about class and racial difference, the stakes of defining fusion cuisine along racialized lines come into focus. If Indian food is denigrated for its excess, it is startlingly evident that the real contribution of fusion for those who are invested in articulating its shape and meanings is in allowing Indian flavors to enter the realm of sophistication and quiet dignity—descriptive categories most typically reserved for whiteness. For Indian food to acquire cultural capital, it must be fused; moreover, it cannot be fused with Blackness except at a nominative level. To add Blackness to Indianness is to merely add another level of excess to Indian food. To rid Indian food of its excessiveness—its spiciness, its oiliness, and its pungency—it must go through a process of what Koichi Iwabuchi describes as cultural deodorization. For Iwabuchi, "the cultural odor of a product is also closely associated with racial and bodily images of a country of origin" (28). In disarticulating culinary signifiers from the overtly foreign and therefore negative connotations of otherness, fusion cuisine domesticates foreignness, rendering a culturally deodorized end product. In making an entry into America, those ingredients associated with immigrants are cleaned up and deodorized so that only the very best and least offensive from India is transported to American contexts.

To read the emergence of fusion cuisine, particularly fusion cuisine with Indian American chefs at the helm, as a sign of racial acceptance is to thus implicitly endorse the view that consuming Indian-accented food is a catalyst to improving race relations. In essence, fusion cuisine is a culturally odorless form of Indianness that allows goat cheese tikkis, apple samosas, and kachumber coolers to acquire a level of culinary chic at the same time that actual brown bodies are rendered so incredibly suspect because they are seen to embody the type of excess incompatible with what America deems acceptable. Moreover, the extended mediations on food in Jallepalli's, Cardoz's, and Lakshmi's cookbooks do not teach readers how to cook with culinary unmentionables such as dog, or gizzards, or culinary "oddities" such as yogurt and rice. They deal exclusively with wholesome ingredients, strictly adhering to the realm of what is palatable.

As I've argued elsewhere, Asian American legal scholar and cultural critic Frank Wu comes at this question by elaborating on what diversity entails.[7] For Wu, contemporary attitudes toward diversity in the United States are overly simple. He notes, we "only taste diversity" (216), suggesting that it is quite possible to imagine sampling a range of Asian food items including such staples as samosas, fried rice, or even the more "exotic" green tea ice cream at any of the many ethnic festivals organized in towns or cities across the United States, but asks why it is impossible to imagine a food vendor offering up a bowl of dog stew (216). The taboo against dog eating is one site where our principles concerning diversity conflict with the actual practices of tolerating diversity and tastes for what the mainstream might consider intolerable, unethical, unpalatable, and inedible. Wu argues: "our festivals of diversity tend toward the superficial, as if America were a stomach-turning combination plate of grits, tacos, sushi, and hummus. We fail to consider the dilemma of diversity where our principles conflicts with our practices" (216). In any vision of fusion, there is always something that is left out of the equation. But that ingredient that is "left out" cannot merely be ignored. By using the example of dog eating, Wu recasts the terms by which we might understand fusion, including the unpalatable in his frames of reference.

Fusion As an Ethos of Survival

Despite fusion cuisine's currency within the food and beverage industry, the notion of fusion cuisine has been slow to impact the construction of culinary identities within the corpus of South Asian diasporic literature and culture. Even within the larger corpus of Asian American literature, evocations of fusion cuisine are few and far between, even as the trope of fusion carries a particular literary and cultural cachet.[6] The notable and significant exception to this is a novel by Amulya Malladi, a Denmark-based author of Indian origin. Her novel *Serving Crazy with Curry,* though not a literary forerunner among the vast corpus of South Asian diasporic writings, is unique in its evocation of fusion to signify survival in its most basic sense rather than as cosmopolitan chic. Published in 2004, *Serving Crazy with Curry* cautions against the idea that one might necessarily cook one's way into a better future by eliminating all the excess of immigrant taste. This second novel by Amulya Malladi chronicles a tale about Devi, a young Indian American. A self-defined failure, Devi turns to the kitchen as a site of healing after a thwarted attempt at suicide. When Devi unwittingly survives her attempted suicide, she loses her voice. Unable to speak about what motivated her to attempt suicide, she turns to cooking as a source of comfort. Devi, part of the generation of the children of 1965, does not view life as an Indian American through the lens of aggrievement. To be sure, her life bears the traces of the upwardly mobile and assimilated, and is carefully calibrated to diminish the effect and appearance of immigrant excess. But her "failures" seem to emanate from the private, a realm modulated by civic and social excessiveness that threatens to undo the carefully woven life she has established. She can attain success in the workplace, but translating that success into the private realm is less effective. Unable to find a partner, she finds comfort in the arms of a secret lover. From here, the novel unfolds rather predictably. Since Devi's secret lover turns out to be none other than Girish, her sister's husband, it stands to reason that she becomes pregnant. Rather than allow her sister and family to be irreparably damaged by this most intimate of betrayals, Devi opts to terminate her pregnancy. Unable to live with the knowledge and trauma of her transgression, Devi attempts suicide but is derailed when her inquisitive mother visits her unannounced, only to find her youngest daughter limp and lifeless in a bathtub soaked with the blood of Devi's slashed wrists. With her sense of failure doubled (not only did she "fail" at life but also at death), Devi's trauma is heightened to the point that she is rendered speechless. Certainly the trope of silence here bears further scrutiny; so unspeakable is Devi's crime that language fails her; so deep is her sense of failure that she has no words to describe them; and so entrenched in her belief system is the sense that she has committed the unforgivable that she has no capacity to talk about her future. Amid this prevailing mood of abject trauma, the only space of comfort and solace is food. Yet, curiously, Devi has never enjoyed an uncomplicated relationship with food. Within her domestic space, food has always been her mother's forte; in the kitchen "Saroj ruled supreme and no one could bake or anything else there" (70). As an observer of her mother's cooking, Devi's sense of food is governed by her mother's taste. So deep is Saroj's influence that when Devi finally begins to crave food, her mother insists on the tried-and-true recipes. When Saroj arrives at Devi's bedside, armed with samosas and pudhina chutney, Devi thinks, "did her mother really think that she was interested in chutney at this point in her life? And of all the things to cook when your suicidal daughter comes home—the same old mint chutney? Nothing new, nothing different? Nothing to say, *The world has changed. The food in our house definitely has. You can live now?*" (61, emphasis in original). Surviving attempted suicide for Devi means moving beyond the everyday food of her mother's kitchen. Devi observes, "she wanted to eat something else, make something new, start fresh" (71). To make it new becomes Devi's raison d'être. To think of the future demands a reworking of her past. To live means she must find a way to transform the old ingredients into new recipes. To not continue feeling like a problem, she needs to find a new way of being. To live in harmony with her surroundings she must manage the sense of excess in her life.

Perhaps the strategy she employs—trading in old ingredients for new ones in order to create new recipes—might be viewed as simplistic. Certainly there is something overly romantic about the idea of reinventing one's self through new recipes, but cooking takes on a life-affirming quality in this novel that exceeds a simple jettisoning of the old for the new. Oftentimes, a form of assimilation in which South Asian tastes are rendered palatable and domesticated to the Western palate are privileged within narratives of fusion; less common are narratives which imagine the transaction altering South Asian palatal preferences. More often than not the best-selling fusion cuisine cookbooks in the United States allow for a combination of white and Asian, but implicitly disallow fusion between other "colors" or races. The difficulty of imagining Black-Asian fusion cuisine in the cookbook market suggests that in many cases, fusion is acceptable only when it incorporates cultural markers of whiteness.[8] While numerous forms of Chino-Latino fusion restaurants (Chinese-Cuban, Chinese–Puerto Rican) owned by Caribbean immigrants of Chinese origins can be found in New York City, in addition to the Indo-Pak-Bangla combinations Kothari mentions in her autobiographical essay, few of these are considered upscale restaurants serving "cuisine," and most do not command the same prices as "recognizable" fusion restaurants such as Ming Tsai's Blue Ginger, and Floyd Caidoz's Tabla. Chino-Latino and Indo-Pak-Bangla "fusion" restaurants and eateries are generally owned and operated by working-class immigrants who challenge the stereotype of the upwardly mobile model minority. These establishments are thus viewed as serving cheap fast food and not cuisine per se.[8] Food writers such as Diana Kennedy label such versions of everyday fusion—Mexican pizza, fruit-flavored margaritas, and Montezuma croissants—as "'odd, eclectic and ineffective' examples of culinary experimentation gone awry," thereby echoing the sentiment that fusion cuisine is a classed cuisine (qtd. in Gabaccia 216). Culinarily, this rhetorical strategy highlights the difficulty in imagining fusion between Black and Indian, Chinese and Cuban, Chinese and Indian. Lisa Heldke suggests that when the United States is not "Culinary Central," a cognitive dissonance emerges; indeed, when whiteness is not present to mediate "blackness" or "brownness," a culinary dissonance emerges.

Devi's culinary repertoire reimagines fusion, not as a transaction between groups of color, but as a strategy that would "reverse" the direction of fusion. Instead of making Asian tastes fuse into Western cuisines, her cuisine fuses "Western" ingredients into "Indian" dishes. Rather than supreme of pheasant with basmati-truffle risotto or tea-smoked quail with hyderabadi biryani, Devi's more everyday fusion produces dishes like grilled chicken in blueberry sauce, Cajun prawn biryani, and ginger and apricot chutney, dishes that are not unlike the pizza paranthas, vada pav, paneer dosas, and other fusion foods gaining in popularity in Bombay, India (Sinha 47). For Devi, fusion is about positioning Indian food as a canvas upon which to paint other flavors and tastes. The hues and texture of her culinary palate do not emerge solely from the reds of chili powder, the yellows of turmeric, and the green of chilies; rather, she paints a picture of Indian Americanness that also draws from the orange hue of apricots and the blueness of the eponymously named berry. With a more expansive definition of Indian food, Devi can become an Indian diasporic subject on her terms, rather than feeling like a canvas upon whom the colors and tastes of Indian spices alone leave their traces. But more than a simple aesthetic reversal, Devi's quest to cook otherwise is also about coming to terms with the kind of excess that has been so closely managed within her life as an Indian American. Becoming pregnant with her brother-in-law's child, a paradigmatic instance of excess, produces a feeling of lack in Devi. To establish equilibrium, her approach to cooking indulges the desire to be excessive. Malladi conveys this sense of excess in her depictions of Devi's emotions in the kitchen: "unexplained anger bubbled through Devi as she let her hands fly over spices and vegetables while Saroj watched, in wide-eyed horror, as her fridge and spice cabinet went from neat and tidy to something completely the opposite . . . Soon enough Saroj found herself completely kicked out of her kitchen as Devi cooked outrageous meals every day" (77).

Devi's work in the kitchen militates against the benign repetition she associates with the suffocating stagnancy enforced upon the children of 1965. In lieu of being allowed to chart a path of her own, Devi faults the blandness of the model minority ideal for providing her with limited options as to how to live. With the Indian homeland looming large, Devi is subject to the kinds of social censure of diasporic communities. As a diasporic individual, she is already positioned as a poor imitation of an originary Indianness, a failed translation. This perceived sense of lack prevents Devi from translating herself into a psychically complete subject. She works against the sense of loss that accompanies being a failed translation, charting a new path where excess becomes the solution for a life plagued by feeling inadequate. An excess of flavors is brought into her kitchen, metaphorizing her own need for free-spirited excess by which to live. Her old recipes for living produced a staid predictability, yielding a measured sense of blandness, without variety, diversity, or difference. Devi's cooking comes to challenge the ways in which difference is managed to produce palpably monochromatic results. Her understanding of fusion as a mode of survival is not about reducing excess but about celebrating all the ways in which excess can be generative and exciting and vital to survival. For Devi, fusion is about negotiating those flavors which cause unruly immigrant bodies to be viewed with suspicion as a mode of challenging the notion that nondomesticated difference is excessive, aberrant, and unpalatable.

If Padma Lakshmi's, Raji Jallepalli's, and Floyd Cardoz's versions of fusion are about providing solutions to managing immigrant excess, Devi's version of fusion is about insisting on that excess. Put another way, this rhetorical strategy harkens to the legal and ethical construction of the South Asian American subject in the wake of multiculturalism's interest in "difference." In 2000, Vijay Prashad succinctly addressed the place of South Asian Americans in the political-cultural terrain of the United States, posing the question, "How does it feel to be viewed as a solution?"; just two years later, in 2002, in Moustafa Bayoumi's words, we were asking South Asian and Muslim Americans, "How does it feel to be a problem?" Consider how the rhetoric of fusion cuisine becomes the palimpsest upon which narratives of race, assimilation, and otherness are inscribed. What is problematic about South Asian Americans post– 9/11 is their excessive and eccentric location. What is problematic about South Asian food are its extremities and excesses. The culinary, as a conduit into the political, becomes the space from which to imagine and reimagine, buttress and undermine anxieties about racial admixtures. Malladi's novel stages a literary response to the question of feeling like a problem albeit within the realm of the domestic and private space of the home. In the smallest of measures, Malladi's novel exhorts us to examine the failures of multiculturalism and the dangers of considering the culinary as a corrective to the burdens of feeling like the aberrant subject who muddies the meaning of Americanness. If the brownness produced by South Asian Americans that sullies the face of America is only deemed excessive, dangerous, and unruly, the clamor and vitality of the dissonance that emerges from multiplicity is muted. It is this quiet and sanitized version of difference that Malladi's novel asks us to throw into question; it is this form of culturally deodorized difference that Malladi's novel seeks to put into crisis; and finally, it is this version of assimilatory fusion that so carefully scripts the terms under which difference is managed that Malladi's novel militates against, thus producing a poetics of culinary difference that allows us to imagine food as more than a mere portal onto the terrain of multiculturalism.

Conclusion: Room for More: Multiculturalism's Culinary Legacies

The end of an Indian meal, whether consumed in public spaces such as restaurants and small eateries or in private spaces such as the home, is often marked by the consumption of a savory snack designed to promote digestion. Paan, a mixture of betel nut, lime paste, and spices wrapped in a betel leaf, has captured the fancy of travelers and writers alike, inspiring the works of E. M. Forster and Sara Suleri as well as filmmaker Nisha Ganatra, to name a few. In an autobiographical essay titled "Pan," E. M. Forster describes his pleasure and revulsion at consuming paan, describing the taste as akin to feeling one's tongue "stabbed by a hot and angry orange in alliance with pepper" (310). One might conceivably argue that the best kind of social justice within the culinary experience should be about promoting a kind of anger produced through the alliance of rival tastes. Nisha Ganatra's *Chutney Popcorn*, a film about Reena, a queer South Asian American who decides to serve as a surrogate mother for her infertile sister, Sarita, grants a small but significant role to this most poetic of after-dinner edibles. Two moments in particular shore up the notion that the culinary can also be a site of engaged discussion. When Sarita and her mother, Meenu, discuss Sarita's plans to become pregnant, and later when Sarita and Reena discuss Sarita's infertility and her desire to have a child, they do so in the vicinity of an outdoor paan stand in Jackson Heights, an Indian commercial district in Queens, New York. In a fascinating example of how different types of classed immigrant existence converge, these significant discussions about Sarita's inability to reproduce take place within earshot of an Indian paanwalla (seller of betel leaf) who is never directly spoken to during the scene. The scene opens with a shot of Indian storefronts spanning the length of Jackson Heights' crowded streets; accompanying this scene are the sounds of Indian music. The next shot, displaying paan leaves immersed in a bowl of water, cuts to a shot of an Indian man spreading lime paste, areca nut, and other fixings on a betel leaf. As he folds the paan leaf and places it in his mouth, the camera zooms out, revealing the Indian paanwalla's face, the paan stand, and the approaching women. Meenu orders two paan and, in a gesture of paradigmatic heteronormativity, proceeds to offer motherly advice to her daughter about how to become pregnant. It is significant that the two women are completely oblivious to the paanwalla's apparent fascination with their publicly discussed private affairs concerning how Chinese herbal remedies can help Sarita become pregnant. To them, he is an invisible laborer who merely serves them what they wish to eat. Also apparent here is the notion that heterosexual reproduction is the norm. Maintaining its structures and efficacy do not have to be relegated to the private realm in this particular scenario.

But lest we ascribe a kind of heteronormative transparency to the space of this Jackson Heights vendor, the next encounter with the paanwalla upsets the balance between heteronormativity and the ethnic enclave. The scene begins with a close-up shot of the paanwalla preparing paan. But unlike the previous scene, this scene is angled from the paanwalla's vantage point; we do not see him, but we see what he sees—Reena and Sarita conversing. When Sarita dejectedly says, "maybe I wasn't meant to have a baby," she looks at Reena, who appears confused by the dilemmas of her decidedly more conservative sister. Reena, in a gesture of helplessness, turns to look at the paanwalla. As the scene cuts to the next shot, now focused on the paanwalla's face, he is seen shrugging his shoulders in response to Reena's look. He is less upset in this scene than in the preceding one and becomes an interlocutor in this exchange. He may have no response to Reena's dilemma, but he also does not process the information in a way that renders him as a subject vigilant about the affirmation of heteronormative reproduction. That such a seemingly queer moment occurs within earshot of the paanwalla is not insignificant. As I suggested in my reading of "Out on Main Street," the ethnic enclave is often circumscribed by an implicit logic of heterocentrism. It falls to cultural production to imagine such spaces as enabling of queer desire. Anupama Arora's reading of *Chutney Popcorn* signals how the film maps

queer diasporic space, reclaiming spaces associated with heteronormativity with a kind of South Asian diasporic queerness:

> the ethnic space of Jackson Heights in Queens, a largely desi neigh-
> bourhood in New York City, too accrues different meanings as
> lesbian bodies walk its streets and frequent its grocery stores and
> restaurants. This gesture confronts subtly the deliberate political
> invisibility of queer diasporic populations within the ethnic com-
> munity. In one instance, shopping with her mother in an Indian
> grocery store, Reena stuffs a rice-sack into her T-shirt to theatrical-
> ize, perhaps even ironize her imminent pregnancy—as lesbian and
> surrogate. Of course, she is severely reprimanded by Meenu, "You
> should not even think about a child till you have a husband." Thus
> disciplined by Meenu's enforcement of the heterosexual, while Re-
> ena obediently brings the sack of rice to her mother, her playfulness
> has inserted into heteronormative registers and the unspeakable
> has crept into the Indian grocery store, a traditionally heteronor-
> mative environment. (37)

The unspeakable in the grocery store is the queer subject producing a
child outside of the strictures of a regulated heterosexuality. Meenu's
admonishment of Reena's queerness thus contrasts with the paanwalla's
indifference. A mere shrug of the shoulder, while not necessarily a sign of
diffidence, is a gesture that accommodates the possibility of queer desire
and other modes of being and becoming that might be mandated by the
strictures of heteronormative nationalism, of which Meenu is an apparent embodiment. At this site, then, the paanwalla becomes the agent of a
nascent social justice. His labor emerges at the intersection of digestion
and social justice. And what is unspeakable in the grocery store is speak-
able in his vicinity. I do not mean to suggest he is a harbinger of radical
politics but rather that, through his labor producing an edible designed
to promote digestion, he inhabits a subjectivity that can imagine other
possibilities. He becomes part of the site at which queerness is possible;
Jackson Heights becomes the space that allows queerness to emerge
through rituals of everyday life, just as the intimate spaces of the Indian
community in Toronto allow Shani Mootoo's characters to articulate a
queer desire through food.

I allude to paan because it provides a script to think about the intellectual work food can do and to underscore the importance of digesting
ideas, paving the way for what necessarily comes next. The kernel of indi-

gestibility, what might be considered elsewhere as the unpalatable or the abject, becomes the site where the culinary and social justice converge to proffer alternative narratives and possibilities for the work of food studies. In examining the valence of fusion cuisine, an approach that has been much derided because of its seeming shallow take on multiculturalism, we lose a lot in terms of understanding the nuance of racism against unruly immigrant bodies and their cuisines if we don't further scrutinize the stakes of managing excess in order to produce palatability.

To complete the earlier discussion of E. M. Forster's description of how paan is made, it bears mentioning that he also includes a tale about how paan is not always what it might seem. Expanding on the varieties of paan, he notes, "there is Comic Pan which contains salt. It is given to buffoons. Oh how they splutter, sometimes being positively sick! Not even a pun is such fun. And, to end, all, there is Tragic Pan, which contains ground glass, and is given to enemies" (314). In *Meatless Days*, Sara Suleri tells a similar tale about fake paan, "an adult delicacy of betel leaf and nut [which] can be quite convincingly replicated by a mango leaf stuffed with stones" (24). The meanings of fake, tragic, and comic paan converge to symbolically militate against the notion that the meanings of food are singlefold. That this narrative emerges at the end of one so intent on confounding categories of belonging is more than fitting. Analogously, these paan variants and their inner complexities provide a fitting parable for the intellectual labor of food studies. In lieu of promoting a kind of transparency to the meanings of food, the real strength of the field rises from calling for the kind of digestive health that brings a satisfying close to a meal. Meditations on food must go beyond the surface to negotiate the thorny terrain within. Novels like *Pastries*, *Mistress of Spices*, and *Serving Crazy with Curry* too easily get lost amid a sea of exotic detritus if we are not able to delve into the details within to unearth the vision of social justice lodged in each novel. Indeed, many of the culinary narratives, from *Reef* to *Cereus Blooms at Night* and "If You Are What You Eat, Then What Am I" to "The Makers of Chili Paste" and *Mirch Masala* disallow the possibility of feeling unmitigated comfort when negotiating the complex culinary scapes of each cultural work. To work through the complexities of each, food must be cast in a different light; not simply an easily digestible comestible, not simply an item on a menu, food in these works demands a rigorous interrogation of the meanings that can be accrued to food. For in those stones, glass, or salt that complicate easy digestion might be the kernels of a kind of culinary ethos that does not satisfy itself merely by jettisoning the unpalatable, and the objectionable.

Kitchen Poetics

Forget the room of one's own—write in the kitchen.—GLORIA ANZALDÚA, *THIS BRIDGE CALLED MY BACK*

For Paule Marshall, the acclaimed Barbadian American poet and writer, the cultural work of writing begins in the kitchen. Her homage to the women in her family and community of Barbadians lovingly rendered as "poets in the kitchen" speaks to the possibilities for intellectual discourse to emerge within the kitchen space. Marshall cherishes the kitchen poets for "the rich legacy of language and culture they so freely passed on . . . in the wordshop of the kitchen" (12). Thus, the culinary space becomes energized as a site for cultural, racial, and intellectual formation. In rendering the kitchen as a conduit for social interaction, Marshall gives voice to the vital interplay between the sociocultural and the aesthetic as it takes root within the worlds of women of color. A room of one's own à la Virginia Woolf became the conduit for women's writing in the early twentieth century. But for women of color and immigrant women, the kitchen, a largely gendered site, becomes a space of cultural work and cultural production that demands a very real engagement with the dynamics of gender and race. For Anzaldúa, a room of one's own is a luxury not available to all. Intimate spaces of female sociality are also spaces in which a writer can take refuge. The same might be said about Asian American or South Asian diasporic cultural work; to follow a thread developed by Wenying Xu, the culinary as an enunciative site is not governed by a logic to extend the terms of exoticism. The culinary in Asian American literature, as she puts it, works "as a dominant site of economic, cultural, and political struggle, not as a site to produce self-exoticism or food pornography" (*Eating Identities* 14). For Marshall, thinking about writing begins in the kitchen and with the kitchen poets; infused in the patterns of their speech and conversations are the rich flavors of the kind of Caribbean Blackness that would not be legible in other, less domestic spaces. And yet to bring a kind of critical Blackness to the table without reducing Caribbean Blackness to a kind of literary mélange of tropical fruits and pungent spices is also at the center of Marshall's ethical project.

Thinking about race, gender, and ethnicity begins with food, but thinking about food also ends with race, gender, and ethnicity. Beyond this deceptively simple chiasmus lies a structure of aesthetic affect that refuses the simple dichotomies and meanings that have been ascribed to the work of making food and the work food studies can do. And while the epistemology of this kind of cultural work may begin with the kitchen, the meanings ascribed to the kitchen go beyond the literal to name a wider field of signification encompassing multiple realms associated with the culinary. If I have insisted on using the term "culinary," it is to recognize the vital importance of the physical space of the kitchen and the space of consumption and production but also to be very deliberate about positioning the culinary as a site of critical and cultural analysis in lieu of emphasizing food as the primary object d'analysis. While the specific output of a kitchen may be ephemeral, designed for consumption and not for posterity like other cultural products, the work that begins in the kitchen—creative, social, political—resonates far beyond the kitchen table, making itself and its echoes heard and negotiated on other terrain and other sites of analysis. In *A Love Supreme* and *Harold and Kumar*, samosas and hamburgers, respectively, drive the narrative forward, but the meanings accrued to each extend far beyond samosas and burgers; without food, there is no narrative intrigue. But it is only when the food in question is read through the vectors of class and race that the central drama of the narrative becomes legible.

The work of food and the work of food studies within a literary context, if it is to maintain its commitment to transforming the paradigm of food studies, is also about enabling a kind of dynamic collaboration between the political and the cultural. For far too long, food studies has been critiqued as "scholarship lite," producing an understandable but frustrating repudiation of these charges among those of us who work on food. With the possibility of thinking of the culinary as a site of aesthetic and political cultural work must come an acknowledgment of how far the field of food studies has come while paradoxically maintaining its somewhat bewildering status as an interloper in the "real" work of literary studies.

The cultural and political work accomplished by the texts I have surveyed in this book is not unlike the work of other literary and cultural traditions in which the culinary is a governing aesthetic. The "culinary" scripts and undermines particular strategies for thinking about race and ethnicity in the travels of South Asian diasporic literature and culture, unearthing the extent to which questions about food, power, race, gender, and ethnicity animate some of the most vibrant discussions in ethnic American literary studies. But that is also not to say that the work of analyzing the culinary within a specific set of ethno-national parameters can automatically generate questions about, or illuminate the nature of, food and the culinary in other literary traditions as if African American, Asian American, Latino/a were interchangeable; rather, it is to acknowledge the far-reaching consequences of inscribing the culinary into the literary aesthetics of ethnic studies and American studies; to paraphrase the title of a special issue I edited for the *Massachusetts Review* in 2004, food matters, and the implications of placing the culinary as a site of critical interrogation must also go beyond the literary. Historian Vicki Ruiz puts it best in her thoughtful conceptualization of "Citizen Restaurant," a term which "encapsulates racial/ethnic foodscapes as markers of belonging and difference set within a larger frame of U.S. inequality" (3). She concludes her article with a powerful charge for practitioners of food studies and ethnic studies: "we enter Citizen Restaurant not to dine on diversity but to dish up social justice" (18). Dining might be an entry point onto a larger field of signification but should never the end point of a socially engaged food studies. To privilege the ending is to ignore some of the most complicated questions that guide the interior landscapes while negotiating the imbricate meanings of the culinary. For Rachel DuPlessis, "writing beyond the ending means the transgressive invention of narrative strategies that express critical dissent from dominant narrative" (5). I allude to her work here once again to suggest rather simply that food studies must always move beyond the ending to engage issues of social justice. A question that remains is whether it is possible for this engagement of social justice to emerge within a type of writing that has so often been castigated as apolitical and kitschy—an embarrassment alongside the more overtly politicized renderings of difference one finds in the archive of South Asian American transnational cultural production.

Final Course

In this book I have attempted to undertake a kind of intellectual mapping of the culinary, one that necessarily locates the objects and subjects of inquiry—food in South Asian diasporic cultural production in the United States, Canada, and the United Kingdom—at the nexus of Asian American, New American, ethnic, cultural food, and postcolonial studies. Certainly, *Culinary Fictions* crosses genres and time periods through the South Asian diaspora, not simply to consider the provenance of Asian America to be so global and wide-reaching but to more fully attend to the dynamic and changing nature of what constitutes South Asian diasporic culinary fictions. That much of what I consider in this book has grown out of debates and concerns in Asian American studies is in large part a consequence of the nature of U.S. multiculturalism's fetishizing of the culinary as mode of engaging difference. Narratives about culinary practices become enfolded into a kind of multiculturalism that accords a special status to the purported power of food to effect radical social and political change merely by its presence on the cognitive maps of the communities where South Asian transnational subjects make homes, however tentative these might be. Food is part of what makes populations celebrate multiculturalism. For through multiculturalism, populations of color transform the landscape of their communities with the positive addition of "exotic" flavors and palatable difference. In Australia as in the United States, multiculturalism is burdened with the task of making communities of South Asian diasporic subjects palatable to the mainstream. In an article about the state of multiculturalism in Australia tellingly titled "Food's Great, But . . . Evolving Attitudes to Multicultural Australia," Carol Bailey presents the narratives of individual Australians who are both intolerant of, and ambivalent to, Asian immigrants. Encapsulated in the title to her article is the notion that Asian and ethnic foods might be tolerable, even desirable, but the actual bodies that come with those cuisines are not. This tolerance for food, what Stanley Fish dubs,"boutique multiculturalism . . . the multiculturalism of ethnic restaurants" (378), remains vigilant about maintaining the borders of the nation-state such that a mere love for culinary matters does not translate into an acceptance of othered bodies. At stake here is the idea that multiculturalism is about a kind of affective fulfillment in which the varied bodies that make up the nation-state are expected to engage in a kind of happiness. But the culinary is acceptable only when it performs the work of affective fulfillment within multiculturalism to produce a kind of palatable rendering of difference, one in which the excesses of difference are carefully excised to produce a sanitized narrative, enabling rather than disruptive of forms of consumption.

The turn in cultural studies to examining affect in terms of happiness, in addition to trauma, provides an intellectual map to guide this book toward a conclusion. For so many, food is about affective nourishment— it sustains the body, and it allows for a kind of communion and sharing of the spirit that can be affectively cathartic. But multiculturalism can also be about satisfying a kind of hunger to consume the other while being able to keep the multicultural body itself at a safe distance. In both instances, happiness means radically different things. Quite unlike the case of multiculturalism in Australia or the United States, multiculturalism in the British context, as Sara Ahmed suggests, is seen to be a failure unless it can produce a kind of happiness. Immigrants and communities of color who "add" diversity are expected to perform happiness just as the wider communities are expected to be happy about the arrival and presence of communities of color. As she puts it, "multiculturalism is attributed a positive value through the alignment of a story of individual happiness with the social good" (123). Just as multicultural cultural production must convey a kind of happiness in its rendering of difference, so too must the consumer of multicultural work feel happy when engaged in the act of consumption. Put another way, happiness is palatable and expected, whereas melancholia and unhappiness are excessive modes of affect. When one thinks about food, there is an expectation of happiness—food brings people together; food allows people to "experience" other cultures. The practice of "multiculturalist eating" is affectively fulfilling because it satisfies one's craving for otherness while keeping all that is uncomfortable at bay. Thus when multiculturalism takes a turn for the unhappy, articulating the abject or the melancholic, it becomes uncomfortable and is aggressively policed for its articulation of the excessive. Certainly this palatability and promise of a future happiness is exactly what makes critics shudder at the mere mention of novels like *Mistress of Spices*, while others might praise it as a portrait of happy multiculturalism. This promise of a future happiness is also why films like *Harold and Kumar Go to White Castle* are almost universally cherished, whereas the subtext about immigration goes ignored, or, at the very least, undertheorized. In considering the archive of multiculturalist writing about food in a South Asian transnational frame, one necessarily pushes out from the popular to consider where and when the culinary emerges. As such, the intellectual mapping of theorizing food demands a radical reconfiguration of the culinary archive as well the cultural artifacts which might enter into a productive conversation about South Asian diasporic fictions.

I began this book thinking about what was at stake in centering the culinary in diasporic narratives about South Asianness. If there are larger aesthetic and structural threads which braid together the works collectively theorized in this book, it is the discomfort we find lodged within the often palatable narrative that aestheticizes the conditions of migration and diasporic life to the point where differences are flattened. It is also the difficulty in imagining how food can contain anything other than what Ahmed names "happy effects" which has made it so difficult to grant narratives about food a place at the table of radical Asian American inquiry. But as it becomes apparent that ever more examples of South Asian diasporic culinary fictions populate bookstores, it becomes necessary to remain vigilant about how we theorize food.

As popular and critically acclaimed works enter into circuits of cultural discourse, it becomes all that more important to continue to develop our analyses of diaspora, transnationalisms, and South Asian culinary fictions. As such, the way to move forward is to consider the culinary not as an end point that flattens histories of trauma and suffering to render abjection palatable. The way forward involves considering the texture and unevenness of the culinary terrain and remaining vigilant about negotiating the contradictory tastes and aftertastes which emerge from the culinary fictions of the South Asian diaspora. So let us continue to wine and dine, but let's do so in a way that obligates us to keep our critical faculties at the table.

Notes

Introduction

Part of this chapter originally appeared in the *Massachusetts Review* 45.3 (Autumn 2004): 209–15.

1. These terms are also rendered malleable in different strains of cultural criticism. Robyn Morris notes how cultural critic Tseen Khoo "reclaims the term" "banana" in *Banana Bending*, a study of Asian Australian and Asian Canadian fiction. Similarly, the Asian Canadian poet Hiromi Goto reworks the metaphor of the banana in her poem "The Body Politic" (Morris 500).

2. As Lizzie Collingham notes, Noon arrived in Britain in 1970 and worked primarily with the Indian community in Southall. Some twenty years later, his empire extended into British grocery stores as he moved into the business of producing frozen ready-to-eat meals. Such was his success that by 2004 he was among the forty richest Asians in Britain (239).

3. See Elizabeth Buettner (2008) and Ben Highmore (2008, 2009) for rich historical accounts of the emergence of Indian restaurants in twentieth-century Britain.

4. In a subsequent issue of the journal, letters to the editor continued the dialogue initiated by Leonardi's article. The responses to Leonardi's essay included articles that were equally divided between those who welcome opening the doors of literary inquiry to analyses of cookbooks and culinary-themed novels and those skeptical of the implications of this form of canon expansion.

5. Alongside Sau-Ling Wong's study, we can now add Jennifer Ann Ho's *Consumption and Identity in Asian American Coming-of-Age Novels* (2005) and Wenying Xu's *Eating Identities: Reading Food in Asian American Literature* (2007).

6. In her reading of this moment in Mukherjee's narrative, Sumita Lall critiques Jasmine's culinary forays into Elsa County: "[She] runs the risk of replicating the very forms of cross-cultural contact that Mukherjee critiques . . . Why is it that Mukherjee is willing to exalt the virtues of Indian cooking as a cultural symbol of the immi-

grant's old traditions but advocates that immigrants must become American and shed their cultural hyphenations as individuals? . . . food provides a much safer ground of crossing cultural boundaries because it is a marketable commodity that can easily be appropriated by mainstream culture" (50).

7. Opal Mehta, the protagonist of Viswanathan's novel, painstakingly articulates her love for Indian food as a means of chronicling her affinity for her Indian Americanness (130–31); similarly, Dimple Lala, the protagonist of *Born Confused*, frequently questions the role of cooking in her burgeoning cultural identity as a second-generation Indian American.

8. The limited engagement with food in Asian American studies can be found in other contexts. For instance, Donna Gabaccia's otherwise astute analysis of food in ethnic America fails to devote any real attention to Asian America. In particular, the labor of Asian Americans in agriculture and the food service industry is virtually invisible. In addition, Barbara Haber outlines how women's history in the United States can be mapped onto significant moments in U.S. history. Asians Americans, however, are wholly absent from her analysis. A chapter titled "Cooking behind Barbed Wire: POWs during World War II" considers Americans held prisoner by Japanese-occupied Philippines, but it does not consider Asian American foodways.

9. In *Black Hunger*, Doris Witt describes how her interest in African American culinary history was spurred by noticing the centrality of food within contemporary literature by black women writers. While works by Toni Morrison, Gloria Naylor, Alice Walker, Zora Neale Hurston, Ntozake Shange, Rita Dove, and others placed food in a pivotal role, any critical discussion of "black culinary practices were largely absent from African American literary studies" (9).

1 / Culinary Nostalgia: Authenticity, Nationalism, and Diaspora

This chapter first appeared in *MELUS: Journal of the Society for the Study of Multi-Ethnic Literature of the United States* 32.4 (Winter 2007): 11–31. It is reprinted by permission of the journal.

1. Jaffrey also reinscribes North Indian linguistic hegemony. "In India," she notes, "we call our Indian bread *roti*, and we call the *Western-type* loaf a *dubbul* (double) *roti*, probably because of the expansion caused by the yeast" (245) without explaining that *roti* is the Hindi term for "bread" and that Dravidian language (Tamil, Kannada, Telegu, and Malayalam) speakers may not refer to bread as *roti* or *dubbul roti*. Throughout the cookbook, Jaffrey uses English names for recipes; where the original language is provided, it is in Hindi (perhaps because the recipes are from Uttar Pradesh and Delhi, where Hindi predominates), implicitly creating the impression that Hindi is the language of all Indians.

2. See K. T. Achaya, "Bounty from the New World," in *Indian Food: A Historical Companion* (Delhi: Oxford University Press, 1994), 218–38; and Arjun Appadurai, "How to Make a National Cuisine: Cookbooks in Contemporary India," *Comparative Studies in Society and History* 30 (January 1988): 3–24.

3. Ingredients that seem to many to be inextricably part of an Indian diet are not always autochthonously Indian. Cashews, tomatoes, and chili peppers are not native to the Indian subcontinent, but are indispensable in many Indian dishes that were brought to India from South America via Portugal and Spain between the 1500s and

1800s as a result of colonial expansion into the "New World." Such rhizomatic links between Old World and New World colonies are also manifest at a lexicographic level. Words used to refer to food items in Indian languages can be etymologically linked with the languages of the colonized and colonizers in the "New World." Pineapple, known in Hindi, Kannada, and other South Asian languages as *ananas*, is derived from the Portuguese *ananas*; *tamatar*, the Hindi word for "tomato," comes from the Nahuatl *tomatl*; *caju*, or cashew, comes from the Tepic *acaju*; the South Indian *sapota* and North Indian *chiku* are derived from the Meso-American *chicosapote*, and *achar*, the subcontinental referent for pickles, bears a similarity to the Carib term for chile peppers (*axi* or *achi*) (S. Mazumdar 60). Many of Jaffrey's recipes call for ingredients such as chilies, cashews, pineapple, tomatoes—foodstuffs that entered Indian palates through the workings of colonial trade.

4. Although I am aware that separating Sara Suleri as author from Sara Suleri as subject might create a false dichotomy between author and subject, stylistic mechanisms at play in the text by which Suleri as author speaks about Suleri as a child render such distinctions necessary. To avoid confusion, and to distinguish between the construction of author/subject, I refer to the "author" as Suleri and the subject as "Sara."

2 / Feeding Desire: Food, Domesticity, and Challenges to Heteropatriarchy

This chapter originally appeared as "Feeding Desire: Challenging Domestic Heteropatriarchy in South Asian Cultural Production," in "Postcolonial Gay, Lesbian, Queer Writing," special issue, *Journal of Commonwealth and Postcolonial Studies* 10.1 (2003): 34–51.

1. Italicized sections refer to the subtitled Hindi sections of the dialogue.

2. An important precursor to *Indian Cooking* is Meenakshi Ammal's self-published *Cook and See* (1951), a translation of the Tamil *Samaithu Paar*. Since then the book has been translated into English, Hindi, Telugu, and Malayalam and remains one of the most popular guides to home management.

3. "Anglo-Indian" refers to individuals or communities that are biracial or multiracial and claim to be genealogically linked to both Europe and India.

4. The religious significance of the characters' names carries religious-based ideological weight. Within Hindu mythology, Radha and Sita are important female deities; Sita is best known as the self-sacrificing and loyal wife of Rama, and Radha is the devoted consort of the philandering Krishna. Bal Thackeray, the reactionary leader of the Shiv Sena, the Hindu fundamentalist party in Bombay that most vociferously opposed the public screening of *Fire* in Bombay theaters, going so far as to sanction the burning of theaters that screened the film, critiqued the film on the grounds that the names of revered Hindu goddesses were being "defiled."

5. A truncated version of the *Ramayana* enters into the film's narrative when Ashok attends a theatrical performance of the *Ramayana* that pivots around the goddess Sita's trial by fire and eventual expulsion from her royal community. The televised version of *Ramayana* also enters the film in important ways. When Mundu, the household domestic servant, is asked to look after Biji, he often substitutes bootleg pornographic videos procured from Jatin's business for the televised serial version of the *Ramayana*. When Mundu is asked why the mute Biji seems upset, and why he himself appears to be in a sweat, he explains that the *Ramayana*—particularly the scene where

the goddess Sita has been captured by Rama's nemesis, Ravana—is "very emotional," covering up the fact that Biji has been an unwitting—indeed unwilling—audience to the pornographic video to which Mundu masturbates. Later, when Mundu is caught masturbating, he is punished by the family and asked to watch episodes of the serialized version of *Ramayana* as a means of inculcating basic "family values" that he has overlooked by seeking self-gratification.

3 / Sugar and Spice: Sweetening the Taste of Alterity

A portion of this chapter originally appeared as "Culinary Fictions: Immigrant Foodways and Race in Indian American Literature," in *Asian American Studies after Critical Mass*, ed. Kent A. Ono, 36–70 (Malden, Mass.: Wiley-Blackwell, 2005).

1. As Patricia Chu has noted, more overtly political forms of writing are less visible on the Asian American literary landscape. To add to Chu's assessment, narratives about food occupy a similar position to the mother-daughter tale, or the tale of the displaced immigrant's nostalgia. But within critical studies, these narratives are often viewed with suspicion because they are an appealing form of writing that appear to be ethnically affirmative and "merely" cultural, absent of any "hard" political content in order to be "acceptable" to the mainstream.

2. In Chopra's version of pop ayurveda, it is possible to overcome feelings of aggravation by altering one's diet. Chopra advocates using spice mixtures called *churnas*, which are designed to restore harmony and balance. Yet, this search for harmony comes at a price. Chopra explains that such mixtures are complex and therefore "not duplicable at home." Those on the path to spiritual betterment are urged to procure these potent herb and spice mixtures through the Chopra Center for Well Being and its Web portal. Self-improvement within this phase of capitalist Orientalism dovetails with an economy of consumption. In order to find their way amid a world that has lost its bearings, suffering subjects are interpellated as consumers and are urged to spend their money to attain spiritual release.

3. Chitra Bannerjee's personal involvement as a founding member of the Bay Area South Asian women's group MAITRI can perhaps provide an additional point of entry into her treatment of domestic abuse as a structural problem. Literature provided by MAITRI understands domestic abuse as a problem that "cannot be solved by neglect, denial or wishful thinking."

4. The conditions under which their romance transpires in the novel are worth taking into consideration. Khushu-Lahiri and Rao argue, "in the novel the spices shake tectonic plates and cause an earthquake as a karmic punishment for racial hatred" (10). Against this backdrop, Raven and Tilo join forces to bring love back in to the world thus presenting the possibility that the spices enact a form of agency that wreaks havoc on the world when social justice fails to prevail.

5. Khushu-Lahiri and Rao suggest that Mayeda's version of *Mistress of Spices* is far less politically nuanced than the novel. For them, the novel is a complex text able to effect a critique of racism in the United States whereas the cinematic adaptation produces a superficial Indianness in order to capitalize on a narrow vision of multiculturalism (1).

4 / Visualizing Class Critique and Female Labor

1. The unleavened bread chapatti has a number of lexicographic variants. I use "chapatti" unless spelled otherwise in quoted text.

2. See the special issue of *Journal of Asian American Studies* 9.2 (2006), which focuses on the critical and ethical convergences between Asian American and Arab American studies.

3. Similarly, within certain circuits of pop-critical film analysis, food is sometimes used to represent the local "flavor" of a film that does not have any latent connection with food per se. For instance, the term "spaghetti western" references films made by Italian directors and financers; Juzo Itami's hit *Tampopo* was dubbed the first "noodle western"; and Ramesh Sippy's 1975 box-office smash from India, *Sholay*, has been named a "curry western."

4. *Belna, puckni,* and *tawa* translate from the Indo-Caribbean vernacular, respectively, as "rolling pin," "long hollow pipe," and "baking stone." http://library2.nalis. gov.tt/Default.aspx?PageContentID=367&tabid=204.

5. The Airport Authority of India instructs passengers not to carry pickle bottles in their carry-on luggage. This measure, which predates the summer 2006 panic about carry-on luggage, might be read as a preventative measure—one that recognizes how the potency of chilies used to ferment Indian pickles might also serve, creatively, as a weapon. Further, an episode at a U.S. airport in mid-June 2009 attests to the suspicious nature of Indian pickles. A woman travelling from the Columbus airport was held up at security while the contents of her luggage were verified by TSA. As the Associated Press reports, via the *Charleston (S.C.) Post and Courier*, the airport summoned "a bomb squad to detonate a suspicious item that turned out to be pickled mangoes [when] X-ray equipment used by federal security screeners in Columbus could not detect what was inside a sealed canister in luggage being inspected around 7 p.m. Tuesday."

6. Nilesh Patel likens his film to Scorsese's *Raging Bull,* a film that tracks the rise and subsequent demise of boxer Jake La Motta (played by Robert De Niro). Patel's film harkens to Scorsese's film in terms of the mise-en-scène of samosa making. Patel notes, "I have borrowed film techniques [from *Raging Bull*] and used them to show the skill and artistry of women which often goes unrecognized. Cooking here is like a martial art of ballet but with hands instead of feet" (*"A Love Supreme"*).

5 / Eating America: Culture, Race, and Food in the Social Imaginary of the Second Generation

A portion of this chapter originally appeared as "Culinary Fictions: Immigrant Foodways and Race in Indian American Literature," in *Asian American Studies after Critical Mass*, ed. Kent A. Ono, 36–70 (Malden, Mass.: Wiley-Blackwell, 2005).

1. http://travel.discovery.com/fansites/bourdain/about/about.html.

2. The genre of chick-lit has come under fire from feminists, but insights provided by Butler and Desai bring a poignant and compelling nuance to an analysis of the genre. Taking issue with the notion that chick lit is necessarily apolitical, they argue for a reading of the genre that "deploy[s] transnational feminist *critique* as a reading method that attends to and foregrounds issues of race, migration, and political economy" (5).

4. I use the term "white trash" guardedly to refer to the depiction of the characters as such. In the film's reversal of culinary adventuring, the locals who inhabit the wilds of New Jersey assume the role of the backwater locals and uneducated natives dominant in colonial and culinary-adventuring narratives. In this way, their "trashiness" does not disempower low-income rural whites as much as it implicitly critiques how local populations who inhabit rural spaces in the non-Western world are imagined as simple natives.

6 / Easy Exoticism: Culinary Performances of Indianness

Parts of this chapter originally appeared in "Excessively Indian? Navigating the Flavors and Contours of Fusion Cuisine," *Subcontinental: The Journal of South Asian American Public Affairs* 3.1 (Spring–Summer 2007): 13–23. Additional parts of this chapter originally appeared in "Model Minorities Can Cook: Fusion Cuisine in Asian America," in *East Main Street: Asian American Popular Culture*, eds. Shilpa Davé, Leilani Nishime, and Tasha Oren (New York: New York University Press, 2005) and in "Food Matters: An Introduction," *Massachusetts Review* 45.3 (Autumn 2004): 209–15.

1. Justice Sutherland, delivering the opinion of the Court, offers the following reasoning: "What we now hold is that the words 'free white persons' are words of common speech, to be interpreted in accordance with the understanding of the common man, synonymous with the word 'Caucasian' only as that word is popularly understood. As so understood and used, whatever may be the speculations of the ethnologist, it does not include the body of people to whom the appellee belongs. It is a matter of familiar observation and knowledge that the physical group characteristics of the Hindus render them readily distinguishable from the various groups of persons in this country commonly recognized as white. The children of English, French, German, Italian, Scandinavian, and other European parentage, quickly merge into the mass of our population and lose the distinctive hallmarks of their European origin. On the other hand, it cannot be doubted that the children born in this country of Hindu parents would retain indefinitely the clear evidence of their ancestry. It is very far from our thought to suggest the slightest question of racial superiority or inferiority. What we suggest is merely racial difference, and it is of such character and extent that the great body of our people instinctively recognize it and reject the thought of assimilation" (*United States v. Bhagat Singh Thind*, 261 US 204, 1923).

2. http://dsc.discovery.com/fansites/greatchefs/profiles.html.

3. Linda Burum, "Book Notes," *Newsletter: The American Institute of Wine and Food* (Los Angeles chapter) 2 (2000): 3.

4. The seamless entry of Chef Floyd's food into New York's culinaryscape is also made evident through Tabla's affirmation of Jewish culinary rituals. Each year, the restaurant hosts an event appropriately named "The Unleavened Bread Bar" featuring a multicourse Indian-spiced Passover seder. The April 2007 issue of *Gourmet*, for instance, showcases Cardoz's Passover seder and includes recipes for its staple dishes such as matzoh ball soup with spring vegetables and gefilte fish with Goan spices.

5. *Food and Wine* named Thomas John, a native of New Delhi and chef at Mantra, one of the "Best New Chefs" of 2002 (Abdelnour).

6. Among the notable exceptions are David Wong Louie's *The Barbarians Are*

Coming, a novel that chronicles a Chinese American chef's failure to establish himself as a specialist in fusion cuisine (see Mannur, Peeking Ducks"; and Xu, *Eating*).

7. In a special issue of the *Massachusetts Review* devoted to the cultural politics of food, I suggest that Frank Wu's reading of dog eating helps to challenge commonplace understandings of multiculturalism (see Mannur, "Food Matters").

8. The appropriation of Black urban styles, reggae, and hip-hop by Asian American youth exemplifies a very different type of fusion that is marked by an overt attempt to address how the experiences of Black Americans bear on the racial formation of Asian Americans (see Prashad; and Maira).

8. Restaurants like *Hot Wok Village* in Atlanta and Chicago serve the kind of Indo-Chinese fusion cuisine popular in India suggesting that the terrain of South Asian fusion cuisine is beginning to alter. The owner of the restaurant, Sidney Chang, a second-generation Chinese Indian born in Calcutta and raised in Bombay, explains the origins of Indian-Chinese cuisine: "The Hakka Chinese migrated to India from Canton to escape opium warfare and political rivalry. Exposed to the pungent Indian cooking, they borrowed its many spices and incorporated the flavors into their own cuisine."

Bibliography

Abarca, Meredith. "Los Chilaquiles de mi 'ama: The Language of Everyday Cooking." In *Pilaf, Pozole and Pad Thai: American Women and Ethnic Food,* edited by Sherrie A. Inness, 119–44. Amherst: University of Massachusetts Press, 2001.

Abdelnour, Salma. "America's Best New Chefs 2002." *Food and Wine* (July 2002): 123–36.

Ahmed, Sara. "Multiculturalism and the Promise of Happiness." *New Formations* 63.1 (2007): 121–37.

Akhter, Nargis, Naher Alam, and Anannya Bhattacharjee. "Behind Swing Doors: South Asian Restaurant Workers Speak." *SAMAR: South Asian Magazine for Action and Reflection* 12 (Fall/Winter 2000): 13–16.

Allison, Dorothy. "A Lesbian Appetite." In *Trash: Stories by Dorothy Allison.* Ithaca: Firebrand Books, 1988.

"Anatomy of a Genre." http://www.sepiamutiny.com/sepia/archives/002888.html.

Anonymous. "How to Make an Indian Pickle." *Punch,* August 15, 1857.

Appadurai, Arjun. "How to Make a National Cuisine: Cookbooks in Contemporary India." *Comparative Studies in Society and History* 30 (January 1988): 3–24.

———. *Modernity at Large: Cultural Dimensions of Globalization.* Minneapolis: University of Minnesota Press, 1996.

Ashley, Bob, Joanne Hollows, Steve Jones, and Ben Taylor. *Food and Cultural Studies.* London and NewYork: Routledge, 2004.

Bachmann, Monica. "After the Fire." In *Queering India: Same Sex Love and Eroticism in Indian Culture and Society,* edited by Ruth Vanita, 234–43. London and New York: Routledge, 2002.

Banerji, Chitrita. *Eating India: An Odyssey into the Food and Culture of the Land of Spices*. New York: Bloomsbury, 2007.

Bannerjee, Debjani. "'In the Presence of History': The Representation of Past and Present Indias in Bharati Mukherjee's Fiction." In *Bharati Mukherjee: Critical Perspectives*, edited by Emmanuel Nelson. 161–79 . New York: Garland, 1993.

Baudrillard, Jean. *Jean Baudrillard: Selected Writings*. Edited by Mark Poster. Stanford: Stanford University Press, 1988.

Bayoumi, Moustafa. "How Does It Feel to Be a Problem?" *Amerasia Journal* 27.3/28.1 (2001/2002): 69–77.

Bendix, Regina. *In Search of Authenticity: The Formation of Folklore Studies*. Madison: University of Wisconsin Press, 1997.

Bhabha, Homi. *The Location of Culture*. London and New York: Routledge, 1994.

Bhatia, Sunil. *American Karma: Race, Culture and Identity in the Indian Diaspora*. New York: New York University Press, 2007.

Bhatt, Sujata. *The Stinking Rose*. Manchester: Carcanet Press, 1995.

Bhattacharjee, Annanya. "The Habit of Ex-Nomination: Nation, Woman and the Indian Immigrant Bourgeoisie." *Public Culture* 5.1 (1992): 19–44.

Bladholm, Linda. *The Indian Grocery Store Demystified*. Los Angeles: Renaissance Books, 2000.

"Blessings." *Gourmet* 66.4 (2007): 122–31.

Boym, Svetlana. *The Future of Nostalgia*. New York: Basic Books, 2001.

Braziel, Jana Evans, and Anita Mannur, eds. *Theorizing Diaspora*. Malden, Mass.: Blackwell, 2003.

Braziel, Jana Evans, and Katherine LeBesco, eds. *Bodies out of Bounds: Fatness and Transgression*. Berkeley and Los Angeles: University of California Press, 2001.

"Briefly Noted: The Mistress of Spices." *New Yorker,* June 23 and 30, 1997.

Brown, James. *Fictional Meals and Their Function in the French Novel, 1789–1848*. Toronto: University of Toronto Press, 1984.

Buettner, Elizabeth. "'Going for an Indian': South Asian Restaurants and the Limits of Multiculturalism in Britain." *Journal of Modern History* 80 (2008): 865–901.

Butler, Pamela, and Jigna Desai. "Manolos, Marriage and Mantras: Chick-Lit Criticism and Transnational Feminism." *Meridians: feminism, race, transnationalism* 8.2 (2008): 1–31.

Cardoz, Floyd, and Jane Daniels Lear. *One Spice, Two Spice: Indian Flavors, American Food*. New York: Morrow, 2006.

Carter, Mia. "Cosmopolitanism and Communion: Renegotiating Relations in Sara Suleri's *Meatless Days*." In *Articulating the Global and the Local: Globalization and Cultural Studies*, edited by Ann Cvetkovich and Douglas Kellner, 149–83. Boulder: Westview Press, 1997.

Chari, Madhav. "Pundit Coltrane Shows the Way." *Journal of Asian American Studies* 4.3 (2001): 265–83.

Chatterjee, Miabi. "Race to the Bottom: Race and Gender among South Asian Low-Wage Service Workers." Typescript, 2009.

Chatterjee, Partha. "The Nationalist Resolution of the Women's Question." In *Recasting Women: Essays in Indian Colonial History,* edited by Kumkum Sangari and Sudesh Vaid, 233–53. New Brunswick, N.J.: Rutgers University Press, 1990.

Cheah, Pheng, and Bruce Robbins, eds. *Cosmopolitics: Thinking and Feeling beyond the Nation.* Minneapolis: University of Minnesota Press, 1998.

Chin, Frank. *Chickencoop Chinaman and the Year of the Dragon.* Seattle: University of Washington Press, 1981.

Chopra, Deepak. *Perfect Health: The Complete Mind-Body Guide.* New York: Harmony Books, 1990.

Chow, Rey. *Primitive Passions: Visuality, Sexuality, Ethnography and Contemporary Chinese Cinema.* New York: Columbia University Press, 1995.

Chu, Patricia. *Assimilating Asians Gendered Strategies of Authorship in Asian America.* Durham and London: Duke University Press, 2000.

Chughtai, Ismat. *The Quilt and Other Stories.* Translated by Tahira Naqvi and Syeeda Hameed. New Delhi: Kali for Women Press, 1992.

Chuh, Kandice. *Imagine Otherwise: On Asian Americanist Critique.* Durham and London: Duke University Press, 2003.

Chutney Popcorn. Directed by Nisha Ganatra. Performers: Nisha Ganatra, Madhur Jaffrey, Zia Jaffrey. Wolfe Video, 1999.

Clegg, Roger. "Why I'm Sick of the Praise for Diversity on Campuses." *Chronicle of Higher Education,* July 14, 2000. http://chronicle.com.free/v46/i45.45b00801.htm.

Clifford, James. "Introduction: Partial Truths." In *Writing Culture: The Poetics and Politics of Ethnography,* edited by Clifford and George E. Marcus, 1–25. Berkeley and Los Angeles: University of California Press, 1986.

Collingham, Lizzie. *Curry: A Tale of Cooks & Conquerors.* Oxford: Oxford University Press, 2006.

Cook, Robin. "Chicken Tikka Masala." http://www.guardian.co.uk/racism/Story/0,,477023,00.html.

Counihan, Carole, and Penny Van Esterik, eds. *Food and Culture: A Reader.* London and New York: Routledge, 1997.

Curry, Spice and All Things Nice. http://www.menumagazine.co.uk/book/tikkamasala.html.

Cvetkovich, Ann. *An Archive of Feelings: Trauma, Sexuality and Lesbian Public Cultures.* Durham: Duke University Press, 2003.

Dabydeen, David. *The Counting House.* Leeds: Peepal Tress Press, 2005.

Davé, Shilpa, Pawan Dhingra et al. "De-Privileging Positions: Indian Americans, South Asian Americans, and the Politics of Asian American Studies." *Journal of Asian American Studies* 3.1 (1991): 67–100.

David, Esther. *The Book of Rachel*. New Delhi: Penguin India, 2006.

Dayal, Samir. "Style Is (Not) the Woman: Sara Suleri's *Meatless Days*." In *Between the Lines: South Asians and Postcoloniality*, edited by Deepika Bahri and Mary Vasudeva, 250–69. Philadelphia: Temple University Press, 1996.

Deleuze, Gilles, and Felix Guattari. *Kafka: Toward a Minor Literature*. Translated by Dana Polan. Minneapolis: University of Minnesota Press, 1986.

Deutrom, Hilda, ed. *Ceylon Daily News Cookery Book*. Colombo: Associated Newspapers of Sri Lanka, 1964.

Divakaruni, Chitra Bannerjee. *Leaving Yuba City: Poems*. New York: Anchor, 1997.

———. *Mistress of Spices*. London: Doubleday, 1997.

Dornenburg, Andrew, and Karen Page. *Becoming a Chef*. New York: Van Nostrand Reinhold, 1995.

Dunphy, Mark, Nancy Walker, R. Baird Schuman et al. "Recipes for Reading: A Forum" *PMLA* 104. 5 (1989): 903–8.

DuPlessis, Rachel Blau. *Writing beyond the Ending: Narrative Strategies of Twentieth- Century Women*. Bloomington: Indiana University Press, 1985.

Dusselier, Jane. "Bonbons, Lemon Drops and Oh! Henry Bars: Candy, Consumer Culture and the Construction of Gender, 1895–1920." In *Kitchen Culture in America: Popular Representations of Food, Gender and Race*, edited by Sherrie Inness, 13–50. Philadelphia: University of Pennsylvania Press, 2001.

———. "Does Food Make Place? Food Protests in Japanese American Concentration Camps." *Food and Foodways* 10 (2002): 137–65.

Eagleton, Terry. "Edible Ecriture." In *Consuming Passions: Food in the Age of Anxiety*, edited by Sian Griffiths and Jennifer Wallace, 203–8. Manchester: Manchester University Press, 1998.

Eng, David L. "Out Here and Over There: Queerness and Diaspora in Asian American Studies." *Social Text* 52–53 (1997): 31–52.

———. *Racial Castration: Managing Masculinity in Asian America*. Durham and London: Duke University Press, 2001.

Eng, David L., and Alice Hom. "Introduction Q&A: Notes on a Queer Asian America."

In *Q&A: Queer in Asian America*, edited by Eng and Hom, 1–21. Philadelphia: Temple University Press, 1998.

Eng, David L., et al. "What's Queer about Queer Studies Now?" *Social Text* 23.3–4 (2005): 1–17.

Epps, Bradley S. *Intimate Conduct, Public Practice, and the Bounds of Citizenship: In the Wake of Lawrence v. Texas*. Middletown, Ct.: Wesleyan University, 2005.

Espinet, Ramabai. *The Swinging Bridge*. Toronto: Harper Flamingo Canada, 2003.

Espiritu, Yen Le. "Possibilities of a Multi Racial America." In *The Sum of Our Parts: Mixed-Heritage Asian Americans*, edited by Teresa Williams León and Cynthia L. Nakashima, 25–34. Philadelphia: Temple University Press, 2001.

Fairchild, Barbara. "America Goes Global." *Bon Appetit,* September 2001, 42.

Fire. Directed by Deepa Mehta. Performers: Shabana Azmi, Nandita Das. Zeitgeist Films, 1997.

Fish, Stanley. "Boutique Multiculturalism, or Why Liberals Are Incapable of Thinking about Hate Speech." *Critical Inquiry* 23 (Winter 1997): 378–95.

Forster, E. M. "Adrift in India: 5. Pan." In *Abinger Harvest; and England's Pleasant Land,* edited by Elizabeth Heine, 307–13. London: Andre Deutsch, 1996.

Gabaccia, Donna. *We Are What We Eat: Ethnic Food and the Making of Americans.* Cambridge: Harvard University Press, 1998.

Ganguly, Keya. *States of Exception: Everyday Life and Postcolonial Identity.* Minneapolis: University of Minnesota Press, 2001.

George, Rosemary. *The Politics of Home: Postcolonial Relocations and Twentieth-Century Fiction.* Cambridge and New York: Cambridge University Press, 1996.

Ghosh, Amitav. *The Glass Palace.* New Delhi: Harper Collins, 2000.

Giard, Luce. "The Nourishing Arts." In *Living and Cooking,* by Michel de Certeau, Luce Giard, and Pierre Mayol; translated by Thomas Tomasik, vol. 2, *The Practice of Everyday Life.* 151 –70. Minneapolis: University of Minnesota Press, 1998.

Gilroy, Paul. *'There Ain't No Black in the Union Jack': The Cultural Politics of Race and Nation.* London: Hutchison, 1987.

Glissant, Edouard. *Caribbean Discourse: Selected Essays.* Translated by J. Michael Dash. Charlottesville: University Press of Virginia, 1989.

Gooneratne, Yasmine. *A Change of Skies.* Sydney: Picador, 1991.

Gopinath, Gayatri. "'Bombay, U.K., Yuba City': Bhangra Music and the Engendering of Diaspora." *Diaspora* 4.3 (1995): 303–22.

———. "Homo-Economics: Queer Sexualities in a Transnational Frame." In *Burning Down the House: Recycling Domesticity,* edited by Rosemary George, 102–24. Boulder: Westview, 1998.

———. *Impossible Desires: Queer Diasporas and South Asian Public Cultures.* Durham: Duke University Press, 2005.

———. "Nostalgia, Desire, Diaspora: South Asian Sexualities in Motion." *positions: east asia cultural critiques* 5.2 (1997): 467–89.

Guha, Ranajit. *Elementary Aspects of Peasant Insurgency in Colonial India.* Durham: Duke University Press, 1999.

Gunesekera, Romesh. *Reef.* New York: Riverhead Books, 1994.

Gunew, Sneja. "Feminism and the Politics of Irreducible Differences: Multiculturalism/Ethnicity/Race." In *Feminism and the Politics of Difference,* edited by Sneja Gunew and Anna Yeatman, 1–19. Boulder: Westview Press, 1993.

The Guru. Directed by Daisy Von Scherler Mayer. Performers: Jimi Mistri, Marisa Tomei, Heather Graham. Universal Pictures, 2002.

Haney-López, Ian. F. *White by Law: The Legal Construction of Race.* New York: New York University Press, 1997.

Harold and Kumar Go to White Castle. Directed by Danny Leiner. Performers: Kal Penn, John Cho. New Line Cinema, 2005.

Heldke, Lisa. *Exotic Appetites: Ruminations of a Food Adventurer.* London and New York: Routledge, 2003.

Hidier, Tanuja Desai. *Born Confused.* New York: Scholastic, 2003.

Highmore, Ben. "Alimentary Agents: Food, Cultural Theory and Multiculturalism." *Journal of Intercultural Studies* 29.4 (2008): 381–98.

———. "The Taj Mahal in the High Street: The Indian Restaurant as Diaspora Popular Culture in Britain." *Food, Culture and Society* 12.2 (2009): 173–90.

Hirsch, Marianne. "A Mother's Discourse: Incorporation and Repetition in *La Princesse de Clèves.*" *Yale French Studies* 62 (1981): 67–87.

Ho, Jennifer Ann. *Consumption and Identity in Asian American Coming-of-Age Novels.* London and New York: Routledge, 2005.

Hogan, David Gerard. *Selling 'em by the Sack: White Castle and the Creation of American Food.* New York: New York University Press, 1997.

hooks, bell. "Eating the Other: Desire and Resistance." In *Eating Culture*, edited by Ron Scapp and Brian Seitz, 181–200. Albany: State University of New York Press, 1998.

"Hot and Sweet." *Marie Claire India* 2.10 (October 2007).

"Indian Arrival Day: Foods" http://library2.nalis.gov.tt/Default.aspx?PageContentID=367&tabid=204.

Indiana Jones and the Temple of Doom. Directed by Steven Spielberg. Performers: Harrison Ford, Kate Capshaw, Jonathan Ke Quan. Paramount, 1984.

Iwabuchi, Koichi. *Recentering Globalization: Popular Culture and Japanese Transnationalism.* Durham: Duke University Press, 2002.

Jaffrey, Madhur. *An Invitation to Indian Cooking.* New York: Vintage, 1973.

Jallepalli, Raji, and Judith Choate. *Raji Cuisine: Indian Flavors, French Passion.* New York: Morrow, 2000.

Joshi, Khyati. *New Roots in America's Sacred Ground: Religion, Race and Ethnicity in Indian America.* New Brunswick, N.J.: Rutgers University Press, 2006.

Kadi, Joanna. *Food for Our Grandmothers: Writings by Arab-American and Arab-Canadian Feminists.* Boston: South Press, 1994.

Kaimal, Maya. *Savoring the Spice Coast of India: Fresh Flavors from Kerala.* New York: Morrow, 2000.

Kakutani, Michiko. "Wonderbread and Curry: Mingling Cultures, Conflicting Hearts." *New York Times,* April 4, 2008. http://www.nytimes.com/2008/04/04/books/04Book.html.

Katrak, Ketu, "Food and Belonging: At 'Home' and in 'Alien-Kitchens.'" In *Through the Kitchen Window,* edited by Arlene Avakian, 263–75. Boston: Beacon Press, 1997.

———. "South Asian American Literature." In *Asian American Literature: An*

Inter-ethnic Companion, edited by King-Kok Cheung, 192–218.New York: Cambridge University Press, 1997.

Khoo, Tseen. *Banana-Bending: Asian-Australian and Asian-Canadian Literatures.* Montreal: McGill-Queen's University Press, 2003.

Khushu-Lahiri, Rajayshree, and Shweta Rao. "India on a Platter: A Study of Gurinder Chadha and Paul Mayeda Berges' Cinematic Adaptation of *The Mistress of Spices.*" *Postcolonial Text* 4.2 (2008): 1 –13.

Kirchner, Bharati. *Pastries: A Novel of Desserts and Discoveries.* New York: St Martin's Press, 2003.

Kogawa, Joy. *Obasan.* Toronto: Penguin, 2006.

Kondo, Dorinne. "The Narrative Production of 'Home,' Community and Political Identity in Asian American Theater." In *Displacement, Diaspora and Geographies of Identity,* edited by Smadar Lavie and Ted Swedenburg, 7–117. Durham and London: Duke University Press, 1996.

Kothari, Geeta. "If You Are What You Eat, Then What Am I?" *Kenyon Review* (Winter 1999): 6–14.

Kumar, Amitava. *Passport Photos.* Berkeley and Los Angeles: University of California Press, 2000.

Lahiri, Jhumpa. "Indian Takeout" *Food and Wine.* April 2000. http://www.foodandwine.com/articles/indian-takeout.

———. *The Interpreter of Maladies.* Boston: Houghton Mifflin, 2000.

———. *The Namesake.* Boston: Houghton Mifflin, 2003.

———. *Unaccustomed Earth.* New York: Knopf, 2008.

Lakshmi, Padma. *Easy Exotic: A Model's Low Fat Recipes from Around the World.* New York: Miramax, 2000.

———. *Tangy, Tart, Hot and Sweet: A World of Recipes for Every Day.* New York: Weinstein Books, 2007.

Lall, Sumita. "'Subverting the Taste Buds' of America: Transnational Political Agency in Bharati Mukherjee's Novels *Wife* (1975) and *Jasmine* (1989)." *Phoebe* 16.1 (2004): 39–55

Lavie, Smadar, and Ted Swedenburg. Introduction to *Displacement, Diaspora, and Geographies of Identity,* edited by Smadar and Swedenburg, 1–25. Durham and London: Duke University Press, 1996.

Leonardi, Susan. "Recipes for Reading: Summer Pasta, Lobster à la Riseholme, and Key Lime Pie." *PMLA* 104.3 (1989): 340–47.

Lindenfeld, Laura. "Feasting Our Eyes: Food Films, Gender and U.S. American Identity." Ph.D. diss., University of California, Davis, 2003.

A Love Supreme. Directed by Nilesh Patel. Performer: Indumati Patel. Les Beauchistes, 2000.

Lovegren, Sylvia. *Fashionable Food: Seven Decades of Food Fads.* New York: Macmillan, 1995.

Lowe, Lisa. *Immigrant Acts: On Asian American Cultural Politics.* Durham and London: Duke University Press, 1996.

Maira, Sunaina. *Desis in the House: Indian American Youth Culture in New York City*. Philadelphia: Temple University Press, 2002.

Majithia, Sheetal, "Of Foreigners and Fetishes: A Reading of Recent South Asian American Fiction." *SAMAR* (Fall/Winter 2001): 52–53

Makhijani, Pooja. "School Lunch." In *Women Who Eat: A New Generation on the Glory of Food*, edited by Leslie Miller, 41–51. Emeryville, Calif.: Seal Press, 2003.

Malladi, Amulya, *The Mango Season*. New York: Ballantine, 2003.

———. *Serving Crazy with Curry*. New York: Ballantine, 2004.

Manalansan, Martin. "Cooking up the Senses: A Critical Embodied Approach to the Study of Food and Asian American Television Audiences." In *Alien Encounters: Popular Culture in Asian America*, edited by Thuy Linh Yu and Mimi Nguyen, 179–93. Durham: Duke University Press, 2007.

———. "Immigrant Lives and the Politics of Olfaction in the Global City." In *The Smell Culture Reader*, edited by Jim Drobnick, 41–52. Oxford and New York: Berg, 2006.

Mankekar, Purnima. "'India Shopping': Indian Grocery Stores and Transnational Configurings of Belonging." In *The Cultural Politics of Food and Eating*, edited by James L. Watson and Melissa L. Caldwell, 197–214. Malden, Mass.: Blackwell, 2004.

Mannur, Anita. "Food Matters: An Introduction" *Massachusetts Review* 45.3 (Autumn 2004): 209 – 215.

———. "Model Minorities Can Cook: Fusion Cuisine in Asian America." In *East Main Street: Asian American Popular Culture*, edited by Shilpa Davé, Leilani Nishime, and Tasha Oren, 72–94. New York: New York University Press, 2005.

———. "'Peeking Ducks' and 'Food Pornographers: Commodifying Culinary Chinese Americanness." In *Culture, Commodity, Identity: Chinese Diasporic Literatures in English*, edited by Kam Louie and Tseen Khoo, 19–38. Montreal and Hong Kong: Queens/ McGill Press and Hong Kong University Press, 2005.

Mansingh, Lalit. "The Story of the Indian Diaspora Is Compelling and Inspiring." *India Abroad* 34.13 (Friday, December 26, 2003): S13–S16.

Marshall, Paule. *Reena and Other Stories* Old Westbury, N.Y. : Feminist Press, 1983.

Mathieu, Paula. "Economic Citizenship and the Rhetoric of Gourmet Coffee." *Rhetoric Review* 18.1 (1999): 112–27.

Mazumdar, Ranjani. "Dialectic of Public and Private: Representation of Women in *Bhoomika* and *Mirch Masala*." *Economic and Political Weekly*, October 26, 1991, WS81–84.

Mazumdar, Sucheta. "The Impact of New World Food Crops on the Diet and Economy of China and India, 1600–1900." In *Food and Global His-*

tory, edited by Raymond Grew, 58–78. Boulder, Colo.: Westview Press, 1999.

McKee, Larry. "Food Supply and Plantation Social Order: An Archaeological Perspective." In *"I, Too, Am America": Archaeological Studies of African-American Life*, edited by Theresa A. Singleton, 218–39. Charlottesville and London: University Press of Virginia, 1999.

Minhas, Nisha. *Chapatti or Chips?* London: Pocket Books, 2002.

———. *Passion and Poppadums*. London: Pocket Books, 2004.

Mintz, Sidney. *Sweetness and Power: The Place of Sugar in Modern History*. New York: Penguin, 1985.

Mirch Masala. Dir. Ketan Mehta. Perf. Naseeruddin Shah, Smita Patil, Deepti Naval. Channel Four Films, National Film Development Corporation of India (NFDC), 1986.

Mistress of Spices. Directed by Paul Mayeda Berges. Performers: Aishwarya Rai, Dylan McDermott, Anupam Kher, Ayesha Dharker, Padma Lakshmi. Balle Pictures, 2005.

Monsoon Wedding. Directed by Mira Nair. Performers: Naseeruddin Shah, Lilette Dubey, Ishaan Nair. Universal Pictures. 2002.

Mootoo, Shani. *Cereus Blooms at Night*. New York: Harper Perennial, 1999.

———. *Out on Main Street*. Vancouver: Press Gang, 1993.

Morris, Robyn. "Food, Race and the Power of Recuperative Identity Politics within Asian Australian Women's Fiction." *Journal of Australian Studies* 32.4 (2008): 499–508.

Mullen, Bill. *Afro-Orientalism*. Minneapolis: University of Minnesota Press, 2003.

Mudge, Alden. "Family Values: Lahiri Probes the Immigrant Identity in Her First Book."

Book Page. http://www.bookpage.com/0309bp/jhumpa_lahiri.html.

Mukherjee, Bharati. *Jasmine*. New York: Grove, 1989.

Mukherjee, Meenakshi. *The Perishable Empire: Essays on Indian Writing in English*. New Delhi: Oxford University Press, 2000.

Muñoz, José Esteban. *Disidentifications: Queers of Color and the Performance of Politics*. Minneapolis: University of Minnesota Press, 1999.

My Country, My Kitchen—Maya Kaimal. Directed by Irene Wong. Performer: Maya Kaimal. Food Network. 2001.

Narayan, Kirin. "Sprouting and Uprooting of Saili: The Story of the Sacred Tulsi in Kangra." *Manushi: A Journal about Women and Society* 102 (1997): 30–38.

Narayan, Uma. *Dislocating Cultures: Identities, Traditions and Third World Feminism*. London and New York: Routledge, 1997.

Nelson, Cary. "Literature as Cultural Studies: 'American' Poetry of the Spanish Civil War." In *Disciplinarity and Dissent in Cultural Studies*, edited by Dilip Gaonkar and Cary Nelson, 131–48. New York and London: Routledge, 1996.

"The New India." *Newsweek*, March 6. 2006.

Nguyen, Bich Minh. *Stealing Buddha's Dinner*. New York: Viking Penguin, 2007.

Niranjana, Tejaswini. *Siting Translation: History, Post-Structuralism and the Colonial Context*. Berkeley and Los Angeles: University of California Press, 1992.

"Padma's Passport-Aphrodisiacal Foods." *Melting Pot*. Hosted by Padma Lakshmi. Food Network. October 1, 2001.

"Padma's Passport—Indian Feast." *Melting Pot*. Hosted by Padma Lakshmi. Food Network. December 7, 2001.

"Padma's Passport—My Mother's Kitchen." *Melting Pot*. Hosted by Padma Lakshmi. Food Network. October 12, 2001.

Palumbo-Liu, David. "Theory and the Subject of Asian American Studies" *Amerasia Journal* 21. 1 and 2 (1995): 55–66.

Patel, Nilesh. *"A Love Supreme."* http://www.upperstall.com/lovesupreme.html. August 29, 2006.

———. "A Love Supreme and Memory." E-mail to the author. November 11, 2005.

Patel, Vibuthi. "The Maladies of Belonging." *Newsweek* (Pacific edition), September 20, 1999, 60.

Patronite, Rob, and Robin Raisfield. "Bombay Talkie." http://nymag.com/listings/restaurant/bombay-talkie/.

Perri, Lynne. *"Women Who Eat: Two Cups of Love and a Dash of Humor."* http://www.usatoday.com/life/books/reviews/2003–12–08–women-who-eat_x.htm.

Porter, Lewis. *John Coltrane: His Life and Music*. Ann Arbor: University of Michigan Press, 1998.

Primlani, Kala. *Indian Cooking: With Useful Hints on Good Housekeeping*. Translated by R. V. Ramachandani. Bombay: Pearl Books, 1968.

Prashad, Vijay. *The Karma of Brown Folk*. Minneapolis: University of Minnesota Press, 2000.

Probyn, Elspeth. *Carnal Appetites: FoodSexIdentities*. New York and London: Routledge, 2000.

Puwar, Nirmal. "Exhibiting Spectacle and Memory." *Fashion Theory: The Journal of Dress, Body and Culture* 7.3/4. (2003): 257–74.

Rabinow, Paul. "Representations Are Social Facts: Modernity and Post-Modernity in Anthropology." In *Writing Culture: The Poetics and Politics of Ethnography*, edited by James Clifford and George E. Marcus, 234–61. Berkeley and Los Angeles: University of California Press, 1986.

Radhakrishnan, R. *Diasporic Mediations: Between Home and Location*. Minneapolis: University of Minnesota Press, 1996.

Ray, Krishnendu. "Meals, Migration and Modernity: Domestic Cooking and Bengali Indian Ethnicity in the United States." *Amerasia Journal* 24.1 (1998): 105–27.

———. *The Migrant's Table: Meals and Memories in Bengali-American House-holds*. Philadelphia: Temple University Press, 2004.

Reichl, Ruth. "Restaurants: American Food: Indian Spices." *New York Times*, February 24, 1999.

Renan, Ernst. "What Is a Nation?" Translated by Martin Thom. In *Nation and Narration*, edited by Homi. K. Bhabha, 8–22. London and New York: Routledge, 1990.

Rich, B. Ruby. "A Thanksgiving Feast with a Rainbow of Flavors." *New York Times*, November 12, 2000. http://query.nytimes.com/gst/fullpage.html?res=9805E2D81039F931A25752C1A9669C8B63.

"Ring a Ding Ding." *Sex and the City*. HBO. January 27, 2002.

Rodriguez, Richard. *Brown: The Last Discovery of America*. New York: Penguin, 2003.

Roy, Parama. "Reading Communities and Culinary Communities: The Gastropoetics of the South Asian Diaspora." *positions* 10.2 (2002): 471–502.

Roy, Sandip. "Hamburger Curry and Other Films." *India Abroad*, March 22, 2002, M16.

Ruiz, Vicki. "Citizen Restaurant: American Imaginaries, American Communities." *American Quarterly* 60.1 (2008) 1–21.

Rushdie, Salman. *Imaginary Homelands*. London and New York: Granta, 1991.

———. *Midnight's Children*. New York: Penguin, 1980.

Sassen, Saskia. *The Global City: New York, London, Tokyo*. Princeton: Princeton University Press, 2001.

Satyam, Shivam, Sundaram. Directed by Raj Kapoor. Performers: Zeenat Aman, Shashi Kapoor. Yash Raj Films, 1978.

Self Employed Women's Association (SEWA). "'The Burning Falls to Our Share': Women in the Chili Trade." *Manushi: A Journal about Women and Society* 47 (1988): 31–34.

Sen, Samita. *The Indian Women's Movement in Historical Perspective*. Policy Research Report on Gender and Development: The World Bank Working Paper Series No. 9. August 28, 2006. http://siteresources.worldbank.org/INTGENDER/Resources/wp9.pdf.

Sen, Sharmila. "Indian Spices across the Black Waters." In *From Betty Crocker to Feminist Food Studies: Critical Perspectives on Women and Food*, edited by Arlene Voski Avakian and Barbara Haber, 185–199. Amherst: University of Massachusetts, 2005.

Shah, Anand. "Pursuing their Passion" *India Currents*. http://indiacurrents.com/news/view_article.html?article_id=f3a553411c08ea129863b4cf4ee8d854.

Shankar, Shalini. *Desi Land: Teen Culture, Class, and Success in Silicon Valley*. Durham, N.C.: Duke University Press, 2008.

Sharma, Nitasha. "Rotten Coconuts and Other Strange Fruit." *SAMAR* (Fall/Winter 2001): 30–32.

Sharpe, Jenny. "Gender, Nation, and Globalization in *Monsoon Wedding* and

Dilwale Dulhania Le Jayenge." *Meridians: Feminism, Race, Transnationalism* 6.1 (2005): 58–81.

Shih, Shu-Mei, and Françoise Lionnet, eds. *Minor Transnationalisms.* Durham: Duke Univeristy Press, 2005.

Shiva, Vandana "Globalisation: A War against Nature and People of the South." Health Cooperation Papers, vol. 17, August 29, 2006. http://www.aifo.it/english/resources/online/books/other/poverty&health/3–1globalisation-vandanashiva.pdf.

Shohat, Ella. "Framing Post–Third-Worldist Culture: Gender and Nation in Middle Eastern/North African Film and Video." *Jouvert: A Journal of Postcolonial Studies* 1.1 (1997). http://social.chass.ncsu.edu/jouvert/.

Sinha, Suchi. "World on a Platter." *India Today International*, October 29, 2001, 47.

Song, Min Hyoung. "The Children of 1965: Allegory, Postmodernism, and Jhumpa Lahiri's *The Namesake.*" *Twentieth-Century Literature* 53.3 (2007): 345–70.

Spivak, Gayatri. "Can the Subaltern Speak?" In *Marxism and the Interpretation of Culture*, edited by Cary Nelson and Lawrence Grossberg, 271–313. Urbana: University of Illinois Press, 1988.

Srikanth, Rajini. The *World Next Door: South Asian American Literature and the Idea of America.* Philadelphia: Temple University Press, 2004.

Stewart, Kathleen. "Nostalgia—A Polemic." In *Rereading Cultural Anthropology*, edited by George E. Marcus, 252–66. Durham and London, Duke University Press, 1992.

Suleri, Sara. *Meatless Days.* Chicago: University of Chicago Press, 1991.

"Suspicious Item in Ohio Luggage: Pickled Mangoes." Associated Press. http://hosted.ap.org/dynamic/stories/U/US_ODD_SUSPICIOUS_MANGOES ?SITE=SCCHA&SECTION=HOME&TEMPLATE=DEFAULT.

"Tabla Restaurant." 10 March 2007. http://www.tablanyc.com .

Trillin, Calvin. *Feeding a Yen.* New York: Random House, 2003.

Tringali, Juliana. "For External Use Only: Getting in a Lather about the New Trend in Foodie Beauty Products." *Bitch: feminist response to pop culture* 23 (Winter 2004): 34–37.

Tsai, Ming. *Blue Ginger: East Meets West Cooking with Ming Tsai.* New York: Clarkson Potter, 1999.

Unbidden Voices. Directed by Deb Ellis and Prajna Parasher. Women Make Movies. 1989.

United States vs. Bhagat Singh Thind 261 US 204. Supreme Court, 1923.

Visweswaran, Kamala. "Diaspora by Design: Flexible Citizenship and South Asians in U.S. Racial Formations." *Diaspora* 6.1. (1997): 5–29.

Weisberger, Lauren. *The Devil Wears Prada.* New Delhi: Harper Collins India, 2006.

What's Cooking? Directed by Gurinder Chadha. Performers: Alfre Woodard, Julianna Margulies, Joan Chan, Kyra Sedgwick. Lion's Gate, 2000.

Witt, Doris. *Black Hunger: Food and the Politics of U.S. Identity.* New York and Oxford: Oxford University Press, 1999.

Wong, Sau-Ling. *Reading Asian American Literature: From Necessity to Extravagance.* Princeton: Princeton University Press.

Wu, Frank. *Yellow: Race in America beyond Black and White.* New York: Basic Books, 2002.

Xu, Wenying. *Eating Identities: Reading Food in Asian American Literature.* Honolulu: University of Hawaii Press, 2007.

———. "Sticky Rice Balls or Lemon Pie: Enjoyment and Ethnic Identities in *No-No Boy* and *Obasan.*" *LIT: Literature, Interpretation, Theory* 1.1 (2002): 51–68.

Index

Abarca, Meredith, 70
Achaya, K. T., 228n2
affect, 41, 48, 65–67, 159–63, 165–71,
    221–25; and citizenship, 177–78; and
    food, 12, 20, 29, 31–32, 78, 83, 85–86,
    92, 107–8, 179, 184
Afro-Orientalism, 225
aggrievement, politics of, 178, 184, 212
Ahmed, Sara, 225
Allison, Dorothy, 50–52
Ammal, Meenakshi, 229n2
amnesia, historical 46–48
Anglo Indians, 57, 229n3
Anzaldúa, Gloria, 221
Appadurai, Arjun, 8, 55–56, 221n2
archaeological approaches to food studies,
    18
Arora, Anupama, 218–19
Asian Americans: and African American
    Studies, 18, 111, 209–10, 214, 223–24,
    233n8; and "Children of 1965," 177–80;
    and ethnic food pride, 149–50; and
    food studies, 12–16, 223–24, 228n8; and
    food writing, 82–86, 163; and foodways,
    27–28, 174–77, 186–88; and legal
    exclusion, 191–93, 206–7; and literary
    studies, 16–17, 19–22, 29–30, 89–96,
    109–12, 118, 136–37, 167, 212, 221; and
    multiracial identity, 164–65; and race,
    13, 170–71, 178, 206–7; and South Asian
    diasporas, 8–10

Asian Australian Studies, 59–62, 224,
    226n1
assimilation, 90, 100, 150–56, 178, 180,
    187–88, 203, 206–7, 212; and food,
    189–92, 194; and fusion cuisine,
    23, 198–204, 213–14, 216; and legal
    exclusion, 192–93; and immigration,
    59–62, 161
authenticity, 27, 30–35, 39–41, 43, 61, 125,
    177, 181, 187–88, 195–97, 207; and
    diaspora, 42–43; and ethnic identity,
    2–3, 43, 90, 165–67

Bachmann, Monica, 69
Badmash, 181–83
baking, 65, 81, 86, 106–7
Bangladesh: chefs in Britain, 3; American
    restaurant workers, 205
Bannerji, Chitrita, 91
Bannerjee, Debjani, 91
Baudrillard, Jean, 82–84
Bayoumi, Moustafa , 216
Bendix, Regina, 27
Berges, Paul Mayeda, 89–90
Bhabha, Homi, 46–47, 115
Bhatia, Sunil, 150–51
Bhatt, Sujata, 27, 30, 34–35
Blackness, 2, 110–11, 204–11, 221–22
Bladholm, Linda, 88–89
Bollywood, 5, 69, 133, 138, 142
Book of Rachel, 93–94

Born Confused, 207, 208n7
Bourdain, Anthony, 147, 171–72, 174
Bourdieu, Pierre, 11, 207
Bower, Anne, 134–35
Bureau of Citizenship and Immigration Services (BCIS), 23, 187
Braziel, Jana Evans, 48, 84
Brillat Savarin, Jean, 7
Buettner, Elizabeth, 227n3
Butler, Pamela, 231n2

Cardoz, Floyd, 198–202, 206, 208–11, 215–16, 232n4
Carter, Mia, 40
Celebrity Big Brother, 5
Cereus Blooms at Night, 20, 30, 41, 58, 74–78, 81, 220
Ceylon Daily News Cookery Book, 59–60, 62–64
Chadha, Gurinder, 88–89, 119, 166
A Change of Skies, 59–61
chapatti, 115–17, 125, 153, 231n1
Chari, Madhav, 141, 210
Chatterjee, Miabi, 129
Chatterjee, Partha, 34, 51–52
chick lit, 154, 231n2
chicken tikka masala, 3–4, 6
Childs, Lydia Marie, 165, 169
Chin, Frank, 15, 82, 84, 163
Chopra, Deepak, 96–97, 108, 230n2
Chu, Patricia, 231n2
Chughtai, Ismat, 50–51
Chuh, Kandice, 17
chutney, 35, 112, 120; chutney sandwiches, 151
Chutney Popcorn, 120, 217–19
citizenship, 23, 33–34, 157, 186, 191–93, 197, 206; affective, 177–78; autochthonous, 43; culinary, 20, 29, 176, 184; cultural, 171, 203; diasporic, 163; economic, 103–4; 192–93
class: and cultural critique, 22, 118–20, 137; and domestic workers, 36, 39–41; and gentrification, 194; inequities, 101–11, 126–29; middle and upper class groups, 2, 30, 32, 155–56, 166, 175; and managerial ethos, 129; and narrative development, 107–11, 132, 142–43, 210–11; and nostalgia, 48; privilege, 67–68, 72–73, 197–200; and race, 4, 17, 19, 96–100, 109, 136, 192

Clegg, Roger, 189–90, 208
Clifford, James, 16
coconuts, 1–3
Collingham, Lizzie, 227n2
colonialism: and sugar, 81–82
Coltrane, John 139–41, 210; and Ravi Shankar, 139, 141
commodification, 8, 82–84, 108–10, 139, 142–42, 160–61, 183–84
Cook, Robin, 3–5
cookbooks, 19, 23, 29–35, 55–64, 77, 83, 163–70, 184–89, 195–214, 227n4, 228n1
cooking shows, 23, 53–55, 137–39, 142–43, 164–72, 184, 188–90, 196, 201–3
Counihan, Carole 10, 18
Counting House, The 123
cuisine: fusion 22–23, 60, 73, 164–65, 169, 184, 186–216, 220, 232–33n6; labor-intensive, 143
culinary: and the archive 9–10, 59, 223, 225; fictions, 19; metaphors, 2–5, 12; tourism, 163–67
curry, 1, 76, 110, 151, 185–86, 196, 231n3
Cvetkovich, Ann, 177–78

Dabydeen, David, 123
Davé, Shilpa, 24
David, Esther, 93–94
Dayal, Samir, 40
Deleuze, Gilles, 81, 86
Desai, Jigna, 231n2
deodorization, cultural, 211, 216
Deutrom, Hilda, 59–60, 62–64
Devil Wears Prada, The, 185
Dhingra, Pawan, 24
diaspora: conceptual frameworks of, 8–9, 42, 46–49, 131, 170, 223–24; and gender, 35, 41–42; and ideologies about food, 35, 92; and Jewish contexts, 93–94; and labor, 44–45
disability studies, 139
disidentification, 64–65, 67, 77
Divakaurni, Chitra Bannerjee, 13, 15, 21–22, 85, 88–101, 109–13, 118, 132–37
dog eating, 149, 211–12, 233n7
domestic abuse, 75–77, 98–99, 230n3
domestic manuals. See cookbooks
Dornenburg, Andrew, 188
Duplessis, Rachel Blau, 111–12, 223
Dusselier, Jane, 81, 117

Eagleton, Terry, 107
Easy Exotic, 187, 201–4
eating: and enjoyment, 179; and
    hyperreality, 82–83; and
    multiculturalism, 48–49, 225
Ellis, Deb, 118, 126–32, 137
Eng, David, 64
Epps, Bradley, 18
Espinet, Ramabai, 81–82
Espiritu, Yen Le, 165
ethnic enclaves, 14, 87–91, 175, 218–19
exoticism, 82, 85, 91–92, 109, 134, 201–7,
    221

Fairchild, Barbara, 84, 190, 205
fast food, 174–76, 214
fat studies, 84
feminism, 39, 92–94, 124, 134, 231n2; and
    cosmopolitanism, 40–41; and film, 120,
    131, and environmentalism, 123–24;
    and literary studies, 36, 111–12; and
    sovereignty, 93; and translation, 128;
    and women of color, 92–93, 126–27
Fire, 20, 58, 67–73
Fish, Stanley, 224
folktales, 39
food films, 22, 88–89, 118–20, 126–27,
    133–43, 166, 231n3
Food for our Grandmothers, 92–93
food pornography, 15, 21–22, 82, 85–86, 89,
    107–10, 119, 128, 135–37, 142, 161–62,
    221
The Food Network, 163, 171, 188
food studies, 21–24, 220, 222–24; and
    African American Studies, 18, 228n9;
    and Asian American Studies, 12–19,
    21–22, 228n8; and ethnic studies, 224;
    and class, 117–20; and literary studies,
    10–19
Forster, E.M., 217, 220
Foucault, Michel, 56–57
fusion, 22–23, 60, 73, 164–65, 169, 184,
    186–216, 220, 232–33n6

Gabaccia, Donna, 190, 228n8
Ganguly, Keya, 1
George, Rosemary, 52
Ghosh, Amitav,115
Giard, Luce, 27
Gilroy, Paul, 51
Glissant, Edouard, 39

The Glass Palace, 115
global capitalism, 102–7, 109
globalization, 96, 101–4, 131, 175, 184, 194,
    201
Goodness Gracious Me, 6–7
Gooneratne, Yasmine, 59–61
Gopinath, Gayatri, 42, 51, 70–71, 83–84
grocery stores, 88–91, 219, 227n2
Guattan, Felix, 81, 86
Gunesekera, Romesh, 20, 58, 62–67, 73–74
Gunew, Sneja, 149–50
Guru, The, 5–6
gurukul, 94

hamburgers, 171–77
Haney-López, Ian, 193
happiness, 153–54, 174–75, 224–25
Harold and Kumar Go to White Castle, 22,
    171–77, 181–83, 222, 225
Heldke, Lisa, 87, 171, 208, 214
heteronormativity, 50–51, 53, 58, 71, 77–78,
    218–19
Hidier, Tanuja Desai, 207, 208n7
Highmore, Ben, 227n3
Hindu identity, 67, 94; and diets, 46–37;
    as label, 45, 192, 232n1; and the Indian
    Mutiny, 116–17; and rituals, 69, 165–66;
    and pop Ayurveda, 97–98; and the
    Ramayana, 71–72, 229n4, 229–30n5
Hirsch, Marianne, 166–67
Ho, Jennifer Ann, 14, 227n5
Hogan, David Gerard, 175–76
Hom, Ken, 193
homes, 20–21, 59, 61, 142, 215–216, 224;
    and class, 185–86; and cooking, 14, 123,
    147–48, 201–3; and diaspora, 42–43,
    62; and family life, 68–75; and gender,
    19–20, 55–58, 156–63; and immigrants,
    185–86; and nostalgia, 28–35, 48–49,
    69–70; and queerness, 50–53, 63, 67;
    and violence, 75–78
homosociality, spaces of, 53–54, 64, 67–72
hooks, bell 101
hybridity, 61, 180, 184, 197, 207
hyperreal. *See* eating and hyperreality

Ignatieff, Michael, 154
"Imaginary Homelands," 28–29
immigrants, 19, 42, 90, 96–100, 163–64,
    174, 178, 181, 206–7, 211, 216, 218, 221;
    in Australia, 59–62; and the body, 151,

215, 220; in Britain, 4–5; enclaves, 14, 41, 87; entrepreneurs, 4, 175–77, 214; and the everyday, 90–91; and food, 1, 35, 41, 88–89, 154–63, 179, 188, 199, 201–5, 211–12, 224–27, 228n6; and the nation, 42–44; and nostalgia, 14, 20–21, 29–34, 36, 48, 95, 152–53, 230n1; and racism, 190–94; and restaurants, 5–6, 190; and smell, 185–86, 206; subjectivity, 7, 27–29; workers, 13, 16, 90, 108, 126–32, 136

immigration, 22–23, 60, 99, 131, 135, 158–59, 174, 223; and legal exclusion, 190–95; and Nationality Act of 1965, 147, 175–77, 195

indentureship: and domesticity, 76–77; and labor, 45–46, 81–82, 123; and sugar, 45

Indian Grocery Store Demystified, The, 88–89

Indiana Jones and the Temple of Doom, 147–50

Indo-Caribbeanness, 9, 20, 30, 41–49, 81–82, 123–24, 231n4

Indo-Chic, 85, 181–84

Interpreter of Maladies, The, 157–63

intimacy, 20–21, 48–51, 66–71, 76, 81, 134, 154, 212–13, 221

Invitation to Indian Cooking, An, 30–35, 48, 57, 61, 167, 195–96, 198, 199, 201, 228n1, 229n3

Iwabuchi, Koichi, 211

Jackson Heights, 41, 217–19

Jaffrey, Madhur, 30–35, 48, 57, 61, 167, 195–96, 198, 199, 201, 228n1, 229n3

Jallepalli, Raji, 23, 187, 196–97, 201–2, 206–9, 211, 215

Jasmine, 13–14, 90–91, 227n6

jazz music, 139, 141, 210

Jews: and India, 93–94; and Indian-inspired Seders, 232n4

Joshi, Khyati, 150

Kaimal, Maya, 22, 164–71, 176, 179

Kalaria, Honey, 138

Karva Chauth, 68–6

Kadi, Joanna, 92–93

Kapoor, Sanjeev, 53–54

Katrak, Ketu, 27–29, 31, 85–86

Kennedy, Diana, 214

Khana Khazana, 53–54

Khoo, Tseen, 62, 227n1

Khushu-Lahiri, Rajayshree, 94–95, 230nn4–5

Kirchner, Bharati, 13, 21, 85, 101–10, 112–13

Kishwar, Madhu, 69

kitchens, 27, 32–33, 55–57, 60, 193; and domestic space, 14, 68–70, 147–48, 153–54, 156, 159, 165–66, 195, 202–3; and healing, 212–16; and Indianness, 41–42; and poetics, 221–22; and restaurants, 5–6, 13, 120, 126–30, 135, 184, 190

Kogawa, Joy, 108–9

Kothari, Geetha, 22, 153–57, 160, 169, 214

labor, 41, 91, 114, 117, 176, 183–84, 194, 218–20; and Asian Americans, 15–16, 170, 228n8; and diaspora, 44–45, 81–82; and food studies, 21–22; and indentured workers, 45, 123; and outsourcing, 184–85; and women, 52, 56–58, 61, 100, 118–43, 148

Lahiri, Jhumpa, 13–14, 22, 85, 90, 147–48, 150, 157–63, 176, 178

Lakshmi, Padma, 23, 88, 187, 196, 201–8, 211, 215–16

Lall, Sumita, 227n6

Lavie, Smadar, 47

Lebesco, Katie, 84

Leonardi, Susan, 10, 227n4

Lindenfeld, Laura, 118–19

Lionnet, Françoise, 9–10

love cake, 65, 81

A Love Supreme (film), 137–43, 147, 202

A Love Supreme (musical recording), 139

Lovegren, Sylvia, 188, 203–4

Lowe, Lisa, 190–91, 194

Maira, Sunaina, 41–42, 150, 230n8

Majithia, Sheetal, 99–100, 108–9

"Makers of Chili Paste," 21–22, 118, 126, 132–37, 220

Makhijani, Pooja, 22, 152–53, 178

Malladi, Amulya, 13, 23, 110–11, 187, 110–11, 212–16

Manalansan, Martin, 185–86

Mangal Pandey, 116, 120

Mango Season, 110–11

Mankekar, Purnima, 89

Mansingh, Lalit, 1–7

Marshall, Paule, 221
Mathieu, Paula, 103–6
Mazumdar, Ranjani, 125
Mazumdar, Sucheta, 51, 228–29n3
McKee, Larry, 18
Meatless Days, 20, 29–30, 36–41, 48, 220
Mehta, Deepa, 20, 58, 67–73
Mehta, Ketan, 116, 118–26, 130–37
Midnight's Children, 112–13
Minhas, Nisha, 85, 154
minor literature, 81, 86
Mintz, Sidney, 11, 81
Mirch Masala, 118–26, 130–37
Mistress of Spices (novel), 13, 21, 51, 86–101, 107–13, 230n4
Mistress of Spices (film), 89–90, 230n5
model minorities, 23, 95, 185, 192, 198, 203, 208, 214–15
Monsoon Wedding, 20, 52–55, 62, 74
Mootoo, Shani, 20, 30, 41–49, 58, 74–78, 81, 92, 219
Morris, Robyn, 227n1
Mukherjee, Bharati, 13–14, 90–91, 227n6
Mukherjee, Meenakshi, 91–92, 109
Mullen, Bill, 141, 209
multiculturalism, 7, 19, 83, 90, 165–66, 177, 204, 220; in Australia, 62, 224; boutique multiculturalism, 224; in Britain, 4–5, 224–25; and eating, 48, 233n7; and happiness, 224–26; palatable multiculturalism, 108, 162–63, 224; in the U.S., 12, 23, 175, 189–94, 204, 215–16, 224
Muslim identity, 47, 94, 116; Muslim Americans, 22, 206–7, 216; and characters, 39, 50, 96
My Country, My Kitchen, 22, 164–71, 176, 179

Nair, Mira, 20, 52–55, 119, 132
The Namesake, 14, 147–48, 178
naming: and cooks, 39; and ethnic identity, 33–34, 42–44; and foods, 3, 37, 43–44, 228–29; and racial labels, 2–3
Narayan, Kirin, 69
Narayan, Uma, 149–50
nationalism, 93, 99–100, 117, 178, 219, 226
naturalization, 33, 159, 191–93
Nguyen, Bich Minh, 13, 172
Niranjana, Tejaswini, 128
Noon, Ghulam, 4

No-No Boy, 178–79
nostalgia, 19–20, 31–32, 46, 48; and cookbooks, 62; critical nostalgia, 41–42, 48–49; culinary nostalgia, 27–28, 36, 160–61; cultural nostalgia, 139, 159; ersatz nostalgia, 162; immigrant, 29, 41, 62, 95, 160–61, 230n1; and memory, 14, 28–29; and pleasure, 40–41; as problematic, 31; and the second-generation, 176

Obasan, 108–9
odors, 2, 28, 88, 108, 132, 150–51, 154, 159–63, 185–86, 198, 206
Okada, John, 178–79
Oliver, Jamie, 138, 143
Onam, 165–66, 169
One Spice, Two Spice, 187, 200, 210
orientalism, 21, 82, 86–87, 90–91, 94–97, 100, 106, 111, 114, 143, 230n2
"Out on Main Street," 20, 29–30, 41–46, 48–39, 92, 219

paan, 217–20
Padma's Passport, 137–38, 167, 188, 196, 201–3
Page, Karen, 188
Pakistani American contexts, 9, 20, 30, 36–41
Palumbo-Liu, David, 16–17
Parasher, Prajna, 118, 126–32, 137
Pastries, 13, 21, 85, 101–10, 112–13
Patel, Nilesh, 136–43, 146–48, 231n6
Patel, Nimesh, 183
Pickle: as metaphor, 112–16; as weapon, 75–76, 231n5
Prashad, Vijay, 96, 216, 233n8
Primlani, Kala, 55–58
Punch, 114–15
Puwar, Nirmal, 7

"Queer Eye for the FOB Guy," 181–84
"Queer Eye for the Straight Guy," 181–83
queerness, 51, 53, 77; and diasporic fictions, 20; and dress, 44; and food, 52, 54, 58, 59–78; and kinship, 50; and subjectivity, 41, 54–55, 58, 217–19
"The Quilt," 50–51, 62

Rabinow, Paul, 16
race, 2–3, 8, 24, 47–48, 87, 89, 97,

192–95, 201, 221–23, 231n2; and Asian Americans, 13, 170–71, 178, 206–7; and character development, 111; and class in Britain, 4–5; and class in the U.S., 117–19, 128–29, 199; and critical race studies, 98–99; and disability, 139; and food, 3–5, 16–19, 91–92, 109, 142–43, 154, 158–59, 163, 166, 185, 189, 211, 214–16; and the immigrant body, 151–53; and multiracial identity, 164–65; and Orientalism, 21

racism, 5–7, 17, 87, 94–99, 108–10, 117, 150, 178–79, 220

Radhakrishnan, R., 33–34

Raji Cuisine, 23, 187, 196–97, 201–2, 206–9, 211, 215

Ramanujan, A.K., 69

Ramayana, 72–72, 229–30n5

Rao, Shweta, 94–95, 230nn4–5

Ray, Krishnendu, 160–61

Ray, Rachael, 199

recipes, 31–33, 56–61, 103–4, 161–68, 187, 189, 195–97, 200–205, 228n1, 229n3, 232n4; as metaphor of survival, 99, 213–14

Reef, 20, 58, 62–74, 77–78

regionalism, 91, 164; and culinary difference, 33, 1–92; and Kerala cuisine, 163–71; and symbolic identity, 35

Reichl, Ruth, 199–200

Renan, Ernest, 47–48

restaurants, 7, 138, 190, 200, 228n3; and labor, 5, 13, 15, 22, 118, 120, 126–32, 184–85, 205–6; and fusion cuisine, 23, 187–88, 190, 194, 196–200, 207–10, 214, 232n4, 233n4; and opportunity, 72–74; and racism, 5–6, 185; and smell, 1, 185

romance, 90, 99–101, 108–9, 111, 230n4

Roy, Parama, 21

Roy, Sandip, 120

Ruiz, Vicki, 221

Rushdie, Salman, 28– 29, 31, 85, 112–13

Sassen, Saskia, 103–4, 194

Self-Employed Women's Association (SEWA), 134

Sen, Samita, 124

Sen, Sharmila, 44

Sepia Mutiny, 110

Sepoy Mutiny. *See* Indian Mutiny

Serving Crazy with Curry, 23, 187, 212–16, 220

Sex and the City, 1, 5, 185

sexuality, 19–20, 29, 44, 47, 50, 53–54, 74

Shankar, Ravi, 139, 141

Shankar, Shalini, 151

Sharma, Nitasha, 2

Sharpe, Jenny, 52–53

Shetty, Shilpa, 5

Shih, Shu-Mei, 9–10

Shiva, Vandana, 103, 123

Shohat, Ella, 131

small businesses, 86, 98, 103–7, 111

Solomon, Charmaine, 61, 81

Song, Min, 178–80

South Asia, definition of, 8

spice trade, 228 and 229n3

Spices, See Mirch Masala

Srikanth, Rajini, 8

Sri Lankan cultural production, 9, 20, 58–73, 81

Stewart, Kathleen, 31–32

suicide, 212–13

Suleri, Sara, 20, 29–30, 36–41, 48, 217, 229,n4

"Sushila's Bakhti," 45–48

Swedenburg, Ted, 47

Tasty, Tangy, Tart and Sweet, 204–5

Thanksgiving, 165–66, 169

Thind, Bhagat Singh, 191–93, 232n1

Third World: and aesthetics, 131; and excess, 199; exploitation of, 131; and women, 36

Top Chef 196

tourism, culinary, 163–77

translation, 127–28, 135–37, 165; and failure, 215; of food terms, 44, 228–29n3

transnationalism, 9, 60, 92, 103, 205, 226; and Asian Americanist critique, 9; corporations, 100; and feminism, 231n3; and labor, 183–84; minor transnationalism, 9–10; and South Asianness, 9–10, 119, 224–26; and translation, 137

Trillin, Calvin 147, 172–77, 205

Tringali, Danielle, 84

Tsai, Ming, 189, 193, 196, 214

Unaccustomed Earth, 151

Unbidden Voices, 22, 118, 126–32, 135–37

Van Aken, Norman, 188